Language and Human Nature

Mark Halpern

Language and Human Nature

Mark Halpern

Art is Man's Nature
– Burke

Regent Press
Oakland, CA

ISBN-13: 978-1-58790-089-1
ISBN-10: 1-58790-089-0

Library of Congress Control Number: 2006920647

Manufactured in the U.S.A.
REGENT PRESS
6020-A Adeline Street
Oakland, California 94608
www.regentpress.net

To Phyllis
sine qua …

Contents

A Preface by Jacques Barzun

There is one domain, surely, where discrimination is not only allowable but required. That is the domain of Words. In some situations you may be tempted to exclaim: "So the old codger kicked the bucket!" But if what brings the thought is your friend's telling you that his father has just died, you really must find some other way to express yourself.

This choice, of course, would — or ought to — be automatic before speaking. But going from ordinary and colloquial occasions, when we know at once what is and is not appropriate, to equally frequent others, calls for taking thought about words. The dinner table with guests, the business office, the phone and the computer linked to strangers, the board meeting, the memorial service, the Oval office in the White House, the desk of the journalist, novelist and playwright writing news or dialogue, and the poet's when composing memorable lines, all are settings for continuous verbal discrimination.

The word *discriminate* is derived from the idea of differences measured on a scale. The ability to read the fine scale of expressions in one's language depends not only on knowing their precise meaning and what connectives they require. It also depends on knowing their force, their overtones, and their changeableness under the influence of their close neighbors and even of others at a distance. Again, in language for spoken delivery, sound and rhythmical fitness in the sentence affect how readily the sense is grasped. The same is true in print: the silent reader responds to these features as if hearing the words.

All this is a matter of course; it used to be taken for granted under the name of correct expression. But nowadays there is among us a group of highly intelligent persons, who call themselves scientists (*social* scientist, when one of them has a touch of modesty) who deny the need for fussing in the ways just described. They are the linguists, students of language native and foreign, past and present. They argue that correctness, which consists in applying the knowledge detailed above, is an old prejudice to be discarded. The scientific attitude — and democratic sentiment, too — command the practice of speaking and writing "as it comes." So-called mistakes do not exist; people just speak differently and should not bother to change, because the "life" of the language depends on its free development, as shown by its endless alteration over time. It has been due to the rich supply of mistakes, some of which turned out to be improvements. Others, such as confused or reversed meaning, we now accept as "correct." It will happen again, is happening, and trying to stop "life" is futile.

This is the state of affairs that has long engaged Mr. Halpern's attention as a professional writer and editor, and he has found that it has consequences overlooked by the linguists and the public generally. The author invites the reader to discover here what these are, in hopes that the high cost of the linguists' laissez-faire philosophy will become plain. The reader will find, to begin with, a full account

of the linguists' position and intention. He will learn among other things what one does not expect from a science, that it warrants propaganda, often in the form of attacks on whoever maintains and gives reasons for believing that the principle and practice of correctness are desirable.

The present book is, to the best of my knowledge, the first thorough discussion of the pros and cons of this debate. The author explains how the scholarly study of language began a couple of centuries ago and produced findings valid today and as important as they are interesting; next, how out of that discipline linguistics, the new name adopted in place of *philology*, which meant love of words, to stress scientific rigor arose toward the end of the 19th century and has developed the fighting spirit just referred to.

Mr. Halpern then takes up the assumptions of the doctrine and the difficulties it inflicts on all users of the word—the citizen in daily life and the professional who writes or speaks for a living — journalist, editor, lawyer, writer, preacher, advertiser, televiser, and politician. To illustrate by an instance typical of only one sort of difficulty: Should a writer use *disinterested* in its still-used sense of "not partial from interest" (= selfish motive) or as a synonym for "uninterested," a duplicate not needed? Multiply the examples of such doubt and blurring of expression by the number of tolerated misuses and double senses, and you face "the problem of communication," so repeatedly invoked to excuse blunders in business, medicine, education, and government.

Language did not come into being by sudden inspiration; it had to be invented, with much effort, to give form to ideas and to convey them from one mind into another. It would therefore seem best to keep the working pieces of the device sharp, well-oiled and moving along the right path.

In describing the various aspects of the predicament and its cause, the following pages should not be expected to read like a good many books of these days that are addressed to "dummies" and talk down to the reader in colloquial words. Mr. Halpern hammers away at his main points in one context after another. He avoids technicalities, but in my estimation he does not trust his audience enough, no doubt because he is aware of the strength of the prejudice he has chosen to contest. He might have relaxed his tone and his pace if he had reflected that the popularity of syndicated columns about usage in newspapers and magazines, and the publication of books on how to write well prepared a group of readers for him. True, the dictionaries have gone over to the enemy and become guides to what is being said and printed in the press, rather than what the most admired writers still prefer. Still, let us hope that because or in spite of Mr. Halpern's relentless exposition, the happily careless and the converts to the linguistic creed, who feel guilty for preferring correctness, may themselves become crusaders for the better cause.

Author's Introduction

Plan and content of the book

This book is an attempt to expose a century's worth of bad thinking about language, to exhibit some of the dangers it presents, and to suggest a path to recovery. It begins by examining the causes of changes in the English vocabulary, which sometimes take the form of new words, but more often that of new senses for old words. In the course of this examination I discuss a wide variety of verbal solecisms, vulgarisms, and infelicities generally, but my objective is not to deplore such things (although many are deplorable) but to expose the reasons for their existence, the human traits that generate them. These reasons, which I review in some detail, are very different from those suggested by the academic specialists in language, the *linguists*.

A large part of this book is devoted to contesting the claims of academic linguists to be not only experts in the study of language change, but scientists bringing to bear on language the same attitudes and methods that physicists bring to the study of atoms or astronomers to stars. I contest them not because I have some personal quarrel with linguists, but because I think their claims are profoundly wrong and dangerous: language is too central to civilized life to be so deeply misunderstood without causing a multitude of troubles throughout our culture. And we are currently experiencing such troubles, a number of which are examined here. The exposure of the linguists' misunderstandings is not an end in itself, but a necessary first step in recovery from the confusion we are now enmeshed in.

The false picture of the relation between words and thoughts that is part of the vain attempt to deal with language "scientifically" — which means in practice dealing almost exclusively with syntax and phonology — is at least partly responsible for some further dangerous cultural developments. The attempt by linguists to treat their subject scientifically makes them see meaning as an irritating complication to be ignored if possible, rather than as the *raison d'être* of language, and the aspect of it that should be the chief object of linguistic study. It turns them into formalists who try to understand language by studying its physical representations, visible and audible, with resort to semantics only when unavoidable. With words practically stripped of their role as bearers of meaning, it becomes easy to see them as unimportant, and correctness and facility in their use a frivolity important only to esthetes and pedants. And so it seems to a great many today, including, shamefully, some teachers, editors, and writers.

The degree and type of responsibility linguistics bears for those troubles varies; for some of them it is directly and wholly responsible — the uselessness of much modern lexicography, for example. For others, such as the disrepute into which rhetoric has fallen, its responsibility is less direct; these troubles spring not from any explicit linguistic doctrine, but just from the general decoupling of words and meaning that modern linguistics fosters. And there are still others, such as the startling decline in literacy among people born since roughly 1960 — a decline that has colleges and even graduate schools attempting to teach their students what they should have learned in elementary and high school — whose connection to linguistic doctrine is still more indirect, but quite real nevertheless.

Finally, I examine some problems that are rooted in what I call "language decadence," which means using words not so much to describe, model, and master experience as to build an alternative reality that is more important to the victim of decadence than the world most people see and live in. There are a few who succeed in transmuting such a verbal obsession into the gold of poems and stories, but there are many more who are simply captivated by words, and whose obsession has no effect other than to make their behavior in the sublunary world inappropriate, sometimes to the point of madness. This last type of problem is the responsibility of linguistics only in the sense that a properly oriented study of language would be dealing with just such problems, but cannot come into being until today's wrong-headed linguistics is pushed aside to make way for it.

The changing character of the language

A full understanding of these bad and occasionally bizarre consequences of the linguistic view of language requires in addition an awareness of a profound cultural development that has not received anything like the attention it deserves. Over the last few hundred years language has been moving from being a part of Nature to being a part of Culture. It is no longer simply the tool we use to communicate on subjects of interest, or to "express ourselves," it is, increasingly, a prize to be sought for; no longer a part of the intellectual commons that all use freely and without responsibility, but an asset whose acquisition would be greatly rewarding to its proprietor. In Schiller's terms, language has passed from the naïve (the simple, direct, and unembarrassed) to the sentimental (the self-conscious, self-regarding, and ironic); so far from being a neutral medium for the conveyance of ideas, it is now seen to be a source of power, and many of us are trying to enlist it in our causes. And since we are taking conscious control of language, it is vital that we understand what we're doing, and make sure that the wardens of language have our interests at heart.

Language manipulation in the interest of this faction or that is already a commonplace. Practiced by public relations agencies for the benefit of individuals and private-sector institutions, and by the Ministry of Information when backed by the power of the state, the increasingly common attempt to control language and bend it to one's special purposes, whatever the harm done to it as a neutral medium of communication, is a development that must not be allowed to take place unscrutinized and uncriticized. But just such an uncritical attitude prevails today, and here too linguistics is part of the problem: the necessary scrutiny and criticism is being thwarted by those who should be the first to insist on it, the professional students of language.

The offenses of language manipulators of all kinds, ranging from the relatively harmless salesman who calls a used car *pre-owned* to the despot who calls his murderous regime *guided democracy*, are in their various degrees troubling, but probably within our power to resist. What makes our efforts to resist them much harder — perhaps so much harder as to make us fail — is that they have the effective support of linguists, who should be our main defenders against them. Linguists are not, of course, particularly concerned to help car salesmen or dictators, but their aspirations to the status of scientists cause them to insist, for reasons that will be explored in some detail later, that language is a natural phenomenon. That being so, they further insist, attempts at guiding it by writers, editors, and teachers constitute "interference" with nature and with the scientific study of language — and in so arguing they are providing cover to all the scoundrels and ignoramuses who are busily making it harder and harder to discuss public issues clearly and disinterestedly.[1] The gist of my complaint against the linguists is that in fostering a false idea of language, they undermine our defenses against the evils that follow from abuse of language.

It may seem at first glance that the relatively trivial sins against language that are examined in some detail in the early part of the book are very far from the really harmful offenses and corruptions studied in the latter part. They are indeed of very different magnitudes — but they are all part of a single spectrum, differing greatly in degree but not in kind. And for that reason, the minor faults, when uncorrected, lead by easy stages to the serious abuses; to connive at those minor errors, to fail to correct them whenever possible, is to be complicit in those abuses. A principal objective of this book is to display language abuse as a continuum in which the most trivial offenses, although they may directly trouble only a minority, pave the way for the most serious offenses, those that victimize us all. Becoming sensitive to mere solecisms increases one's sensitivity to language in general, and is a big step in learning to detect and resist dishonest and tendentious language.

A personal note

My involvement in the issues dealt with here came about as a by-product of my work as writer and editor. I had had a smattering of linguistics while doing graduate work at Columbia in English, taking an introductory course in the subject, and another in which I learned a little of what was then called Anglo-Saxon. But it was not until I noted many years later that linguists were, however unintentionally, protecting the language corruptors that I began to read widely in the subject. As part of my self-education I engaged several eminent linguists in debate on the relevant topics, some in private correspondence and some in public media. I found that many of them had notions that were not merely disputable, but so glaringly false as to make me wonder how anyone could entertain them at all, let alone expound them in public. Examples of these bizarre notions: that standard English is nothing more than the dialect of the ruling class, and is forced on others simply for that reason; that Eskimos have no more terms for snow and ice than anyone else, and that it is racist to suppose that they do; and that all change in language is natural and inevitable, and not to be opposed by anyone for any reason, however regrettable its consequences.

I published some attacks on these views, and several linguists fought back, again both privately and publicly. The result of their efforts has been to reassure me that my arguments are sound. When leading academic linguists, including the president of the Linguistic Society of America, their professional organization, can do no more than misquote an opponent, mount *ad hominem* attacks on him, and occasionally even insult him, you can be sure that they cannot refute his theses. This is of course gratifying to the debater, who wants to win, but saddening to the serious critic, who wants his arguments squarely confronted and rationally examined, and his points either refuted or accepted. A very few of the linguists with whom I have exchanged views have been honorable enough to concede a few of my points, and if this were a personal memoir I would name and salute them. But for the most part my opponents, while often showing in their later exchanges with me that they had tacitly accepted some points I had made earlier, have resolutely refused to say *touché*. This does not increase one's respect for their profession.

I have tried to serve two types of reader: first, the one who wants to read straight through without the distraction of footnotes or other digressions, and does not require, at least not immediately, the exact source of quotations, the identification of persons mentioned in the text, or other such scholarly apparatus. The second is his opposite: the reader who demands immediate support and source for every assertion and allusion, and wants details of every topic that is raised at all. My way of trying to serve both readers is to keep the main text as free as possible of what the general reader might think of as distractions — there are no footnotes — while supplying all the details the critical reader might require, but relegated to endnotes, appendices, and other such ignorable features. One special point: I refer throughout to *prescriptivist* and *descripitivist* positions on language usage; those who are unfamiliar with these terms may want to start by reading the first few pages of Chapter 4, where they are discussed, along with my own position in the conflict between them.

A word of explanation about the serpentine structure of some of what follows: in correcting the linguists' standard view of language, much of what needs to be done is purely destructive — the clearing up of a mess. And that process is itself messy; one has to deal with confusion largely on its own terms, finding and cleaning it up wherever the confused have created it. The project is more like bringing order to a teenager's room than conducting an argument with a philosopher, in which one moves with dignity from premises to conclusions. This is also what accounts for the instances of repetition that I have reluctantly permitted to stand; the same point sometimes has to be made in several different contexts, and a writer has the choice of repeating himself or referring the reader back to its original appearance. In such cases I have preferred committing the sin of repetition to the even more irritating one of asking the reader to turn back to an earlier page to refresh himself on some point made there.

Finally, this is primarily a work of criticism, directed mainly toward the exposure of what I see as error, and is therefore necessarily "negative in tone." But there are throughout at least hints, and in the final chapter explicit suggestions, about what I think should be done to correct the errors I point to. From these hints and suggestions I think any reasonable reader can infer the course of action I would urge upon my allies: that is, upon those who see language as neither a natural phenomenon whose laws are to be sought in the laboratory, nor a sales tool or weapon to be seized and exploited before a competitor does so, but rather as our greatest common treasure and the prerequisite of truly human life. This book, then, is preaching to the choir — to readers who are already in sympathy with its views. It could hardly be otherwise; I find it impossible to imagine any other kind of reader picking the book up, sticking with it to the end, and allowing himself to be won over by it. It was not with any such expectation that I wrote it, nor does it have to achieve that impossible goal to be effective. What I hope it will do is encourage my natural allies, strengthen their hearts, and arm them better for battle with the adversary. And that is no modest goal; those allies, if acting whole-heartedly and with a common goal, will prevail.

Acknowledgements and thanks

I'm grateful first of all to Anne Fadiman who, as editor of *The American Scholar*, printed the essay that is the core of the first chapter of this book; without her enthusiastic acceptance of it I might have written no further on the subject. I owe a debt of gratitude to Bryan A. Garner, author of *Garner's Modern American Usage*, for some useful comments on the first several chapters, as well as for face-to-face discussions on usage in which we found ourselves almost always on the same side. I owe another such debt to my friend Lucian Endicott for reading this book in a slightly earlier version, going through it thoroughly even though its subject is not one of his principal interests, and perhaps for that very reason being able to make many useful suggestions. I have been helped and encouraged by my old high school classmate Bill Safire, who astonished me some years ago by calling from Washington to congratulate me on one of the essays whose substance is incorporated into this book, and who put me in touch with the late James McCawley, a professor of linguistics at the University of Chicago with whom it was a pleasure to correspond. To my friend Jacques Barzun my debt is so great that if he were to call it in, I would have to declare bankruptcy. He urged me to write this book, gave me detailed comments on various drafts of it as it was written, and supported it in every possible way — all at a time when he was often suffering some degree of disability, and laboring to meet various other obligations. The only anxiety I have about this book is over his opinion of it; if he thinks it worthy of the time and trouble he has spent on it, I will feel fully rewarded for the labor of producing it, whatever the rest of the world may think.

My wife Phyllis has supported the writing of this book for far longer than either of us supposed it would take, and it would not exist at all if not for her willingness to see it through to the end.

The Question of Change in Language

We know, of course,
that it is not the English language
which does something when it changes.
We know that this has something
to do with the
people who use it.
But what?
– Rudi Keller[2]

The root of the confusion: why does language change?

The educated speaker of English today, especially one "fascinated by words," is almost certain to hold the view that language is and must always be changing, and that change of any kind is a Good Thing. There may be particular changes he is not happy about, but he is not likely to try to oppose them; he is persuaded that resistence to lexical changes is both futile and something close to politically reactionary. And he will have gotten that idea, directly or indirectly, from the professional academic students of language called *linguists*. There are many schools of linguists, and they can be quite sharp in criticizing each other, but they are as one in holding and propagating a view of language change of which the layman's version is a somewhat degraded copy. (By "language change" and similar expressions I will mean, unless otherwise stated, changes in the English vocabulary: newly coined or imported words, or old words in new senses.) Linguists indiscriminately accept the idea of change, seeing it as springing from "the genius of the language" expressing itself through the speech of the common people. They see resistance to any particular change as springing from ignorance and old-fogeyism, if not elitism and racism, and as in any case futile, since change will always prevail. But even while enthusiastically embracing change in their role as linguists, they are not always so welcoming of it in their private capacities; they often refuse to adopt in their own writings changes they have defended in that of others — more on this later. The standard response that one hears when any such change is questioned is some variant of *Language is a living, growing thing, and all living things change. Don't interfere with life!*

The dogma that language is a living, growing thing has been repeated so often that it has become virtually the one thing that everyone "knows" about the subject — which makes it especially unfortunate that it is false.[3] This metaphor may once have served some useful purpose; today its effect is to stifle rational discussion. It is heard whenever Mr. A questions a usage of Mr. B's: someone, usually Mr. C, will counter the criticism by reciting this one thing everyone knows — and with that remark, reason flies out the window. Do you, A, raise your eyebrows at B's use of *reticent* to mean *reluctant*? think him ignorant for using *disinterested* to mean *uninterested*? groan because he speaks of *running the gauntlet*? "I, C, tell you in response that language is a living, growing thing; thus I refute pedantry — and carry the day."

So enthralled are we by this cliché that it is almost painful — like massaging back to life a leg that's fallen asleep — to force oneself to recognize that every word of it is false. Language is not living, not growing, and not a thing; it is a vast system of social habits and conventions, inherited from our forebears, and showing every sign of being an artifact rather than an organic growth. Certainly languages, or at least some aspects of them, exhibit some changes over time — but then, so do the Dow Jones Industrial Average, barometer readings, and the Oregon coastline, none of which we characterize as living or growing. The changes exhibited by our language in historical times make it plain that it changes only when it is changed by us, its users, and never of its own accord, since it has no accord. It is, in a word, *inert* — we cannot call it *dead,* primarily because it never lived, but also because we have, rather tellingly, reserved *dead language* for one whose *native speakers* are dead.

It is only the liveliness of its users that makes the attribution of life to inert language so nearly irresistible; languages seem to have many of the marks of living, growing things because they are bound up so closely with beings who are indeed alive and growing. And in the 19th and earlier 20th centuries the triumphs of linguistics,

4

or at least that branch of it called *phonology,* seemed to lend support to the notion that languages possessed lives of their own, and were not simply reflections of human needs and desires. In sound changes, at least, they seemed to follow their own developmental laws, independent of our wishes and efforts, and much was built on that early promise. But that historical moment, which will be discussed later, has passed, and with it any excuse for succumbing to the *Fallacy of Linguistic Autonomy.*

A modern language changes when we change it, and the metaphor that makes it autonomous only obscures our real task, which is to consider just why and how we do so. Language has always changed for perfectly understandable human reasons, although until recently those reasons operated without serious examination and therefore with little control. But over the last few centuries, we humans have begun to take charge of our languages as we took charge of our food supply in going from plant gathering to agriculture, and as we will shortly be taking charge of our genetic makeup. And just as taking charge of our food supply and our genetic makeup requires that we become much more aware of how those matters developed before we consciously intervened, so taking charge of our language requires that we understand clearly how it has developed and changed so far. What follows is at least the beginning of an answer.

Six common ways in which we change language

By far the most common kind of change we make in our language today is an addition to its vocabulary, made for the excellent reason that a new creature has been observed in Eden, and Adam is called on to perform again his onomastic function: naming the beasts. There may be occasional objections to the particular token Adam chooses, but no one objects in principle to the coining of new words for new things. And apart from this unexceptionable and linguistically uninteresting kind of change, innovations in language are almost always the result of one of six human traits or motives: *Simple Ignorance, Social*

Climbing, Semantic Inflation, Group Solidarity, Journalistic Convenience, or Effort Minimization.

Simple Ignorance is a mistaken but entirely forgivable reason for making a change in the language — at least I hope it is excusable, because I have been guilty of it, and fear that I may be guilty of it again. My personal errors may not have misled anyone else, but they illustrate one way in which errors arise, and how some errors of this kind go on to become accepted usage. For some years I thought there was a form of light called *infrared* (rhymes with *impaired*), because I had seen *infra-red* spelled without the hyphen, and failed to recognize it. For years I gave full value to the syllable -*is*- in names like Salisbury. I supposed for some time that *internecine* referred to something that happened between two parties of Necines — the Necines being a clan apparently more tense and peculiar even than the Oedipuses,[4] ones so given to fighting among themselves that their name gives us the standard term for such intramural conflicts. And so on; the list of my errors is a long one. (I intrude my personal failings into this discussion because I would have no one think that Simple Ignorance is a bludgeon that I have created to beat others with.)

If Simple Ignorance is considered to subsume Temporary Confusion, it can been seen in a newspaper piece[5] that claimed that when W. H. Auden visited Yale around 1973, Edward Mendelson (later his literary executor, then an undergraduate), served as his *chaperone*. The thought of Auden needing — and accepting — a chaperon (if Mr Mendelson filled that role, it should be so spelled) so bemused me that it took a few moments before I realized that the writer meant *cicerone*. Since then I've seen the same blunder elsewhere, and no wonder: two uncommon, Mediterranean-looking words, both referring to specialized kinds of escort, both starting with 'c' and ending with 'on[e]' — like twins, they seem born to be confused with each other.[6]

Most of the time Simple Ignorance can be corrected without arousing hostility in the Simply Ignorant; if the correction is made tactfully, most of the S.I. will accept it without resentment, sometimes even gratefully. But sometimes the would-be benefactor is told that he is a pedant, a reactionary, or some other kind of villain for presuming to correct a free-born, native speaker of the language. And while he is no villain, it is true that he is sometimes a hero come too late.

It is clearly too late, for example, to correct the almost universal notion that *ilk* means *type* or *class* or *kind* or *category*, or that a *cohort* is a *buddy, partner, sidekick* or *colleague*. But if we give up on these points, it is not a triumph of the new and improved over the old and obsolete, nor even a replacement of the old by something just as good — it is simply loss, and a capitulation to ignorance. The new usage does not even offer the stimulation of novelty, because its users are not aware that it is new; we have all lost, and no one has won. Two penalties will have to be paid for this surrender: we will have lost good words for our own later use, and we will have lost yet another small connection to the literature of our language. Losing *ilk*, we will not be able to say "Campbell of that ilk" to convey that we are speaking not of just any Campbell, but of *the* Campbell, nor will readers fully understand some passages of Walter Scott's; having lost *cohort*, we will be unable to picture what Byron expected us to when we read

The Assyrian came down like the wolf on the fold,
And his cohorts were gleaming in purple and gold

Why, the thoroughly modern reader will wonder, was it such a big deal when the Assyrian — whoever he was — dropped in with a couple of his pals? And all we will get in return for the loss of either term in its older and distinctive sense is one more loose synonym for a notion already provided with several terms — not much of a testimonial to the worth of a living, growing language.

Even biblical phrases are subject to inadvertent change of meaning at the hands of those who are not familiar with the source; here, for example, a journalist quotes an authority on his subject without noting any problem:

Notes Lawrence Levine, an employment communications manager whose defenses against passive-aggressive employees haven't been terribly successful: "Only the quick and the dead have avoided passive aggressives."[7]

Mr Levine evidently meant that of the living, only the fleet of foot can hope to evade passive aggressives; what he has succeeded in saying, for those who have met the phrase "the quick and the dead" in its original context, is that everyone, living or dead, can do so, which would make the passive aggressives a hollow threat. In this case it is clear what the speaker meant despite what he said, but in many others the result will be ambiguity or — what is much worse — a wholly mistaken belief on the reader's part that he understands what was said.

But to the linguist such losses are negligible (if he acknowledges them as losses at all). He sees them simply as necessary consequences of change, inevitable as well as a sign that the language is alive. When linguists deign to reply at all to protests about specific changes, they do so by treating them as if the matter were already decided, and the protestors were trying to undo the past and bring back the dead. This is Linguistic Triumphalism: it contents itself with pointing out that once a change is accepted by enough users of a language (where "enough" seems to mean "enough to satisfy linguists"), it becomes part of the language, and those who opposed it have lost — and then treating this tautology as if it were the whole story. What it leaves out is that if a change is *not* accepted by enough users (particularly writers and the most prestigious speakers), it does *not* become part of the language, and those who opposed it have *won*. And such rejection of change has occurred many times in the history of the language, probably far more often than the universal acceptance of a change.[8]

Changes in usage of the kind caused by Simple Ignorance do not occur instantaneously; they start off slowly, often in some remote (very lofty or very lowly) and marginal part of the cultural arena, and are quite vulnerable during their infancy and minority. During that period at least they are subject to criticism and defeat, and indeed the infant mortality rate among linguistic innovations is quite high, as is clear from a glance at yesterday's slang and catchphrases and smart talk. Much of it is now incomprehensible, and many even of those examples that can still be understood strike today's ear as quaint. Linguists are fond of producing lists of words that are now accepted parts of the language despite the efforts of "purists" to kill them; what they fail to do is acknowledge all the words that purists opposed, and have since passed into oblivion.[9]

"When is misuse not misuse?" asks one eminent linguist, Peter Trudgill (Professor of English Language and Linguistics at the University of Lausanne) rhetorically, and answers, "When everybody does it."[10] Agreed — but what about when only a *few* are "doing it"? Is it futile, or in some sense improper, to oppose a usage that only a handful have so far adopted? If not, at what point does it become futile or improper? For example, is it too late to correct the error, noted earlier, of using *reticent* for *reluctant*? It is still new, far from universal, and thus not yet incorrigible. It popped up only in the last quarter of the 20th century. It is not limited to the uneducated — the first time I heard it, it was uttered by a computer-industry executive who had been a professor of computer science at the University of California at Berkeley — but it is still far from widely accepted. This, I contend, is an error that one should be able to oppose without incurring the scorn or exasperation of linguists.

One form taken by Simple Ignorance is hypercorrectness, which turns a commendable desire to be correct into a new kind of error, that of obeying a rule where it has no application. It produces such locutions as "Mommy gave some ice-cream to Debby and I," and "...he is a former All-Star whom the Knicks apparently feel can help them contend for a title." Hypercorrectness can also spring from Social Climbing (on which see the next entry in this list) when speakers see certain hypercorrect locutions as the mark of superior people, but for the most part it results from misunderstood rules. The typical perpetrator of the hypercorrectness fault has been chided for using "me" when "I" is required, or "who" when "whom" is required, and has come away with the notion that "I" and "whom" are intrinsically better than their alternative forms. As a result he falls off the grammatical tightrope on the left rather than the right, unaware that it is just as far down to the ground on one side as the other.

9

Social Climbing (which includes simple Showing Off) is a less innocent but still forgivable cause of language change. Into this category fall all the usages that we adopt in the hope that they will cause others to think more highly of us: the fancy, half-understood word; the misspelled or mispronounced French and Latin tags that are supposed to make us sound worldly or learned; the misapplied scientific or technical term that is meant to suggest that we are adepts in one of the modern black arts like electronics or programming; the adoption by whites of the vocabulary and speech patterns of inner-city African Americans in the hope of being taken for street-smart dudes; the insider's term that makes it clear that we are savvy, in the know, wised up, witting, clued in, or otherwise among the cognoscenti.

These variants of Social Climbing differ in the amount of damage they do. It probably costs the community nothing if some members, hoping to be taken for movie-industry dealmakers, talk of *taking a meeting* (or even a *meet*), or *doing* lunch, but there is potential danger when someone talks of making a *quantum jump* when he means a very large, significant jump (see the section on 'Sample applications of the principles, with derivation of secondary rules' in Chapter 10 for further discussion of *quantum jump* and other examples). That practice will cause some to misunderstand the phrase when they see it correctly used, and their misunderstanding could have harmful consequences. There is probably no such thing as an absolutely harmless misunderstanding — given the right circumstances, any error can prove disastrous. The use of *penultimate* to mean something even more final than the merely *ultimate* might under some circumstances cause serious confusion, as might the increasingly common notion that *epicenter* means a point ever so much more central than a mere center; for those of us who live along the San Andreas or Hayward faults it might cause consternation. When the Social Climbing is downward — a yielding to *nostalgie de la boue* — it can have even more serious consequences. When Blacks hear whites try to "talk Black," they may feel contempt for those whites, or feel resentment at having what they thought was their private property co-opted (see Group Solidarity, page 14), or feel rage because they think they are being mocked.

Social Climbing includes all efforts by members of a subordinate group to ape the usages, or even adopt the whole language, of a dominant group. For centuries, the upper crust — or as they would have put it, the *gratin* — of several northern European nations spoke French rather than their national languages, which they felt crude or even semi-barbarous, and fit only for the peasantry. Frederick the Great called the highest decoration at his disposal the *Ordre pour le Mérite,* and as recently as World War I some Germans received this Francophile medal for killing Frenchmen. (Of course this phenomenon produced a reaction and a resistance movement in many of the nations it appeared in; a hard core of speakers of, for example, Welsh and Gaelic fight to this day to preserve their mother tongue from complete replacement by English.) And this adoption of a foreign language by the royal courts and the nobility of some nations in centuries past is to be distinguished from the current widespread adoption of English by the masses in many nations (including France); this modern displacement of one language by another is not due to social climbing, but to a desire to participate in the modern international technologically-driven economy and culture.

Semantic Inflation is what people in a hurry or at a loss for words indulge in when they become aware that figures of speech, like all artifacts, wear out and lose effectiveness over time; that countless voices are competing for public attention, apparently making it necessary to scream if one would be heard; and that the substance of what they have to say is an insipid dish that seems to need the hottest, most piquant sauce we can make. Aware of this problem, but unable to find a more graceful way of dealing with it, many such writers are constantly in search of verbal novelties and new levels of hyperbole and strained metaphor to give their utterance some chance of winning our attention.

This is the quest that causes so many to call perfectly ordinary things *awesome, devastating,* or *divine;* that uses *genocide* for any random massacre, or even for social or political events that involve no deliberately inflicted deaths at all. It has produced a generation that has never seen *wicked, sinful, depraved, outrageous* or *decadent* in print except to describe chocolate confections on archly playful dessert menus, and might be surprised to learn that they once played other roles. Then there is the writer who, knowing he is using a thread-bare figure of speech, makes things worse by insisting that it is not a figure at all: "I literally exploded with rage!" One bad effect of this practice is to make the speaker or writer ridiculous in the eyes of many whose respect he hopes for; another, more serious for the rest of us, is to rob us of the use of the inflated terms for their original purposes.

There are a few variants or sub-genres of Semantic Inflation that are worth mention before we pass on: one is the turning of what was a merely factual term into a reproach; another, the mirror image of the first, is the dimming of what was a euphemism into a merely factual term. As an illustration of the first, consider the career of *stereotype*. Once merely a technical term for a kind of mechanical copy, then a near synonym of *cliché*, it has become a condemnation of any attempt to generalize about any human group, particularly one felt to be in need of protection, with a meaning lying somewhere between *unwarranted generalization* and *false accusation*. This represents something close to a complete reversal in meaning: where *stereotype* once meant a characterization that, although trite, was probably true, it now means one that is perhaps provocative, but false. Here, for example, is a contributor to an Internet discussion group, objecting to a description of librarians as harsh enforcers of the rule of silence: "News flash! The grim librarian is a stereotype." The speaker felt no need to specify that it is a *false* stereotype, since *stereotype* now includes, indeed consists mainly of, the notion of falsity. Another, even more explicit example (emphasis supplied):

> None of our usual sports metaphors for business teamwork invokes the "female" traits — *real* or *stereotyped* — of empathy and social cooperation.[11]

Agenda, too, is in danger of losing its basic sense through its use as a euphemism; it now means, in popular usage, sinister ulterior motives. When you hear "He has an agenda!" these days, you are not hearing that the person so described is admirably well organized and prepared for business, but that he has alarming plans that you had better be on your guard against.

The opposite type of change — call it Semantic Deflation — in which a once effective euphemism loses its euphemistic power and becomes merely the standard term for the unpleasantness it once tried to shield us from is illustrated by the career of *misunderstanding*. Would-be spreaders of oil on troubled waters have called so many conflicts *misunderstandings* where the combatants had a perfect understanding of each other's intentions (as when two dogs fight over a bone) that the term has lost all its power to soothe, and is now, for many, just the ordinary term for a quarrel.

Another variant of Semantic Deflation worth noting: Jespersen points out[12] that words can be used falsely so frequently that the false meaning becomes their true meaning. For example, the words *soon, presently,* and *anon* all once meant "right away," but were so often used to buy time by people who really meant "in a little while" that that is what they came to mean formally. (The loss of those words in their original sense had among other effects the partial revival of Latin; attending physicians who need something done for a hospital patient instantly use *stat* to convey that, counting on the deadness of Latin to keep that term, too, from being eroded into yet another version of "at your earliest convenience.")

With increasing frequency, however, words are knowingly corrupted and destroyed in the name of higher values. At some point in the 20th century, for example, some champion of education told us for the first time that children have a *right* to the best possible education. When first uttered, this was a conscious piece of hyperbole; neither children nor any other class of citizens have a right, at least in the United States, to anything but life, liberty, and the pursuit of happiness. It was harmless in itself because it was understood to be simply a dramatic way of declaring that it was vitally important that children be well educated; a rhetorical trope like calling one's sweetheart a red, red rose. But such an outburst in such a cause raised the rhetorical bar; could the next advocate of children's education say anything less? Could one revert to merely pointing out, calmly and rationally, the social advantages of giving all children good educations after the heady concept *right* had been introduced into such discussions?

Clearly the answer is no, and the imaginary right to education, now joined by rights to privacy, self-esteem, and many other highly desirable things, has become a staple of political speeches, party platforms, and commencement addresses. Passionate and excusable exaggeration has hardened and shrunk into standard boilerplate and literal fact, and the lover who charmed us by calling his beloved a red, red rose is now terrifying us by approaching her with secateurs in hand. Presumably we will restrain the literal-minded lover before he prunes her, but it is not clear how we are to convey, except by clumsy circumlocution, the idea once conveyed by the now eroded term *right*. There are those who will say that the importance of good education for children is worth the sacrifice of the term, and that if its loss increases in the slightest degree the likelihood that children will get such an education, the loss is acceptable. That position is a logically tenable one, but the loss is nevertheless real, and damage to our language is something one would have thought more troubling to those who are so keen on education.

Group Solidarity is deliberate language change, made for the purpose of affirming our identification with or support of some group at odds with mainstream society. Does that society say *homosexual*? *We* say *gay*. Do you speak of *women*? We insist on *womyn*. Do we suspect that people call us, in private, *niggers*? Then we will defuse the word by calling ourselves that *in public*. Are we afraid that mean-spirited "nativists" will deport poor people who entered this country without going through the officially prescribed procedures? Then we will refuse to call them *illegal aliens,* and refer to them as *undocumented workers,* although not all are workers, and some have copious if forged or illegally obtained documentation. Are we horrified by the way the tribal peoples they found in this land were treated by the European settlers of North America? Then we will make amends by

reserving the term *native American* for them, unconcerned about implying that the fifth-generation descendent of one of the settlers, born in
Kansas, is a foreigner or at best a naturalized citizen. Did we in the
bad old days of colonialism call certain northern peoples *Eskimos?*
Let us now call them the *Inuit,* even though that is a misnomer, since
the Inuit are just one tribe or group of the people in question. Are we
concerned that the authorities may treat the people who used to be
known as junkies, cokeheads, and addicts as criminals rather than
victims or patients? Then let us call their practices *substance abuse,*
a term almost unique for vapidity and misdirection. And so on. These
language changes are political acts; whether one sympathizes with
them or not, they are not primarily *linguistic* phenomena, any more
than throwing a bomb is primarily an exercise in ballistics.

Sometimes political disapproval takes the form of a refusal to get
someone's name or title right. For example, the inability of so many
American writers, and even quite a few British writers, to grasp the
most elementary facts about British titles of nobility and honor is so
egregious as to make it clear that it springs from something more positive than natural ignorance. The finer points of the system of honors
and titles and forms of address do verge on the esoteric, and even educated Britons might have to turn to *Debrett's Correct Form* when writing to the widow of a Scottish highland clan chief. But it does not seem
too much to ask of the educated anywhere to grasp such simple rules
as that when John Smith is knighted, he becomes not Sir Smith but
Sir John, and that when Fred Jones is created a baron, he becomes
not Lord Fred Jones, but Lord Jones, although their wives are Lady
Smith and Lady Jones. And is it asking too much to expect the enthusiasts who created a Web site devoted to the life and work of the
novelist Anthony Powell to know that Powell's wife was "Lady Violet"
because she was the daughter of an earl, and not a holder of that title
"in her own right"?

Apparently it *is* too much to expect, since such errors are common
among writers who never commit such errors as *knots per hour* or *it
happened light years ago.* The only way to account for the refusal of
so many educated writers to acquaint themselves with the rudiments

of the system governing titles and forms of address is to suppose that there is a good measure of willfulness in it — they are showing their refusal to be impressed by ribbons, orders, and all such baubles. Kind hearts are, no doubt, more than coronets, but willfully remaining ignorant about coronets, and flaunting that ignorance, does no honor to kind hearts — or the English language.[13] As misuse of titles is seen more and more in writing, it will infect speech as well, and then guides to usage will tell us, with a sigh, that there is no use resisting the will of the people or the genius of the language. Something very like this has already happened with the adjective *reverend,* which is properly prefixed to Mr or Dr or whatever form of address is appropriate to the clergyman, but not usable as a substantive or as a modifier of a proper name. It is now accepted by almost everyone, including clergymen worried about alienating their flock by insisting on correct form, as itself a form of address, as in "Good morning, Reverend!", which is equivalent to greeting the Pope with "Good afternoon, Holy!"

Journalistic Convenience is the pressure exerted on the written language — and through it on the spoken form — by the exigencies of print, particularly of page and column size, and of course of the speed with which journalism must be written. Spatial constraints present two opposing forces that journalists must deal with: the pressure to compress their words to make them fit within the space allotted to them, and the pressure to expand their words to fill that space completely. To illustrate the first: why do we all now say *gay* rather than *homosexual?* For a few, as just noted, it is to show solidarity with a minority that has suffered oppression, but for most it is because we have become accustomed to seeing *gay* in the daily paper. A boon for page-layout editors and compositors, perhaps, to have a three-letter word rather than a 10-letter one, but perhaps not so convenient for the rest of us. When we see the story head "A raps B," experienced readers know that they are probably going to read merely that A has criticized B, or even just declined to endorse B's position unreservedly, but it takes a while before one has fully grasped that most print organs carry headlines that fit the space more than the story.[14]

The slow and subtle corruption of the language that takes place every time a busy editor uses the wrong word in a heading because it fits the column better than the right one generally has only a long-term and very gradual effect, but I predict that the practice will eventually cause the shedding of blood. When the United States launches a reconnaissance satellite, or deploys an aircraft whose function is observation and intelligence-gathering, news stories will almost invariably talk about a *spy*-satellite or *spy*-plane; so much more easily fitted in — and exciting — than the inconveniently lengthy and un-English term *reconnaissance* aircraft or the even more awkward *intelligence-gathering* aircraft, you see. But there is a price for that little bit of compositorial corner-cutting that someone else down the road may have to pay: a spy is not protected by the Geneva Convention, and if captured is often put to death by his captors. This is too bad, because the pilot of a U-2 aircraft, for example, is actually far more like an American military attaché in the country in which he is stationed; both of them exist quite openly to collect intelligence, and the foreign country in which they are performing their task is similarly represented in the United States. The worst that can happen to a military attaché, even if caught red-handed trying to acquire top-secret information by bribery or other impermissible means, is to be declared *persona non grata* and expelled from the country he has offended. But someday a U-2 pilot, or someone in a similar role, will be captured by a country that wants to get tough with us, and they will subject him to abuse up to and including death, justifying their actions by pointing out that even American news media have identified him as a spy.

Apart from the constraints of the narrow column and other formatting exigencies, there is a whole sub-vocabulary that is virtually confined to journalism — where but in periodicals do we find the regular use of such space-saving but otherwise unheard-of terms as *nary, festoon, mulls, opts, eyes* (vb.), *sports* (vb.), *garnered, poised to,* and *ensconced*? And there is the license given to slang and even near-obscenity by newspapers like *The New York Times* that were once chaste, even prudish, in diction, in the forlorn hope that by lowering their standards they will appeal to a younger and broader public, but the reward they get for sacrificing their reputation is meager; aspiring to vulgarity, they achieve incoherence.

But just as often as he needs to compress a story to make it fit within the area left free by ads, the journalist needs to pad it so as not to leave embarrassing blank space (or if a radio or television journalist, so as not to leave 'dead air,' the primal sin of either medium). This is in part the explanation of the comic vocabulary that journalists so often have to resort to to stretch a piece to the required length. It is not only what Fowler called *elegant variation* that is responsible for restaurant reviews that call oysters "succulent bivalves."[15] And is there a journalist anywhere who can resist dubbing any new trend the "brave new world of ..."? For the most part, speech leads in the production of new locutions, and the printed word follows — but as noted earlier in the discussion of the use of "Reverend" as a personal title and form of address, the traffic is not all one way. One occasionally observes some term that is usually confined to print, and journalistic print at that, invading the speech of impressionable readers; it is a curious experience to hear otherwise normal people utter in conversation such stilted locutions as *interestingly enough* and *ironically.*

Effort Minimization is the pressure exerted on the spoken language — and through it on writing — by the desire to speak without exerting ourselves more than necessary. Our desire to have our tongue move smoothly from one consonant to the next conflicts with the full pronunciation of *arctic*, for example, so many people adopt the relaxed pronunciation *artic*, and a few have now begun to spell it that way.[16] Similarly, we insert auxiliary vowels — "epenthetic sounds" — where necessary to make pronunciation easier; as in *athalete, joolery, nucular,* and *realator.* Another form taken by Effort Minimization is ellipsis — the omission of words that we trust will be understood by our listeners. For example, in weight-conscious America, *diet,* unless emphatically and explicitly modified, is taken to mean *weight-loss diet.* In many cases speakers are unaware that the term is elliptical, so that when they hear the phrase *bulking-up diet,* they feel it as a self-contradiction. Similarly, many are confused at hearing *asylum* used without reference to insanity. *Discrimination,* once the name of an admired intellectual faculty and practice, has been used so often as short for *racial discrimination* or *bigotry* that its use in its own right is imperiled; here is a typical modern and 'progressive' use:

> It is wrong for the police to pull a car over just because its black occupants are driving in a rich white neighborhood. It is discrimination.[17]

(The corruption of *discrimination* is especially dangerous, because it fosters the notion that the very act of distinguishing between one person or practice and another, no matter on what basis or for what purpose, is reprehensible.)

And sometimes the quest for Effort Minimization has been so successful that not one in a thousand would even understand the full original expression for which we have adopted a convenient short form; imagine asking a doorman on a rainy day to get you a *taximeter cabriolet.* I do not suggest we try to revive the old, full term — if we did, we would get drenched before we could articulate it, and get the doorman to understand what we were talking about — but simply offer it as an illustration of my point that short forms may so completely succeed that the original forms are irretrievably lost.

All these mechanisms, of course, change merely our vocabulary or minute and localized points of usage, and should therefore be of little interest in the eyes of linguistic science — mere froth on the surface of the ocean of language. Just before insistently defending such changes, linguists usually protest that of course these are trivial, not the sort of deep matters that they deal with professionally. But the surface is where most of us sail, and we are rightly concerned with its state; its changes are the ones that exercise the public, including linguistic scientists when they are acting simply as citizens and controversialists; they are the ones that cause debate and conflict. What linguists regard as really deep language change, such as a drift from agglutinative to analytic syntax, is, like geological change, something that very few people other than specialists are even aware of, much less passionate about. The changes that excite both the linguists and that fragment of the educated public that cares about language are the surface ones, the ones that shouldn't concern scientists at all — but somehow do.

Why linguists are champions of change

Few human actions are taken for just one reason, and linguists' insatiable appetite for change in language is undoubtedly another phenomenon for which there is a mixture of reasons, but among them one is surely fundamental: without change, an important group of linguists would have little fresh material to study. Rudi Keller, himself a linguist in good standing, has said as much:

> Historians of language have traditionally focused on the aspect of change, perhaps tacitly assuming that 'Where nothing changes, there is nothing to be explained.'[18]

Among the other reasons why linguists approve of change, two may be worth mentioning here. First, there is the history of their subject: the greatest triumphs by linguists have been the finding of regularities in sound changes, and finding more of them is their fondest hope — more will be said about this in the proper place. Second, objection to specific changes is typical of popular usage critics — they seldom bother to comment on changes unless they strongly disapprove them[19] — and such laymen need to be put in their place, and made to acknowledge the authority of the specialist in all matters to do with language. Geoffrey Nunberg, sometime professor of linguistics at Stanford, and senior member of the staff at Xerox's Palo Alto Research Center, wrote in a landmark essay that will be examined later that "it is impossible to talk intelligently about the language nowadays without having an idea of what the program of modern linguistics is all about…,"[20] and this is from one of the most tolerant and open-minded of the experts.

How linguists account for the usability of language despite constant change

Some opponents of change, or at least of particular changes, are supposed by enthusiasts for change to be worried that a perpetually changing language might make clear communication difficult or impossible, so linguists have attempted to reassure them by saying that there is a mechanism within language that maintains coherence even while it is in constant flux. Here are such reassurances from two eminent specialists in language change — one of them Peter Trudgill, and the other Jean Aitchison, Rupert Murdoch Professor of Language and Communication in Oxford University. Trudgill tells us that:

> Language change cannot be halted. Nor should the worriers feel obliged to try to halt it. Languages are self-regulating systems which can be left to take care of themselves. Languages are self-regulating because their speakers want to understand each other and be understood. If there is any danger of misunderstanding, speakers and writers will appreciate this possibility and guard against it by avoiding synonyms, or by giving extra context, as in the well-known *"I mean funny ha-ha, not funny peculiar."*[21]

This attempt at reassurnce fails. It is less than comforting to be told that there is no reason for us to be concerned over ambiguity, because people will always come up with some sort of workaround, however clumsy. Nor are makeshift *ad hoc* explanations normal *context,* any more than an artificial leg, however technically advanced, is a normal limb. For one thing, people do not always recognize that their words are ambiguous until their audience has reacted in a way that they did not intend. When I shout "Fire!" it is rather important that those addressed know immediately whether I mean "Run for your lives!" or "Pull the trigger!", for by the time I've noticed that their reaction is inappropriate, and supplied them with "context," untoward events may have occurred. In some cases an ambiguity will cause unintended consequences that cannot even be traced back to the original misunderstanding, let alone remedied. But even disregarding such cases, why should we willingly put up with situations in which verbal bandages have to be applied to bind up a wound that needn't have been suffered? Even if waste of time and energy were the only penalty for lexical ambiguity, why accept it cheerfully? Time and energy are our most valuable resources, and what wastes them wastes us.

The most striking point of the Trudgill passage, though, is his offhand description of the mechanism he has postulated: the way in which languages are "self-regulating" turns out to be that we speakers and writers regulate them. The truth that Trudgill is really describing under the euphemistic label of "self-regulation" is that speakers and writers will just have to keep compensating as best they can, in often awkward and verbose ways, for those changes that have diminished language's expressive power. If we speakers and writers bear the responsibility for regulating language, as Trudgill tells us we do, isn't it possible that rejecting some changes, at least while they are still young enough to be successfully opposed, is one of the ways in which we might carry out our regulatory function?

When we turn to Professor Aitchison, wondering whether she will have something more illuminating to tell us about how language coherence is secured even while change goes on ceaselessly, we find her saying

> Some inbuilt property in the human mind maintains all languages, everywhere.

"Some inbuilt property"? — that sounds even less scientific than Trudgill's explanation; in fact, it is uncomfortably reminiscent of the "dormitive power" that one candidate for admission to the medical profession offered to explain the soporific action of opiates.[22] In the absence of a rigorously scientific explanation of how languages somehow remain usable even while changing, I venture a suggestion: could this mysterious property in the human mind be what is sometimes called *critical intelligence or discrimination*?

It is symptomatic of their confusion that both Trudgill and Aitchison go on to invoke the thermostat as an example of what they mean by self-regulation. But thermostats do not regulate themselves; they regulate heating systems; they themselves are regulated, or set, by human beings. Once so set, they turn the furnace on and off to keep the temperature where their human masters want it, but they cannot turn *themselves* on and off, nor do anything other than the simple switching action some human has ordered. The thermostat analogy, like so many of the analogies offered by linguists, works against them, showing clearly where they have gone wrong. In their attempts to explain how language is stabilized, and in the thermostat analogy they offer to clarify it, they both offer vague and essentially meaningless verbiage to account for the phenomenon in question rather than accept the simple and obvious answer: human beings are making choices, some good, some bad.

If linguists approve of all changes, why don't they adopt them?

I said earlier that many linguists, though prepared in their official "language scientist" role to champion almost any change against the attack of prescriptivists, grammarians, and purists, wouldn't dream of accepting some of those changes for themselves, refusing to let them appear in their own writings. Here are a couple of examples:

Geoffrey Nunberg claimed[23] that the transformation of *disinterested* into a synonym for *uninterested* was a *fait accompli,* something no sensible person would waste time trying to resist any longer, even supposing that such resistance had ever been called for. But after all Nunberg says about the death of *disinterested* in the sense 'having no personal stake in the matter,' that's exactly how he uses it himself. In an e-mail message, we find him saying "I am far from a disinterested contributor to this thread [of conversation], since I wrote the usage notes to the AHD3 in my capacity as usage editor...."[24] — and it is fair to guess that he would be embarrassed to be caught using that word to mean "indifferent, unconcerned."

And Professor Trudgill, after pooh-poohing at some length the idea that it is important to distinguish between *imply* and *infer* — in almost every case, he claims, context makes it perfectly clear what is meant, so why make such a fuss about using these terms "correctly"? — creates for himself an opportunity to use *infer* in order to drive home the fact that he is quite aware of the meanings of the two terms, and uses them correctly:

> Now, it is undoubtedly true that if you use *infer* in this way [i.e., to mean *imply*], there are people around who will infer that you are uneducated or careless.[25]

And elsewhere he praises those who use the terms interchangeably as brave pioneers:

> but [Halpern] seems not to share my respect for individuals who happen to be in the vanguard of any particular change at any one time.[26]

So the man who misuses *infer* for *imply* is, in Trudgill's view, simply in the vanguard of an inevitable change that we will all go along with eventually, and is hence worthy of respect rather than scorn, and deserving of emulation rather than correction. I doubt that we will all fall in behind this "vanguard," but if Trudgill really believes what he says, why has he not shown his own respect for this brave pioneer by joining him in this new usage, rather than going out of his way to show that he, Peter Trudgill, knows very well how to use *infer*? It is typical of the descriptivists to pat the uneducated on their heads and assure them that some poor usage is just fine, even if they would never dream of employing such usages in their own work. On this basis they plume themselves on being 'democratic,' and charge their prescriptivist opponents with elitism.

It is also worth noting that in his discussion of the *imply-infer* confusion, Trudgill no longer maintains that a usage becomes part of the language only when "everybody does it" (see the quotation from him toward the end of the Simple Ignorance section). Now the usage is also to be accepted even if only a few use it, if those few are seen as a "vanguard" by some unspecified vanguard-spotter — a change must be accepted, it seems, in just about any case. Trudgill not only attempts to stack the deck so that he must win, but presumes to foretell the future as well. It is only long after the event that we can say that some small group of innovators constituted a vanguard, as opposed to a coterie of misguided and now forgotten cranks.

A review[27] by Tom Shippey, Professor of Humanities at St. Louis University, of a modern history of the English language (David Crystal's *The Stories of English*) notes this trait in his author:

> There is indeed a major contradiction in the whole work, which is that while it celebrates diversity [of usage] in every possible way, it is written throughout in flawless Standard English, with only the very occasional token "you ain't seen nothing yet" to break the flow. This is in a sense inevitable — the book wouldn't get printed otherwise — but one may also feel that the author is only theoretically sympathetic to non-standards.

One reply sometimes made to this charge of refusing to accept for themselves usages that they accept enthusiastically for others is that, as linguists, they are writing on highly technical matters, and have to observe conventions and distinctions that ordinary folks need not, and indeed might be better off ignoring. But note that the terms whose usage is under discussion, such as the *infer* & *imply* pair, are rather learned and literary words that most speakers of English go through life without using. The comparatively few who do use them are almost always writers who are trying to construct serious and sustained arguments addressed to the educated — writers who have to use these terms correctly if they want to be understood and respected by their readers. These words are, in fact, just such words as linguists themselves use virtually always correctly; if *they* find it necessary to observe the conventional rules when using them, to whom are they granting a license to use *infer* and *imply* interchangeably? The learned use these words correctly; the common folk don't use them at all — who's left?[28]

Change versus *changes* — too subtle a distinction?

Quite a few of the skirmishes between today's academic language specialists and their critics might be avoided if the specialists were fully alive to the difference between *change* and *changes*. When critics and usage guides protest a particular change, the specialists think they are seeing a rejection of change in general, and react with the scorn that might appropriately be directed toward such indiscriminate negativism. But none of today's critics or prescriptivists is actually against all change, or even most changes — something linguists could easily observe if they paid as close attention to their critics as they do to native informants. I think they react in this near-panicky way because defense of change is so important to them that they have quite lost the coolness necessary to make careful distinctions; speak up against any change, and they see the fundamental data of their discipline being taken away from them. What makes the situation especially regrettable is that there is no need for academic language specialists to protect the few usages that critics would like to discourage; there is no rational reason why those specialists should not study such changes even though critics are arguing agains them — there is no reason, in fact, why the specialists could not actually join those who would like to see a particular usage forgotten even while studying its origins and circumstances.

As should be clear from what has been said so far, a reasoned attitude toward change is one of critical discrimination: some changes are to be resisted with all our power; some ignored; and some welcomed gladly. Indeed, there are some changes that we critics of the linguistic attitude would ourselves introduce and institute if we were able to — criteria for deciding which changes fall into which category will be discussed later. That this attitude toward language change is the one taken here should be easily inferred, but it must be stated explicitly because linguists are very prone to describe their critics as stone-walling conservatives or even reactionaries who are against all changes, just as they themselves are in favor of all.

CHAPTER 2

How **L**anguage
is Studied
Today

Building
on air:
phonology as the
basis of
'linguistic science'

The scholarly study of language seems to have begun — we are dependent here on such texts and inscriptions as happen to have survived — millennia ago, reaching a very high level by the fourth century BC in the work of the Sanskrit grammarian Pāṇini in ancient India. Linguistics in the modern sense, however — linguistics not as grammatical scholarship in the service of religious ritual and the preservation of sacred texts, but as an aspirant to the status of science — dates from the late eighteenth century. A generally accepted starting point is the recognition in 1786 by Sir William Jones of the relationships among Latin, Greek, and Sanskrit that led to the idea of what is now called the Indo-European family of languages. That recognition inspired a century-long effort on the part of linguistic scholars to find other such relationships and families, and that effort bore so much fruit that nowadays the marvel is to find a language, like Basque, that seems to have no relatives.[29]

The triumphs of the great 19th-century pioneer linguists were almost entirely in phonology, the branch of linguistics that deals with the sounds by means of which words are conveyed in speech, and especially with the question of how these sounds change from one era to another, and one language to another, related one. Their studies, triumphs of imagination and learning, culminated in the various laws that summarize the great phonetic changes that have been observed in the Indo-European languages — Grimm's and Verner's Laws being the best-known (more about this in Appendix A). These substantial accomplishments seemed to establish the claim of linguists to be practicing a science — a discipline dedicated to discovering the laws that govern an order of nature. And so it seemed, for several exciting decades in the latter half of the 19th century and the first half of the 20th, that linguistics, now founded on rock, was taking its place among the natural sciences, and could soon be expected to produce the kind of rigorous and illuminating results that the others did. But although departments and journals of linguistics sprang up everywhere, the results achieved by what seemed in the early decades of the twentieth century a promising science have been disappointing. No findings even remotely comparable to the triumphs of nineteenth-century linguistics have been made, no great new principles have been formulated, no epoch-making discoveries have been announced.

The cause of that disappointment is, I think, easy to identify: it is the almost exclusively phonological character of these early achievements. The sounds used by the speakers of any particular language, interesting as they may be in some ways, are neither intrinsic nor universal characteristics of language in general; they are merely accidental and local features of one natural language or another. We know that a dog is just as much a *chien,* a *hund,* a *perro,* as a *dog,* which means that none of these names is the one true name of all canine creatures — all are aliases, none is the name Adam uttered when he first saw a dog. These various names are the result of thousands of historical events having no *linguistic* significance: displacement of one people by another as a consequence of conquest or natural disaster, migrations of tribes to richer grazing or hunting grounds, emulation of social superiors by subordinates. The linguistic consequences of these events may provide valuable evidence to historians, but tell us nothing about the essence of *language.* And if such temporally and geographically parochial names and the changes they exhibit and testify to are insufficiently general to lead to a deep understanding of language, the sounds we utter to convey them to others' ears are still less significant for that purpose. To believe that one has turned the study of language into a science because one has found some regular relationships among the sounds used to carry words is unwarranted.

But that belief underlies standard linguistic doctrine today: the claim of linguists to be practicing a science is based on the achievements of 19th-century European scholars in formulating the laws of sound change, mainly in the Germanic and Romance languages, and using these results to help establish the genealogical relationships among those languages. These were truly impressive results; they were roughly analogous to Darwin's preparatory work in collecting and classifying masses of information about the distribution and development of animal and vegetable species — but they were not followed, as Darwin's preparatory work was, by a momentous theoretical concept that subsumed and organized a great deal of existing knowledge, and pointed the way to the acquisition of much more. Linguistics has instead since the early 20th century dissipated its energies in pursuit of dozens of ever more divergent investigations and projects, with no sign of convergence into a unified vision like that of evolution by natural selection. One can understand today the elation of the early linguists as they began to make a little order in a subject that had been just a wilderness of anecdotes and random observations until their time, but while one can easily forgive them their exuberance, one must also acknowledge that their hopes have not been fulfilled, and one can see why.

The sound and the fury — does it signify anything?

In giving phonology so central a position within linguistics, linguists are making the best of what material they have. Phonology is where they have had their best if not their only triumphs, and they are understandably proud of them and eager to build on them. But the early linguists worked in that subfield of linguistics because little else was possible for them. The path of early linguistics, like that of any infant discipline, was determined less by what the pioneers' ultimate goals and interests were than by what their methods and data enabled them to do. What the pioneer linguists were able to do was to find regularities in the sound changes exhibited by the languages about which they had sufficient information, and, as noted, to arrange many of those languages in family trees — and they did this admirably. But those achievements were supposed to be only very preliminary steps, a clearing of the ground for investigations into the real mysteries of language, which are all concerned with *meaning,* not sounds. The question of how one sound evolves into another over time, or is replaced by another, is two removes away from what the world is really interested in: how thought generates words, and words in turn stimulate thought.

The eminent linguist Noam Chomsky, whose work will be discussed in some detail later, has offered a defense of the emphasis on phonology by linguistics, and the relative neglect or even shunning of semantics:

There is a widespread feeling that semantics is the part of language that is really deep and important, and that the study of language is interesting primarily insofar as it contributes to some understanding of these questions of real profundity. There is some merit to this view. Thus, the questions having to do with what people say and why, questions that relate to the "creative aspects of language use," are surely of great intrinsic interest, and are also invested with great mystery, in a sense in which the principles of rule ordering in phonology are not. Analogously, we might say that questions of human behavior are intrinsically interesting to us in ways in which the behavior of inanimate objects is not — but we would not therefore conclude that physics is superficial, in that it confines itself to inanimate matter and abstracts away from human acts (say, from the fact that the predictions of physical experiments can be falsified by human intervention, a fact that cannot be accommodated within physical theory, so far as we know). The significance of physics does not derive from the intrinsic interest of its subject matter; no one cares what happens under the exotic conditions of physical experiments, apart from the relation to physical theory.

Physics is significant, applications aside, because of its intellectual depth, and if it were to turn out that the principles of phonology are considerably more sophisticated and intricate than those of semantics, that they enter into nontrivial arguments to explain surprising facts, that they give us much more insight into the nature of the organism, then phonology will be a far deeper theory than semantics, despite the more limited intrinsic interest of the phenomena with which it deals.[30]

Chomsky has done us a service in reminding us that we are often wise to attend to the ultimately rewarding rather than the immediately gratifying step, and to pursue pure rather than applied research. And, he tells us, if phonology is what really explains more about hujman behavior than its superficially more attractive sister study, semantics, then it is phonology in which we must invest our resources. In saying this, he shows himself more clear minded and fair minded than most of his colleagues, who generally refuse to acknowledge that phonology is not, on its face, a promising avenue of approach to the deeper mysteries of language, and that it must earn its way by yielding impressive results. What Chomsky says here is, I believe, indubitably true, and his saying it is a credit to his integrity as an investigator.

But there are two problems with this argument of Chomsky's: first, his analogy is unsound; second, the possibility he asks us to entertain is so far-fetched as to tempt a critic to make a flippant reply. Physics is not and never purported to be an approach to the understanding of human behavior; it is an entirely separate study of an altogether different domain. There are those who are not interested in physics, and might strongly resist being made to study it, but no one, I think, would say "I regard physics as a failure because it isn't psychology (or sociology or history or any other study of human behavior)." Phonology as a component of linguistics, by contrast, does claim to be at least a stepping stone to the understanding of an aspect of human behavior — linguistic behavior — and is rightfully judged by what, in the end, it contributes to our understanding of that behavior.

So Chomsky errs when he suggests, in effect, that phonology is, or at least may be, to semantics as physics is to humanistic studies.

Then there is his suggestion that if phonology should somehow prove more illuminating than semantics, it, not semantics, would be the deeper, more important study. This is close to being tautological, and so of course true — trivially true. But it invites the sort of response that Hotspur gave to Owen Glendower. It might fairly be asked whether, so far from leading the investigation into the innermost nature of language, phonology has provided any illumination about language since it helped the 19th century pioneers of language study build a tree of language relationships. And if the answer is No, the further question of whether much more attention should be paid it arises, with the burden of proof lying squarely on those who would answer that it still deserves serious attention. (Of course phonetics may well deserve further attention for its value in speech therapy, theatrical training, and the like; what is being questioned here is just its continued relevance to linguistics.) Chomsky does not himself shoulder that burden in the book just quoted from, or anywhere else so far as I know, but he makes a real contribution by forthrightly declaring that linguistics must do so.

The demeaning of meaning

Words are interesting only because they convey meanings; speech sounds are interesting, insofar as they are at all, only because they convey words. What all of us who are not linguists (and even a few who are) are ultimately concerned with is, in the broadest sense, semantics — meanings. All other aspects of language are peripheral and ancillary. Unfortunately, linguistics has little to offer us here. There are of course many books on semantics, and countless papers in the linguistic journals, but their authors are far from claiming to have come up with *scientific* findings, even to the small degree to which phonology can boast of having done so. And this failure has resulted in a paradoxical situation: semantics, which is concerned with what should be the central issue for linguistics, is almost ostracized by mainstream linguistics, and for most linguists just barely hangs on as an auxiliary linguistic tool.

Here are a few comments by linguists, as reported by the semanticist Stephen Ullmann; examples could easily be multiplied:

> Ever since scientific rigor became the main aspiration of linguistics, the 'unscientific' nature of meaning brought that concept, and with it semantics at large, into disrepute. A leading American structuralist [Charles Fries] recently admitted that 'for many linguistic students the word *meaning* itself has become almost anathema'. The situation has been ably summed up by Professor W. S. Allen in his inaugural lecture at Cambridge: 'Meaning, as at least one linguist has expressed it, has become a "dirty word"; but if the name tends to be avoided, there is no doubt that every linguist employs the concept, although some would be unwilling to admit to such improper thoughts. And surely, without meaning linguistics cannot exist.'[31]

And later in the same book:

> The future of semantics will largely depend on its *status* within linguistics. There is no doubt at all that progress in this field was retarded, and at times almost brought to a standstill, by the climate of linguistics in the late 1930s and in the 1940s, when anything connected with meaning was frowned upon, or looked at askance, by many leading structuralists. ... This taboo has now [1962] been considerably relaxed, but there is still a marked reluctance in some quarters to handle problems of meaning. ... On a more theoretical plane, the same bias is seen in the marginal place which some linguists would assign to semantic studies.[32]

Ullmann goes on, immediately after this passage, to paraphrase Charles F. Hockett's division, proposed in his *Course in Modern Linguistics,* of linguistic topics into 'central' and 'peripheral' ones, with phonology (along with grammar and the morphophonemic system)

35

being central, and semantics (along with the phonetic system) being peripheral. He then quotes Hockett on the reason for this relegation of semantics to a secondary position:

> The peripheral systems are just as important as the central ones; the fact is, however, that they are much harder to study and that, so far, less has been learned about them.

Hockett's demotion of semantics to 'peripheral' status might seem strange to a lay observer, given his handsome admission that it is 'just as important' as, say, phonology. If subject A is just as important as subject B, but is harder to study and less understood, that would seem good reason to invest in its study resources at least equal to those devoted to B, rather than to demote it to 'peripheral' status. But linguistics is still in the primitive stage where the course taken by a discipline is almost entirely dictated by what its tools will let it do, and what linguistics can do does not include dealing with meaning, so meaning is neglected. One's only reservation about Ullmann's remarks applies to his claim that "the taboo has now been considerably relaxed." If mainstream linguists seldom say derogatory things about the study of meaning any more, it is because they long ago won their campaign against it, and feel no need even to mention it now. Something they call "semantics" is now admitted to a role in linguistics, but, as will be shown, it is hardly what has been traditionally known by that term.

The project of modern linguistics: building the Golem

To understand the state of linguistics today, in the early years of the 21st century, the major developments of the last century must be kept in mind. I've said that linguistics has split into at least a dozen distinct sub-disciplines whose respective practitioners usually have little to say to each other. But those who are generally regarded as mainstream linguists, and the direct heirs of the great 19th-century founders and giants of the field, are the transformational generative grammarians, and unless otherwise indicated, they are the ones I will mean henceforth when I say "linguists." They are the ones who try to answer such questions as how children learn languages so easily, how all of us can immediately understand and produce utterances that neither we nor anyone else have ever heard before, and how all of us, almost always, understand immediately anything said to us in English words — even, in most cases, when the words are not conventionally organized. Their efforts are now primarily devoted to the construction of a set of rules that collectively discriminate between acceptable and unacceptable sentences; that is, a virtual or "software" machine that would, for example, accept as correct the most complex sentences written by Henry James and postmodernist academics, but balk at "the cat on the mat sat."[33] And this machine is not seen by them — that is, by Chomsky and his school — as merely a "black box" that happens, in its own perhaps very different way, to analyze those sentences given it so as to yield the same judgments about their correctness that human minds arrive at. It is seen by them to constitute, to the degree to which it is perfected, a window into the workings of the human mind, almost a schematic of the actual wiring of the human brain.

At this point a terminological difficulty must be dealt with: the linguists who are trying to build such a machine call each successive approximation to it a "grammar" — a term so misleading that one wonders how people professionally concerned with words can bear to let it be so used. "Grammar" in ordinary usage refers to the rules we're taught in school: don't use double negatives, make sure your verbs agree with their subjects in number, use 'who' when it is the subject and 'whom' when it is the object, and so on — rules that are simply a miscellaneous collection of edicts of widely varying cogency and usefulness, and that do not aspire, as the new "grammar" of the linguists' does, to constitute a complete system for discriminating between acceptable sentences and unacceptable ones, much less an explanation of how the brain works with language. Chomsky acknowledges this quite explicitly:

... ordinary grammar books are concerned with a domain of facts that is virtually complementary to what is most significant for the project I have been discussing [of Universal Grammar, or the principles underlying all human languages].[34]

The result of using 'grammar' for both of these very different things is to cause frequent misunderstandings between linguists and laymen, and sometimes even among linguists themselves. I have no hope of persuading linguists to cease this offense against clarity, and when quoting them I will, of course, reproduce their *ipsissima verba;* otherwise I will use my own term. Since what the linguists are trying to create is a virtual machine that will show that it "knows English" by recognizing among the examples submitted to it all and only those that are good English, I will call it the Good Language Machine, or *Golem* for short.

Not all linguists would maintain that our heads actually contain a Golem — not all, that is, are followers in this respect of Chomsky — just as not everyone imagines that a baseball outfielder is actually engaged in solving differential equations as he runs to the spot where a fly ball will descend to where he can catch it. For many of them, the rules that constitute the Golem are meant only to be the formal equivalent of whatever goes on in our heads when we hear or read someone's English utterance, just as the equations of kinematics are simply the formal equivalent of whatever went on in the heads of Willy Mays or Joe DiMaggio as they robbed some batter of a base hit.

But while the Golem is for these less radical linguists only formally equivalent, not actually identical or analogous in full detail to the processes that go on in the human mind as it deals with language, it *is* supposed to be at least the full functional equivalent of what goes on in the head of a competent speaker of English as he decides whether some utterance is good English or not. But the best Golem that could be built by the linguists of the first half of the 20th century, the structuralists, was very far from being able to do that (the linguists of that era did not think of themselves as trying to build the Golem — the explicit acknowledgment of that goal had to await the coming of Chomsky — but that is what they were in effect doing.)

Their attempts took the form of analyzing sentences to yield diagrams — *trees,* in the technical jargon — similar to the sentence-parsing diagrams that used to be assigned as a standard exercise in English composition classes in elementary schools, and perhaps still are in some. Each of the words in their sample sentences would be labeled as to part of speech; then related words would be clustered and labeled as noun phrases or verb phrases or whatever type of syntactic unit they formed, and so on through clauses and, finally, complete sentences. As these diagrams became more technical and sophisticated in the hands of the structuralists, and were applied to more and more sample sentences, patterns of general acceptability and non-acceptability were observed and were collected and organized as small steps toward a general grammar of the language.

But these diagrams were restricted to dealing with nothing beyond the actual words of the sample sentences and the standard grammatical categories that school grammars had always recognized, and very little insight into the general patterns of acceptable and non-acceptable sentences could be discovered from that sparse base. Structuralists felt that going further than the words before their eyes, and what could be immediately inferred from them, was going beyond the evidence. As a result, their grammars — Phrase Structure Grammars, as they were called — were not fundamentally different from the tree diagrams produced in the schools for pedagogical purposes, and while analyses at this level may have been useful for giving high school or elementary school students some feeling for the structure of English sentences, they were totally inadequate to creating the Golem.

Such was the state of affairs in linguistics when, in 1957, the young Noam Chomsky burst on the linguistic scene with a proposal that linguists go far beyond such methods — a proposal that introduced the ideas of *generative grammar, deep structure,* and later *transformational grammar.* Chomsky, who had been trained like every linguist of his generation in standard structural methods, was the first to fully recognize their radical inadequacy, and to put forth an idea that got linguistics moving forward again. That idea was that the data linguists should be concerned with must include far more than the actual words of their samples and the standard grammatical labels for them and the simple phrases they formed — the "surface structure," as he called it. The evidence to be used must include, he contended, concepts that were drawn from the general body of knowledge about language usage that all articulate humans possess — what he called "deep structure."

He supported his proposal by showing that by using such additional information, one could define further rules, *transformations* as he called them, that enable the grammarian to deal with some of the problems found intractable by the Phrase Structure Grammars. A "transformation" is a restructuring of a sentence that moves words from one position to another; deletes a word or phrase, or replaces it with another; and so on — so as to convert the original sentence to another, semantically related one. A transformation might, for example, convert sentences in the active voice to their equivalents in the passive, or interrogative sentences to the declaratives that are their answers. What saves transformations from suspicion of being nothing more than *ad hoc* devices (like Ptolemy's equants and epicycles) for forcing a wanted result is that they work not just with selected examples, but with fairly broad classes of sentences, suggesting that they really reflect the way speakers form the required sentences.

Further technical details of Chomsky's work[35] are not relevant here (see Appendix D for more about his work); what matters for present purposes is that Chomsky broke the impasse in which linguistics found itself at the midpoint of the 20th century by liberating it from the idea that only the words immediately before one's eyes, and something close to standard schoolchild diagramming, could be used to analyze a sentence. So revolutionary were Chomsky's proposals, and so wide and deep their effect on linguists, that it would hardly be an exaggeration to say that mainstream linguistics has been ever since a series of footnotes to Chomsky. Of course much work has been done in the half-century since the Chomskyan revolution, and some young linguists now regard him as an old fogy, as is perfectly normal in the progress of any discipline, but whether linguists agree with him fully, partially, or not at all, they all still define their positions with reference to his.

Chomsky's greatest contribution may turn out to be the explicit setting of a goal for linguistics: that comprehensive and detailed set of rules or transformations that would collectively amount to the infallible discriminator between acceptable and non-acceptable sentences that I have called the Golem. What is important for present purposes is that the "grammar" so arrived at is still not enough — nowhere near enough — to constitute the Golem. Chomsky greatly enlarged the world of theoretical devices, if not evidence, that linguists could legitimately draw upon in constructing the Golem But it is still far from enough, as linguists recognize; probably no issue of any linguistic journal, or session of a linguistic conference, fails to include at least one example of a usage that the present approximation to the Golem cannot handle — and the finding of exceptions seems endless. Linguistics is back in an impasse, though at a higher level than it was when Chomsky first appeared.

After Chomsky's, what must the next revolution be like if linguistics is to make any further progress? I suggest that what is needed is a new conception of human communication,[36] and the role that language plays in it. In making Golem-building their project, linguistics seems to have conceived of communication between humans as an event in which a speaker encapsulates a complete thought in a tissue of words, and launches the resulting package at a recipient, who uses his grammatical knowledge — and only that — to unwrap the package of words, and thereby get the meaning that they carry. But this is an altogether misleading picture of what really happens. (I do not suppose that many linguists, when off duty, entertain so simple-minded a view of communication — but linguistic theory does.) The truth is that even the most explicit and detailed message from one human to another requires its recipient to bring to bear on it a tremendous body of preexisting knowledge, and make an effort of his own that is just as great as — sometimes even greater than — that made by the sender of the message.[37]

Verbal messages, even the most explicit and detailed, are of necessity highly concentrated shorthand, containing within themselves only a small fraction of the information needed to understand them; they work by evoking and activating the appropriate parts of their recipients' store of existing knowledge. This, by the way, is one of the most valuable lessons to be learned form the various attempts, during the last half of the 20th century, at realizing Artificial Intelligence and Machine Translation. What those projects did was to demonstrate just the point that a vast infrastructure of shared background knowledge must be available and put to use in order for a recipient to understand even the simplest kind of message (more on this point in Appendix C). The Machine Translation projects of the 1960's, which had as their goal not true comprehension by machine of the complete range of human utterances, but the much simpler one of translating strings of words in language A into equivalent strings in language B, failed, and in failing should have taught us that practically no human message — particularly no spoken message — can be translated with nothing more than a dictionary and a grammar, because the messages themselves do not contain all the information necessary for their comprehension. But unwelcome lessons like this one are never learned once and for all; they need frequent repetition. And this lesson about the major role played by the recipient, the apparently passive partner in any act of communication, is one that seems particularly in need of being re-learned today.

Chomsky has, however inadvertently, performed such a service for us in showing that the whole project of building a Golem is a dead end. And he seems to have recognized very early that that's what he might be accomplishing; in the book that first presented his new ideas to the world, he said:

> Precisely constructed models for linguistic structure can play an important role, both negative and positive, in the process of discovery itself. By pushing a precise but inadequate formulation to an unacceptable conclusion, we can often expose the exact source of this inadequacy and, consequently, gain a deeper understanding of the linguistic data.[38]

I think that the transformational model that Chomsky introduced has performed the service that he describes in the words just quoted;

it can teach us — but only if we are prepared to learn — that the amount of information that has to be available to the recipient of verbal messages is nothing less than the entire body of knowledge normally possessed by human beings, and the deeper understanding of language that Chomsky said would be our reward for pushing an inadequate model to the point of failure is now ours, if we wish to claim it: it is simply that the linguistic data — the actual words of the messages before us, augmented by all the explicit transformations of those words that our ingenuity can come up with — is radically and incorrigibly inadequate, and that the further pursuit of that model of linguistic understanding would be unrewarding.

Symptoms of trouble in the Golem project

What is accepted by all contemporary mainstream linguists is a fundamentally *formal* strategy for achieving understanding of language — one that minimizes, if it cannot altogether eliminate, *meaning*. The reason for this shying away from what is regarded by the rest of the world as the property that makes language interesting and important is one that does linguistics credit: if you want to show that language is amenable to scientific study, then you must restrict yourself to using scientific tools and methods, and no such tools or methods are available for the study of meaning. No doubt many linguists are aware that their discipline has not reached the heart of their subject — they surely realize that phonology and syntax are at most the suburbs and outskirts of language, while its citadel has barely been approached. But they would rather achieve scientifically sound results, even if in just peripheral and minor areas, than grapple directly with the core of language using inadequate tools. Such a strategy is sometimes mockingly described as looking for our lost keys under a lamppost, not because it is where we probably dropped them, but because the light is better there — but it is quite in order when we begin to study a department of nature; better to come up with small results that are solidly founded, and hence usable as stepping stones to further results, than to produce exciting but untestable speculations about one's ultimate objective.

But language is not a department of nature, and not amenable to scientific study at all, if only because it is not a body of phenomena that can be usefully studied in isolation. (See Appendix A for more on this.) To be fair, the more moderate defenders of the scientific pretensions of linguistics concede that it may not yet be a true science, and point to other studies that evolved from being jumbles of magic and superstition into true sciences: alchemy evolved into chemistry and astrology into astronomy. But the implied analogy does not hold when we turn to linguistics, the study of that aspect of human behavior that is speech and writing. The price of turning alchemy into chemistry was the giving up of the dream of acquiring wealth by transmuting base into noble metals; that of turning astrology into astronomy was giving up the dream of predicting a man's destiny from his natal date. If in both cases the price was high, what was purchased was so valuable that most of us are content with the bargain. But when linguistics asks us to defer or abandon the hope of understanding the way we form utterances, and the way they affect us, it offers us nothing we see as compensation — a scientific linguistics promises no great rewards, even if it succeeded far beyond the point it has so far. In the transformation of alchemy into chemistry and astrology into astronomy, getting rid of the "human element" was just what was needed to turn muddle into science; in linguistics, getting rid of the human element is what has kept the study from yielding anything of value.

Geoffrey Nunberg has offered us the following as a sample of the conundrums that a scientific linguistics will be able to solve for us:

> ... the rules of English allow us to say *Everyone has taken his coat* but not *Everyone left, didn't he?* Linguists have puzzled a great deal over examples like these, in an effort to understand the basic workings of English syntax; it is small wonder that they should have little patience with popular grammarians who blithely proclaim that the whole problem is simple, except for the thickheaded.[39]

Perhaps there is something important about this point of syntax that linguists have puzzled over, but if so Nunberg has not made it clear to us. There is the possibility, either unnoticed or dismissed by Nunberg and his colleagues, that there is no general rule or deep significance hiding behind this example — it may well be just one of the innumerable little special cases and irregularities that so much of language, like life, consists of. But let us suppose for argument's sake that enough puzzling would eventually yield a rule — say, "*Everyone* can be the antecedent of a singular pronoun in a declarative sentence, but not in an interrogative one" — what would be our gain? The linguist who first formulated the rule might enjoy a sense of accomplishment, and get a published paper out of it, but what would it contribute otherwise? It would be of no concern to the public, even the highly educated part of the public; it might not even interest the discoverer's colleagues. Is this a trivial example, not really representative of the profound issues that generally engage linguists? Perhaps, yet it is the one Nunberg chose in order to show us what linguistics does. I don't know any popular grammarians who have proclaimed, blithely or somberly, that "the whole problem is simple"; my own reaction to Nunberg's example is that linguists have their work cut out for them just to establish that it is deserving of the name *problem.*

Since the project of building the Golem — that system of rules that will distinguish good sentences from bad — is clearly in trouble, linguists have unbent so far as to admit some small amount of semantics into their councils as a possible help. So in one quite special sense semantics has been rehabilitated: orthodox linguists have found ways to make use of it, or at least of something they call by its name, in their traditional models of language. A landmark event in this development was the publication in 1971 of a 603-page collection of papers[40] under the title *Semantics: An Interdisciplinary Reader in Philosophy, Linguistics and Psychology.* Given the subtitle, one might expect to see the three disciplines mentioned there all contributing to semantics, but something close to the reverse is the case. For the linguists the point is rather to see how semantics can help them out of the new impasse they seem to be stuck in, without giving it an inch more. In their clearly demarcated third of the book, they make little or no use of the insights supposedly supplied by their colleagues in the other two disciplines. No great surprise here; a reader with any familiarity with the linguistic literature observes immediately that the linguists represented are among the established leaders of the Chomskyan school: Chomsky himself, Jerrold Katz, George Lakoff, James McCawley, Uriel Weinreich, and so on. And the papers themselves bear out one's expectation that all that these writers will try to do with semantics is, at most, to use meaning to fill in the gaps of the standard syntax-based model that most of the profession accepts and tries to build on in one way or another.

They are all members of the school that would ideally deduce which are the permissible word strings in the language and which are not from purely formal, meaning-free patterns found within the body of utterances they consider. Since such attempts quickly run into a stone wall — since they discover, that is, that one cannot do even the most elementary kind of sentence parsing without relying, openly or covertly, on the meanings not only of the words involved, but of the meaning of the sentence as a whole — it is little wonder that linguists have been forced to admit some token meanings into their model; they would be utterly bogged down if they could not.[41]

But it must not be supposed that linguists have finally welcomed semantics wholeheartedly into full membership in the profession, or indeed that any of the three disciplines represented in the *Reader* shows much use for any of the others. The book is, in truth, three distinct works bound together in one pair of covers. The names mentioned in the several papers, and the books and papers cited in their reference lists, testify to their fundamental independence of each other. The Philosophers refer almost exclusively to other Philosophers, the Psychologists to other Psychologists, while the Linguists largely confine themselves to arguments with other Linguists. When any of the three parties refers to either of the others, it is usually no more than a polite tip of the hat; little or nothing is made of their findings or arguments.

Are sentences regular components of speech?

Further difficulties confront the Golem-building enterprise. A fundamental one is that what linguists are trying to teach the Golem is to recognize sentences, when sentences are not characteristic of speech — they do occur frequently, indeed almost to the exclusion of other structures, in that quite different use of language, writing, but seldom in normal speech.[42] The true unit of spoken communication is the "minimal complete utterance": any utterance that is found meaningful by its recipient; any utterance that a speaker's interlocutor would recognize as a return of the conversational ball, or an answer to his question. The Golem, whose sole function is to discriminate between those utterances that are well-formed sentences and those that are not, is looking for something quite different from what human conversationalists regard as acceptable. The Golem is looking for utterances that satisfy a set of rules or transformations rather than those that succeed in conveying their intended messages to the intended recipients.[43] Whether a string of words that passes the Golem's test would in fact convey its intended message to a human being is of no concern to the Golem; it knows only that the string in question meets its mechanical criteria. The emphasis I am placing on communicative success as the criterion that should be used, a success that calls for a substantial contribution by the recipient of an utterance, is fully intended. Much of what is unsatisfactory in the standard linguistic picture of language use is, as I have said, its failure to see how greatly communication by language is dependent on a listener or reader who is as much concerned to understand as the speaker or writer is to be understood.[44]

In normal spontaneous speech, the occurrence of complete, well-formed sentences is exceptional, and when we do speak in complete sentences, they tend to be short, simple ones that exhibit very few of the intricate structures and convolutions that are needed to test the Golem. This is especially so in the highly informal and elliptical mode of speech that we adopt when among our family and close friends. When among our intimates, we speak in fragments, sometimes not even in words but just in grunts or other such noises; syntactic considerations are almost totally replaced by the right tone of voice and the private vocabulary that is possible within a circle of those who know each other very well.[45] But even when speaking to more general audiences, where we are on our better grammatical behavior, we are not really much bound by syntactic considerations. I offered earlier "the cat on the mat sat" as an example of the kind of ill-formed expression that the Golem would presumably filter out, while allowing all proper sentences to pass through unscathed. But in fact no speaker of English would have the slightest problem understanding this "ill-formed" sentence, even though he would take it as either an attempt by the speaker to be funny, or a sign that he was probably a recent immigrant who hadn't fully mastered English yet.

So in building the Golem the modern transformational grammarian is trying to produce a machine whose design is not only far beyond his present powers, but is not even directed toward the right end: it is being designed not to recognize instances of actual speech, but only highly idealized and contrived instances. This means that the Golem enterprise is, by the linguists' own standards, misconceived. Virtually all linguists agree that speech is linguistics' true subject matter, yet even though it is observable that sentences are not what speech is principally composed of, they are building a system to discriminate among just such structures.

But there is, of course, as just noted, a mode of language use that *does* produce such utterances as the Golem is built to discriminate among: writing. Written utterances are a rich source of just those full sentences and elaborate constructs that the Golem would look for with little success in speech. And in fact the Golem, if the practice of current linguists is any guide, would be fed a diet of written sentences masquerading as transcriptions of speech — actual speech samples, whether transmitted aurally or after transcription into some other system of signals, would leave the Golem famished. But more important even than the alimentary needs of the Golem, there are general considerations that strongly recommend that linguists pay far more attention to language in written form.

As we know, speech is normally accompanied by all sorts of ancillaries to help it with its communicative task — tone of voice, gesture, facial expression, body posture, immediate feedback from its recipient—that are not available to written communications.[46] (Dependence on these semantic auxiliaries is so much the rule that one commonly observes users of cell phones gesturing, smiling, and otherwise acting exactly as if their conversational partners could see them.[47]) But written words get no such help: they stand alone, bearing the whole burden of communication, and writers have to pay far more attention than speakers to their diction, and have to use a much richer array of linguistic resources to convey their ideas.[48]

In contrast to speech, then, the written form is language fully mobilized, deploying all the resources its writer commands, and showing what it can do without help from outside. If *language* is to be studied, surely this is the form its students should look to for their primary material. And in fact, by taking as "data" contrived sentences that bear little resemblance to normal speech utterances (see any modern linguistics study for confirmation), linguists have tacitly recognized this — but only tacitly. Linguistic doctrine still insists on the primacy of speech as grist for the linguistic mill, and linguists still routinely assert that they are trying to demonstrate the relationship of meaning and *sounds*.[49]

Perhaps linguists have taken the fact that speech precedes writing in the history of both the race and the individual — a precedence that we will not dispute, even though the available evidence is all on the other side[50] — as establishing priority in *importance*. If so, they are misled; the baby talks long before it even begins to learn to read and write, but this does not mean that speech is really language in full flower, any more than the baby's appearance or behavior are good indications of what to expect from an adult. Adding to the pressure on linguists to see speech as real language, and writing as little more than its shadow, is the fact that everyone talks, but few write unless they have to — which makes it natural for linguists, as "progressive" as most academics, to see speech as The People's use of language, and writing as the unnatural practice of an elite.

49

Does ambiguity present opportunities
for Golem-building?

Modern linguists, although they regard speech as primary, and writing as secondary, seem not to have noticed that when we talk to one another, language is only one, and not necessarily the most important, of the communication tools we are using. A symptom of this unawareness is the heavy use that linguists make of ambiguous sentences — ambiguous syntactically or lexically — in constructing the Golem. To enable it to recognize the two or more possible constructions to put on such a sentence, they augment it with the transformation rules that seem to be needed for the purpose. In doing so, they are overlooking or disregarding the obvious: the problematic sentences they contrive in order to pose interesting problems would present no ambiguity if actually uttered in a real conversation because, first, they would be embedded in a context that would usually make their meaning clear, and, second, they would be supported by all the non-linguistic communication devices listed earlier.[51] The Golem, having no access to such devices, is forced to try to account by endless proliferation of rules for what humans need no rule to understand, because they are getting further, and usually decisive, information through other channels.

Is it a virtue in a grammar to be
infinitely productive?

So central to the modern linguistic program is the contention that *A natural language comprises, at least potentially, an infinite number of sentences* that this proposition is called by one writer highly sympathetic to Chomsky "Chomsky's Axiom."[52] I think this proposition, so far from being axiomatic, is fallacious, and if it is taken as axiomatic, that is indicative of another trouble at the root of the Golem project. When Chomsky and his school insist that there is no end to the number of distinct sentences producible by a natural language, they are confounding the observable language with their model of it, the Golem. It is not the English language as we know it that is capable of generating an infinite number of sentences, it is only the Golem that can do so — but the Golem's behavior, for linguists, is apparently what counts. If in fact the Golem can generate an infinite number of sentences, that is a fault, due to an oversight: no one has gotten around to building into it an explicit rule against doing so.

Recall that the Golem is nothing more than a collection of the rules that make explicit the deep, largely subconscious knowledge or intuitions about their language shared by virtually all speakers of English. If all such speakers would agree that no natural English sentence can exceed (say) 10,000 words, why does the Golem incorporate no constraint, no negative transformational rule, that says so explicitly?[53] If someone, whether as a joke or as an attempt at a serious refutation of such a rule, were to generate, probably by means of a computer, a sentence that broke the rule, a critic could raise the ante, and make the limit a million words, or whatever number is needed to defeat the critic. And a string of words that long would count as a sentence only if one ignored the communicative function of sentences, and the role of the recipient in an act of communication: no string of words is a sentence if no one lives long enough to read it, let alone understand it.

The defender of Chomsky's Axiom might argue that while it is true that no one ever will generate an English sentence of 10,000 words, this is a merely contingent fact; in principle, he would say, English *can* generate such a sentence. But why are the limitations of human short-term memory, patience, and ultimately life span, negligible for linguistics? Such considerations have, in fact, influence on every aspect of language, including what Chomsky regards as fundamental to it, namely syntax. It may well be that in deciding that English can do whatever the Golem can, we are excluding from our study some of the most important facts about language.[54] Inferring the characteristics of the actual language from those of the model one is attempting to build of it is letting theory invent whatever facts it needs to survive — an especially unsound method to adopt when the theory itself is far from satisfactory.

CHAPTER 3

Linguistic Authority: Rules, Dictionaries, and Teaching

Rules
in the
classroom

Another fallacy about language, the
Fallacy of Pedantic Persecution, springs from a myth of the kind
that we freedom-loving Americans are especially susceptible to: the
myth holding that the language and its users are born free and
naturally creative, but are everywhere in the chains of pettifogging,
narrow-minded, reactionary, and mean-spirited pedants, sworn to
thwart aspiring young writers, to blight literature with oppressive and
irrelevant rules, and generally to take the bloom off the linguistic and
literary roses.[55]

This fantasy rests, in part, on the prime delusion that language is
a living, growing thing, so it is a derivative of the Linguistic Autonomy
fallacy. But it is so pervasive and hardy that it must be attacked in
its own right, treated as if it were an independent axiom of the
system. As the literate public must be convinced that language is
merely an aspect of human behavior, not an independent entity —
that it has no nature, no destiny, no desires, no "genius," no yearning to be free — so it must be convinced that schools, teachers, and
rules are not dedicated to the thwarting of literary genius, nor instrumental in doing so.

These delusions are reinforced when linguists and their allies in
academia warn us that we are beleaguered by schoolmarms threatening to crack our knuckles if we split an infinitive, use a double
negative, or commit any of the other solecisms that 19th-century teachers were so alert for, and which, no doubt, a few in the 21st-century

may still be. This delusion, in turn, fosters the suspicion that there are many potentially great writers who have been crushed and silenced by the strictures of these pedants, and that we have been deprived of many a masterpiece by such oppression. The best short retort to these fevered imaginings is that of Flannery O'Connor:

> Everywhere I go I'm asked if the university stifles writers. My opinion is that they don't stifle enough of them. There's many a bestseller that could have been prevented by a good teacher.[56]

Unfortunately there are not enough good teachers, and those angry rebels who would free language from the shackles of the pedants are often rebelling against an early bout with bad teaching. Not that the teaching need be bad to arouse student hostility: there is frequently a conflict between the young writer, who generally wants to write stories about himself and his feelings, and the teacher — the possibly very good teacher — who is more interested in teaching him the craft of writing than in giving him an opportunity to "express himself." That good teacher may seem to the adolescent writer to be just the stifling pedant that popular fantasy paints, but what the young Great American Novelist does not know, and his teacher does, is that in a few years his early Sturm und Drang productions will embarrass him to the point where he will try to destroy all copies of them. The lessons taught by his old teacher, on the other hand, will come to seem more and more pertinent and useful, and he will often feel gratitude later in life for just those precepts and comments that enraged him as a student.

Some of the hapless instructors whose job it is to try to turn semi-literate and even positively anti-literate adolescents into tolerable writers fall back, in desperation, on rules as a way of breaking their students of at least their worst practices — they know that no body of rules will ever turn a bad writer into a good one, but the sheer number of poorly-prepared and often hostile students they have to cope with forces them to reach for the crudest and nearest of tools. So they tell their charges not to use the passive voice, or not to end a sentence with a preposition, or not to start a sentence with *and*, and so on. These rules

— even the few for which there is some rational basis — do not help the poorer students, and they depress or even infuriate some potentially good ones. And many of these last will store up lifelong resentment against all rules and all authority on the foundation of the frustration they experienced at school.

These schoolchild grievances remain smoldering in many adult minds, and need only a whiff of oxygen to flare up even after many years. When some time ago I incidentally said a good word about rules in a magazine article,[57] a number of readers demanded that I specify just what rules I had in mind, or, assuming that I must be championing the very rules that they had been tormented with as schoolchildren, simply poured scorn and outrage on me for defending such foolishness or wickedness. My suggestion that there might be a place in language usage for rules, to judge by the mail the article provoked, exercised my readers far more than all the rest of my points taken together, controversial though they were. Clearly there is something very troublesome to many English-speakers about rules, and much of the trouble is due to poor understanding of what rules are supposed to accomplish.

The proper role and use of rules

I think there are three general points about grammatical rules that need to be grasped: they are artifacts, they are not intended to produce good writers, and they are not lessons but reminders.

1: By *rules* I don't mean *laws,* such as those that linguists find in the history of sound changes. A grammatical *rule* is an edict intended to regulate writers (and to a lesser extent speakers) of English, not to discover what they have done or are doing; its aim is prescriptive, not descriptive. I'll use *laws* when discussing the regularities found by linguists, *rules* for the judgments laid down by grammarians. Some protest against rules, calling them *arbitrary;* I can accept that description, but only with the understanding that *arbitrary* does not in such a context mean *mindless, capricious,* or *oppressive,* it simply means a *convention,* something that does not claim to have been discovered in nature. It is instead a judgment or decision taken by some authority, declaring some form of behavior to be acceptable or not. It is almost always the result of much debate and balancing of equally desired but mutually exclusive goods — if it is arbitrary, it is so in a sense closely related to *arbitration:* a way of resolving disputes on complex matters in such a way as to preserve civilization, which cannot survive without them.

The classic example from outside the linguistic world of a rule is the injunction to keep to the right when driving. We know that it is only a convention, but it is none the worse for that — it does sort us out on the road, and virtually eliminates the head-on collisions that would result

from allowing drivers to decide for themselves, as free-born citizens, which side of the road they would keep to. If a critic were to protest this rule on the grounds that it was — in the bad sense — arbitrary, and that no objective grounds could be found for preferring the right to the left here, he would find little support; it is accepted universally that while it matters not at all whether we all keep to the right or the left, it matters a great deal that we all keep to the *same* side — and the rule accomplishes that, while not, so far as we can see, infringing on anyone's rights. One would not have infringed on the rights of Buridan's ass by giving him a shove to one side so that he'd have a reason to go to the bale of hay on that side, rather than starving for want of good grounds for a preference.

(But note that even so widely accepted a rule can breed misunderstandings in the minds of those who are determined to see design or natural law behind all phenomena. A Martian sociologist observing North Americans from his flying saucer might conclude that it was a law of nature that we Earthlings drive on the right, and might hypothesize a connection between our driving on the right and the right-handedness of most of us. His colleague, whose saucer was hovering over London, would likewise believe he was observing a law of nature at work, but would find himself embroiled in scholarly quarrels with the first observer when they got back home. Luckily for Martian academic peace, they could at least agree that stopping at a red light was an undoubted law of nature on this mysterious planet.)

Grammatical rules are attempts to regulate linguistic traffic so that we don't collide with each other. They are neither divinely inspired nor scientifically founded, but they are necessary for civilized life. Some of them are faulty, just as some traffic regulations are faulty — every driver has encountered unrealistic speed limits and badly placed stop signs. Similarly, many grammatical rules that once commanded respect and obedience we no longer observe: the prohibitions against splitting infinitives, ending a sentence with a preposition or starting it with *and*, and others like them, have been, as it were, repealed. But to conclude that rules as such have been discredited and should be ignored is wrong and dangerous.

2: An argument frequently made by linguistic freedom fighters is that rules don't make good writers. Of course they don't; they were never intended to. They do for writers what pitons do for mountain climbers: they work to prevent mistakes from becoming disasters. Teachers are particularly prone to disparage rules for not making good writers, because teachers in America are being asked to turn the unwilling and the unable into writers, and this impossible task makes them desperate for an answer, which the rules disappoint them by not supplying. What makes a good writer — apart from the innate qualities involved — is good reading and much writing. Neither of these preparations can be realistically required of the unwilling — a category that includes the great majority of students today. As noted earlier, huge numbers of students today are positively anti-literate, feeling genuinely aggrieved when asked to read or write. And even if one could somehow induce them to do either, it would do them no good; no transmitter, however powerful, can get through to a receiver not tuned to the right frequency.

The hardest thing of all for teachers to face is that the students who refuse to learn to read and write in any except the most rudimentary way are bearing witness to a truth that the education establishment averts its eyes from: they would be wasting their time on books. They know, even if their teachers don't know — or cannot admit — that reading and writing will play very little part in their lives; they get little enjoyment or profit from reading, and as for writing, they don't need it because they have nothing to say. Why labor to master the art of good writing unless one feels that one has a vision or a message of importance to impart? It is futile to try to force anyone to exert himself to acquire a skill for which he feels no present need, and rightly foresees no future need, unless you are prepared to use measures as harsh as those used to motivate unwilling scholars a century and more ago.

Given the hordes of recalcitrant students they have to deal with, and the impossibility of actually teaching them to be good writers, many teachers fall back, in desperation, on inculcating rules instead. True, it won't improve the students' reading and writing skills, but then nothing (at least nothing politically possible) will do that — and driving rules into their heads may just possibly get them to avoid some solecisms, and — an important consideration — it is something they can be tested on. This is an enormous waste of time, talent, and energy, but that's not the worst of it; it also has the effect, as we noted, of instilling a contempt for rules — any and all rules — in those students, and helps them grow up to be instinctive anarchists who believe that all rules were created simply to frustrate and torment them. And all this is the predictable result of a "politically correct" refusal to recognize that not all are equally educable, and that the attempt to educate everyone in the same way and to the same degree is a disservice to all, including the supposed beneficiaries of that policy.

3: An evil that follows from neglecting point 2 is that rules are presented as lessons instead of what they should be, reminders. To the average student of our time, rules are utterly arbitrary (in the pejorative sense), pills that have to be choked down along with all the other meaningless things he has to swallow in school. The better student may wonder briefly *why* he mustn't split an infinitive or use the passive voice, but he is not likely to wonder long, and if he does persevere long enough to ask, he is not likely to get a satisfactory answer, because the average teacher isn't sure himself. And this is inevitable, because even the best rules are not *meant* to explain or teach anything. They are not enlightenments, just reminders, short-hand mnemonic devices, for what a student is supposed to have absorbed through much reading, and through the comments he's received on his essays — by themselves they do little or nothing to make a good writer, any more than a book of recipes can make a good cook. Offered to students who have not done that reading and seldom got good editing for their writing, they are meaningless and useless. Instructions to restaurant staff to wash their hands before returning from the bathroom to the kitchen would be similarly incomprehensible to those who hadn't learned about germs and disease.

You do not understand a rule until you know when to ignore and disobey it. It may be that the circumstances in which it would be best to ignore it are very rare, and one may never need to do so, but there is a great deal of difference between obeying a rule blindly, and obeying it because you know that it makes sense in present circumstances — but would not in others. And to put a rule in someone's hands without making sure he understands it is to put a dangerous device in the hands of a child. "Shun the passive voice!" many authorities tell us. What they really mean — if they have any sense — is "Make the active voice your normal, default choice; use the passive only where it is clearly called for — but then use it without hesitation," and if we know this, we may get some benefit from the rule; at least we won't be harmed by it. But if we take the rule on faith, and simply eliminate the passive from our rhetorical resources, we partially disable ourselves as writers, and turn out some deformed and maimed sentences. ("Shun the passive voice!" is itself a mild example of the distorted emphasis caused by refusal to use the passive voice; rhetorical logic would demand "The passive voice is to be shunned!") An example will be offered in the course of examining the rules proposed by George Orwell.

We know what results in public life from following or enforcing rules literally and mindlessly: disaster. In some industries, employees who want to put pressure on their management often do so by "working to rule"; that is, by following every rule and regulation absolutely and literally, untempered by common sense — with the result that the business or other enterprise affected slows down to the point of collapse. In the anarchistic story *The Good Soldier Schweik,* the hero defeats his military superiors by carrying out their orders to the letter. The results of blindly following "the rules" — even the best of rules — in writing and editing is no less destructive.

Orwell's rules: the exception to the rule?

Virtually all the usage rules proposed over the years, whether by private grammarians or official academies, have been disregarded and even derided by the writers and speakers who were supposed to follow them; the very idea of rules has been discredited among most intellectual workers of the Western world. The rejection is particularly drastic in the English-speaking countries, where it is led by academic linguists like Jean Aitchison, whom we have already been introduced to. So it is most remarkable that she should quite happily make an exception of one set of rules — that proposed by George Orwell — and it is instructive to see what kind of usage rules win the approval of a specialist who is otherwise among the most implacable enemies of rules. In the essay cited earlier[58] she reprints Orwell's rules in what she calls "slightly rephrased" form; I reprint them here as Orwell wrote them:

1. Never use a metaphor, simile or other figure of speech which you are used to seeing in print.
2. Never use a long word where a short one will do.
3. If it is possible to cut a word out, always cut it out.
4. Never use the passive where you can use the active.
5. Never use a foreign phrase, a scientific word or a jargon word if you can think of an everyday English equivalent.
6. Break any of these rules sooner than say anything outright barbarous.

It is an example of the justice, or perhaps the sense of humor, of Providence that someone who generally disdains rules should, when making her one exception, fall victim to one of the weakest sets of rules ever proposed. I much admire Orwell, and I think that his instincts about language are as sound as his political instincts — indeed, they are just two aspects of the same good sense — but even his rules, as I try to show in the critique that follows, are useless or worse.[59] Orwell himself may be forgiven much, since he was much provoked, but for descriptivists like Aitchison to cheer for his rules is simply a symptom of confusion.

The first of Orwell's rules, trying to prevent us from sounding "bookish," forbids us to use almost anything we have seen in our reading. (Aitchison, in her rephrasing, makes his prohibition even stronger; she simplifies it to "Never use a metaphor you've seen in print.") But what if we have been reading books by authors who write clearly and simply — books like Orwell's, for example? And if we read widely, there are very few useful figures of speech that we are not used to seeing in books — this rule would make it virtually impossible to write at all. What he is doing here is using his own youthful experience as the basis for a far-reaching rule, and that experience is much too narrow to support the rule.

He was an Edwardian by birth, and with his interest in the rough side of life, must have found little of interest in the kind of heavily "literary" writing that was the staple of the period. But by the time he formulated his rules, Modernism had been in full swing for a generation, and the leading writers much preferred being thought barbarians to being thought genteel — it was early in the '20s that the literate began to prefer Caliban to Ariel. Accordingly, his prohibition against using the figures of speech found in books was even when he issued it an anachronism; if he were living today, he would be appalled at how few are literate enough to write bookishly or in any other intelligible way.

His second rule sets up a spurious opposition between "a long word" and "a short word" — spurious because one virtually never meets in practice a choice between one long word and a fully equivalent short one; what one has to choose between is almost always one long word and *a string* of short ones — and there's no way of saying, in general, which is best; each case is unique. And even in the uncommon case when we do have a long and a short word that are close enough in meaning to make either acceptable, the choice is not automatic. It is not true, despite what Orwell seems sometimes to suggest, that the short word, of good old Anglo-Saxon stock, is always more pungent and effective than the long Latinate word, even though the long one may have been adopted originally as a euphemism.

When a euphemism has been in use long enough to take on the connotations of the simpler, shockingly direct word it replaced — which it inevitably does, even though it was adopted just because of its freedom from those connotations — *it* becomes the term of power, the term that reaches our gut. Tell me that Marie Antoinette or Jayne Mansfield had their heads chopped off, and I remain unaffected; your expression is so crude, so cartoonish, that it leaves me untouched; tell me that they were *decapitated,* and I feel that frisson that means I have fully taken in the reality. In a world where the fearful and the shameful are regularly described in euphemisms and bland circumlocutions, it is euphemisms and circumlocutions that terrify us; a simple blunt word is almost a relief.

The third is Occam's Razor, applied to words rather than concepts, but just as useless: *when* is it possible to cut a word, assuming it had some function to begin with? Another rule that requires so much interpretation that it becomes mere excess baggage.

The fourth advises changing the passive to the active voice whenever possible — which is to say, always. But as writers keep discovering, the passive has a unique and important function: it is the voice that meets our needs whenever we want to focus attention on an action or its object rather than the actor or subject, and to force such an utterance into the active voice is to distort and falsify our meaning. Here is a writer making an important distinction by means of the passive; try to make the point as sharply and economically without it:

What is important is not that I should correct and explain Juvenal, but that Juvenal should be corrected and explained...[60]

It is true that the passive is to be used with discrimination — but then, what feature of the language is not?

To understand why Orwell formulated so silly a rule, recall that he was writing in an era that was, and not only to him, one of unparalleled deceit and muddle.[61] Torrents of official lying and evasiveness during the years leading up to World War II had driven him to propose extreme measures in his campaign to restore decency and clarity to public discourse. One of the standard devices of politicians and bureaucrats seeking to evade responsibility is the passive voice, with its reticence about just who said or did the thing in question — "no names, no pack drill," the civil servant mutters as he issues a press release saying "mistakes were made." Orwell, in his zeal to end the abuse, proposed the drastic measure of rejecting the passive voice altogether. But this is the remedy that kills the patient along with the disease: the passive is an irreplaceable resource of the language; forbidding it will not diminish human dishonesty or muddle-headedness; and the *maxim abusus non tollit usum* — "the abuse does not invalidate the proper use" — holds in language as in law.

The fifth mixes several quite different things: for real scientific words there are no everyday English equivalents — that's why scientific terms are coined. Jargon? Sometimes quite in place, as when one is talking shop with colleagues, and even for some special rhetorical purposes when writing for a more general audience. The foreign term? Sometimes pretentious verbiage, sometimes the *mot juste* (see Appendix G). Here as elsewhere, Orwell is so determined to get rid of impediments to clarity that he throws out baby, bathwater, and the tub as well.

The sixth, which some admirers of Orwell's rules think his masterstroke, is the final seal on his failure; all the rules just given, it turns out, are to be ignored if they violate an implied rule against the Barbarous — a concept about which we are given no information whatever.

If even so admirable a writer, critic, and moralist as Orwell cannot state a rule that is of much use, are we to conclude that there are no good rules, and that the effort to formulate them is simply a waste of time? I think not; I think that rules are in fact of the highest importance, and that the effort to formulate good ones should never cease. (Some good ones are to be found in Graves & Hodge 1943.) I will not pursue the topic any further here, profoundly important though it is; I have dealt with it to the extent I have only because I think it important to show how, on the subject of rules, an eminent academic linguist is at least as lost as the typical layman, and far more so than the working writer.

Dictionaries and usage guides: filling the power vacuum

Next in this survey of attitudes toward language, consider the *Fallacy of Linguistic Anarchism*. In matters of language usage, as in religion, morals, and politics, the trend of our time is revolt against authority. Contemporary man is resolved that nothing and no one is going to tell him what to do — not church, king, parent, community, school, or books. His sovereign will alone determines what he does and thinks, and as for what his will will will, that is no one's business but his, or its, or — well, whatever. I am not concerned here with the effect this doctrine has on other aspects of human life, but its effect on speech and writing has been what one would expect of a determination to saw off the branch on which one sits.

It has made us simultaneously bold and timid: we want to be the final judge of how we say our say, but we also want to be correct — we want to do as we please, but we also want our audience to both understand and respect us. So we demand of our dictionary, for example, that while not daring to tell us explicitly what is correct and incorrect, it should nevertheless guide us to the usage that will achieve for us our double goal of being understood and respected. (See *A step toward rescuing the dictionary*, below, for how one dictionary attempts to do this.) Our double demand of our dictionaries is rather like our double demand as children that our parents should not restrict us in any way, but should nevertheless protect us from danger, hardship, and embarrassment.

In questions of language usage, the demand that we shall eat our cake, have it, and not grow fat, is especially difficult to meet, because even those who are most militant in the fight against the notion of "correct" English sometimes need to use words that will mean the same thing to others that they do to themselves. And at least on such occasions we find ourselves wanting to know what is correct, and we look for the dictionary that we know is around somewhere. But when we find it, our problems are compounded. Until well into the twentieth century, dictionaries, grammars, and other such guides and reference books were forthrightly prescriptive — they made no bones about telling their readers "This is right" and "This is wrong." Starting about the middle of the 20th century, however, these authorities lost their nerve, and for the most part have stopped making such explicit judgments about our speech and writing. The cause of their surrender of authority was two-fold: academic linguists often were successful in undermining the traditional lexicographers' pretensions to competence at their business (and with it, their self-confidence), and champions of the common man protested any attempt to lay down rules on matters of usage to free-born citizens.

The result is that many books that inexperienced readers still regard as authoritative are merely stenographic: they no longer profess to offer expert opinions and judgments, they merely record the phenomena. Their compilers read the books and articles that come their way, listen to the speech they hear the public utter, and record the usage they observe in those sources as closely as possible in their own books, passing no judgment on any of it. So when the reader turns to one of these works for a rule or at least advice on what he should say or write, he is not consulting an expert, he is merely looking into a mirror.

Sometimes readers realize that they are being denied guidance, and complain; more often they don't, and take the presence of some locution in such a book for approval. Thus, they may be led by some supposedly authoritative guide to think that *imply* and *infer* mean much the same thing, or that *reticent* means *reluctant,* and the like. The readers are mistaken; the compilers of these books are merely saying that they have found those terms used that way in some of their sources, and that they are not presumptuous or courageous enough to call such uses wrong.

The immediate problem caused by this abdication of authority — an abdication largely unnoticed by the general public — is that the common reader often thinks his questions have been answered when they have in fact only been thrown back at him: he asks, "Is it OK to use *imply* for *infer?*", and echo answers "...use *imply* for *infer.*" The longer-term problem is what follows all abdication of authority in the absence of a legitimate successor: it does not mean that we are now free; it means only that a new authority, probably less legitimate and less restrained, has silently taken over.

Somebody or *something* is going to determine the way we speak and write; *somebody* is going to make decisions on usage — there is no such thing as a vacuum or moratorium in language use any more than in politics. We must keep speaking and writing; we cannot defer usage decisions while waiting for linguists or anyone else to carry on further research and arrive at a consensus, nor can we, alternatively, invent for ourselves a language and a set of rules for using it. We can only choose among authorities, and only among those we know of. And if the authorities on usage are not to be the best writers of the recent past and present, and the critics and teachers with whom we study them, who are they to be? Television personalities? Rock stars? Gangbangers? Funeral directors? Gossip columnists? Telemarketing consultants? Or will we settle for the judgment of Sir Echo, soothingly confirming all our choices?

The linguistic libertine, who wants the advantages of absolute freedom plus those of the coddled child, invariably falls into the hands of one or more of the familiar figures listed above. Children whose parents have refrained from teaching them a code of behavior, so as to allow them to choose one for themselves when they reach their majority, do not in fact remain in a limbo of manners and morals until then, but join the local gang and adopt its code; a dog left masterless does not live independently, but joins the local pack of feral dogs, and submits to its alpha male.

A dialogue with a dictionary editor

Not long ago a professional lexicographer was provoked by an unfavorable review of a dictionary into responding to criticism at some length — an uncommon occurrence, and one that sheds light on the way academic linguistics has influenced lexicography. The provocation occurred when Robert Hartwell Fiske, the editor of the on-line monthly *The Vocabula Review*, reviewed for the conservative journal *The Weekly Standard* the new (eleventh) edition of *Merriam-Webster's Collegiate Dictionary*, and found severe fault with it. In response, Erin McKean, editor of another on-line journal, *Verbatim*, and — more important — senior editor of American dictionaries for the Oxford University Press, wrote the following letter to *The Weekly Standard*:

I began Robert Hartwell Fiske's review of the MW11 with great interest, but ended it with an even greater incredulity.

Fiske argues that lexicographers are adding ephemeral and "illiterate" words to their dictionaries, and that by doing so that they are encouraging illiteracy. As an example he cites the conflation of "disinterested" and "uninterested" — but neglects to mention the nearly twenty lines (a great deal of space for a college dictionary) that the editors of MW11 have included at "disinterested" explaining the development of meaning of these two words, the historical basis for using "disinterested" to mean "not interested in," and the fact that actual evidence shows that the meaning "not having a selfish motive or interest" is, in fact, the most used sense — so that the "vanished distinction" that Fiske laments is actually alive and well.

Fiske's other examples are similarly straw men; he cannot seem to grasp that the modern dictionary is not a portrait of the language, idealized by a sycophantic painter, but instead a mirror held up to show what the language actually looks like, warts and all. Thanks to vast improvements in the collection and analysis of language data, lexicographers can now report what people actually write (and, to a lesser extent, say), instead of what people think they write and say (and any scientist will tell you that self-reported data is at best

misleading and at worst worthless). Even a dictionary with a relatively small collection of language data, or a collection that's mostly
citations instead of running text, such as *Merriam-Webster's*, can now
rely on actual evidence instead of upon the introspection of lexicographers, who, if they were average speakers of English, would not
be lexicographers.

Would Fiske complain that the phone book lists the numbers of
shady businesses and people who are not nice to know? That the
almanac persists in listing facts about Iraq and North Korea, and
that his map refuses to obscure the roads in the red-light district
of his town? All of those reference tools provide many fewer helpful warnings to their users than a good dictionary.

Many of the "solecisms" Fiske rails against have a history of use
in educated, edited English going back hundreds of years, and some
have been used by well-respected and much-admired authors. Most,
if not all, of them are mere shibboleths, or at best, matters of taste
where people in good conscience can differ.

If Fiske wants a book to guide users as to what is the highest
generally-accepted standard of educated English, I recommend a
good usage manual (such as Bryan Garner's *Dictionary of Modern
American Usage*). He should leave the lexicographers to do their
jobs — reporting the facts, however ugly they may be to his eyes.

Sincerely, Erin McKean

This letter is a precious document, exemplifying very nearly all the
important fallacies on which modern English language dictionaries —
that is, those compiled since *Webster's Third New International Dictionary*
appeared in 1961[62] — are based. To begin with, it shows that McKean
suffers from the same disability that afflicts virtually all academically
trained linguists when confronting critics of their views on language
usage: they find it so impossible to believe that anyone of sound mind
can knowingly differ with those views that they simply ignore plain statements to that effect. Thus, McKean writes that Fiske "cannot seem to
grasp that the modern dictionary is ... a mirror held up to show what
the language actually looks like, warts and all." On the contrary, that

is what Fiske has grasped very firmly — and what he is attacking: the very policy that McKean boasts of, and rather patronizingly thinks he needs to have called to his attention. Several passages in Fiske's review show that not only is he aware of the lexicographic policy McKean thinks he's ignorant of, but wrote his review precisely because he knows about it, and opposes it. Here are three of those passages, taken from various places in his review[63]:

> "Laxicographers" all, the Merriam-Webster staff reminds us that dictionaries merely record how people use the language, not how it ought to be used.

> And if there are enough uneducated people saying *disinterested* (and I'm afraid there are) when they mean *uninterested* or *indifferent,* lexicographers enter the definition into their dictionaries.

> All it takes for a solecism to become standard English is people misusing or misspelling the word. And if enough people do so, lexicographers will enter the originally misused or misspelled word into their dictionaries, and descriptive linguists will embrace it as a further example of the evolution of English.

McKean was doubtless unhappy at the way Fiske put it — she could not have been pleased at being called a *"lax*icographer," and such terms as "solecism," "uneducated," and "misused" make linguists wince — but how could anyone capable of reading at elementary-school level have read the remarks of Fiske's just quoted, and then claimed that their author "cannot seem to grasp" that the modern dictionary is just a mirror of actual speech, not a filter screening out undesirable usages? Unfortunately, illiteracy of this highly selective kind is endemic among linguists and lexicographers.

Not only does Fiske know what modern dictionaries do, he even knows something about them that McKean doesn't: he knows that the users of dictionaries — especially collegiate dictionaries — are not lexicographic researchers or students of linguistics. They do not want or need the raw data whose preservation and presentation McKean regards as the glory of the "modern dictionary." When the buyers of the new Merriam-Webster turn to it, it is either because they have come across in their reading a word that they're unfamiliar with, and want to know what a published writer means when he uses it, or because they themselves are writing, and are looking for guidance on diction and spelling — guidance on how to say something so that their readers will both understand and respect them. Being told what was thought cool by the mall rats of the day — or more likely, of many days ago, when the dictionary they're consulting was compiled — does them no service whatever. The only audience for much of what McKean calls a "modern dictionary" is the linguistic historian who wants a sampling of the jargon teenagers, television show hosts, and other such segments of society employed at some moment in the past. This is a very small and highly specialized audience, and foisting on college undergraduates and other general readers a collection of data valuable — if at all — only to such specialists is fraudulent.

And we need have no fear of depriving that small minority that is concerned with slang of the information they need — slang would hardly go unrecorded if college-level, general purpose dictionaries failed to cover it. Ever since 1785, when Captain Francis Grose's *A Classical Dictionary of the Vulgar Tongue* was published, work after work has appeared expanding on and continuing his work.[64] Grose's own book is in print, and a number of language students, notably Eric Partridge for (mainly) British slang and Wentworth & Flexner for that of the United States (to mention only modern English-language studies), have carried on the task. Partridge's *A Dictionary of Slang and Unconventional English* is only the largest (1429 pages in its 8th edition) of several such collections made by him; others include studies of military jargon, the argot of criminals, and so on. For any serious study of slang, the student would have to consult these specialized dictionaries; the relative handful of slang terms that a collegiate or even general unabridged dictionary could offer wouldn't begin to satisfy his needs. So for almost all users the collegiate dictionary's coverage of slang is wholly unnecessary; for the exceptional reader who really needs to learn about slang, it is pathetically inadequate.

Some linguists and lexicographers take refuge behind cardboard signs reading *Science* and *Democracy* when criticized for their failure to provide dictionary users with the help they want and thought they were going to get when they consult such works. As *Scientists,* they claim they cannot favor some data points and suppress others — that would be to falsify data, the Original Sin of science! — and as champions of *Democracy,* they feel they have no business telling anyone that his usage is wrong — that would be judgmental and elitist! But scientists other than the linguistic variety do not regard it as their obligation to dump their raw research findings on people who want to know, for example, if taking pill A concurrently with medication B will hurt them, and lexicographers likewise have no business dumping *their* raw research findings on people with similar practical questions and requirements in language usage. And if lexicographers refuse to provide the general public with guidance on correctness in usage, others — qualified or not — will gladly supply it.

As for democracy, it is the general public, not elitist intellectuals or snobbish highbrows, who buy all those books by Fowler, Safire, Bernstein, Follett, Garner, and others in an effort to write more correctly. The public is not at all impressed by linguists' protestations that there is no such thing as "correct usage"; the public is usually quite aware that standards change, that the slang of yesterday may either become the accepted usage of tomorrow or be utterly forgotten even by those who reveled in it when it was new — but what they are *definitely* aware of, as lexicographers seem not to be, is that at any one time there are usages that educated readers will understand and respect, and others that they will not. It is in the hope of being guided to the better usages that they turn to a dictionary, and they are finding themselves served worse and worse as dictionaries become ever more "scientific" and "democratic."

McKean asks if Fiske wants phone books, almanacs, and maps to discriminate as he wants the dictionary to discriminate. Her analogy is well chosen from my point of view, showing just where her confusion lies. Dictionaries have been charged with two faults, one of commission — they include information not needed or wanted by their users — and one of omission — they fail to supply forthright guidance on correctness. The reference tools McKean names commit neither fault. They do not burden and confuse their users with extraneous information, but supply exactly what their readers want and expect. Except for highly specialized (and plainly labeled) specimens, they are designed to be used by the general public, not academic specialists; ordinary maps are designed to serve and please travelers, not cartographers; the phone book is published for the sake of subscribers who want to find someone's phone number, not for communication engineers or historians of the Bell System. In short, they offer the information expected by their buyers, unlike the modern dictionary so admired by McKean, which purports to be for college students, but offers, in its slang-of-yesteryear coverage, an inadequate sample of a kind of information needed only by a very few specialists.

And these reference books, although mere compendia of mere facts, cheat no one of guidance, because no one wants or expects guidance from them — no one turns to the phone book to decide which of his friends to invite to a party, or to a map to decide whether it is safe to vacation in Afghanistan. These reference books can be undiscriminating because the necessary discriminations are made elsewhere: the Better Business Bureau and Consumers Union will tell us not to call this roofer or that pet store if we want to be well served; the book reviewers will warn us that such-and-such an almanac is out of date or slanted; the guide books will warn us to avoid certain sections of town if we don't want to be mugged or molested. It is just such guidance that is wanted in language usage, and used to be offered by dictionaries, but no more; lexicographers, long thought harmless drudges, now want to be thought of as scientists — and scientists cannot be troubled with the needs of the reading and writing public. They are too absorbed in stern pursuit of the Laws of Language to concern themselves with the needs of mere users of language; the swineherd is so deeply engrossed in the Higher Porcine Studies that he neglects to slop the pigs.

McKean's attempted analogy fails in another way, too: what Fiske is objecting to in the dictionary's infatuation with slang is not so much the triviality and vulgarity of many of the items it offers — though many *are* trivial and vulgar — as it is their ephemeral character. So brief is the lifetime of most slang terms that by the time a dictionary appears on the market, half its slang entries already seem quaint; by the time the reader consults his five- or ten-year-old copy, almost all its slang entries will be as esoteric as Elizabethan culinary and medical terms. The lexicographer's attempt to be thrillingly up-to-date results in a work that is largely obsolescent on its day of publication; insofar as McKean and her colleagues are right in comparing the "modern dictionary" to a phone directory, it is a directory that lists phone subscribers and numbers as of years or decades ago. As the greatest of textual editors has said, "Now it is the common lot of such works of reference that they begin to be obsolete the day after they are published; but that damage, inflicted by the mere progress of knowledge is inevitable: what is not inevitable is this additional and superabundant damage, inflicted by the mental habits of slaves."[65]

McKean, unusually tolerant as the linguistically trained go, is willing to see the public served in its quest for guidance in usage, so long as they do not demand that service from the dictionary, and she even suggests a resource they can turn to: Bryan Garner's *A Dictionary of Modern American Usage*. It is a good suggestion, but also an amusing one, coming from a descriptivist. Garner is the founder of the H. W. Fowler Society, and is in his disarming way as much a prescriptivist as his mentor and model. If McKean and modern linguists insist on turning our dictionaries into collections of raw (and increasingly out-of-date) data, like obsolescent phone books, and thereby produce snapshots of the language "warts and all," they can only make the common reader let his dictionary gather dust, and turn instead to books like Garner's, which provide what they really need and want — guides in which the warts of language are identified, and ways of getting rid of warts described.

The special case of the OED

Even many who can accept all that has just been said about most modern dictionaries may feel that the *Oxford English Dictionary* is a special case, and exempt from the criticisms just made. It is indeed a special case, and mostly exempt from those criticisms, but it has been used to support its own set of false conclusions. As if to show that nothing can help one who has started with false assumptions, its misuse has given us the *Fallacy of the OED*. An example will make a formal description unnecessary: A decries a usage by a contemporary, B; C rushes to B's rescue by citing the *OED* to show that the usage is to be found in Beowulf, Chaucer, Shakespeare, and Browning.

The *Oxford English Dictionary* has been called, and in many ways

is, the greatest dictionary ever compiled of any language. But if we ever needed to be shown that the devil can quote scripture, the uses to which this great dictionary is regularly put would do it. Many of its users assume that as the "greatest of dictionaries," the *OED* is the greatest of authorities on usage — that is, on how the language should be used. In fact, its greatness and its real usefulness involve its complete renunciation of any claim to authority in that sense. It excels simply as a record of where the language has been; its distinction lies in the fact that it records the earliest use its contributors have found of every sense of every word; that, and nothing more. In doing so, it provides the best available answer to questions of the form, "When did *cattle* start meaning just bovine animals?" and "When did road surfaces start being called *macadam*?"; it is no good at all for questions of the form, "Is it OK to use *infer* and *imply* interchangeably?" or "Is it ever permissible to use a plural pronoun with a singular antecedent?"

All the *OED* can tell you in answer to questions of the latter type is "Well, Shakespeare did it once," or "Browning did it regularly; see *The Bishop Orders His Tomb at St. Praxed's* for the earliest example." These statements, while offering possibly interesting information, are not answers to the questions that were asked; all that these non-answers do is replace one set of questions with another:

"Does Shakespeare's use of such-and-such a construction authorize me to use it now?" and "What does Browning's use of that locution have to do with my situation?" And the answer is that Shakespeare's or Browning's use of some construction or locution has little if anything to tell us about usage today, and for two reasons, either of which would suffice.

First, the authors to whom appeal is being made lived and wrote some time ago, and much has changed since their day: spelling and syntax have been regularized and stabilized by printing, near-universal literacy, public schooling, word-processing programs with spell-checking features, and all the other standardizing institutions and technologies that have in many ways fixed the language. We have decided for virtually every word in the language which of numerous ways of spelling it is correct, and we enforce that decision — in the schools with grades, and afterwards by privately downgrading and, sometimes, publicly humiliating those who use a wrong form (former Vice President Quayle may have lost his chance at the presidency of the United States by misspelling *potato*). We are not quite so settled in matters of grammar and usage, but nearly so — settled enough, at least, to make appeal to the practice of writers of as little as a century ago futile and irrelevant. In short, it simply doesn't matter, for purposes of resolving a dispute over usage today, how Chaucer, or even Dickens, said it.

(There is one way in which the practice of older writers can and should be a consideration in our disputes over current usage: it is good for us to know, say, Shakespeare's usages — that is, to have them in our passive vocabularies — not because his use of them makes them acceptable by today's standards, but because we want to be able to continue to read him with ease. Our delight in Shakespeare and some other older writers is such that those of their usages that would be called errors if employed today are usages that liberally educated moderns should know — but also know enough not to use in their own writing. There is a great difference between those who want to use the *OED*'s Shakespearean citations to defend dubious modern usages, and those who want to use them to read Shakespeare.)

Second, the use to which Shakespeare and Browning (these names are used as examples only, of course) put the language is usually very distant from that to which you are putting it, unless you too are writing poetic drama or dramatic poetry. The use to which language is put in poetry, romances, belles lettres — De Quincey's Literature of Power — is radically different from that in news stories, magazine articles, business reports, scholarly papers, and other non-fiction — De Quincey's Literature of Knowledge; the difference is as great as that between Bernini's use of stone and a mason's use of stone. Even if Shakespeare were our contemporary, then, his use of language — as an art medium — is so different from that of a journalist or academic writer that citing his practice in defense of theirs is ludicrous.

Another error to which *OED* idolaters are prone is that of taking the date of a word's earliest citation in that work as the date of its acceptance into common usage, when it may well be simply the date on which some adventurous innovator tried it out, with no one seconding that use for many years afterward. On the basis of this error, the word in question is then claimed to have been "in use" far longer, or earlier, than the facts warrant, and is deemed to have been a full citizen of the English language when in reality it was still generally unknown, and regarded by most who did know it as an illegal alien.

But despite its irrelevance, the *OED* nevertheless plays a big part in the running battle that has long been going on between the prescriptivists and the descriptivists, because the former sometimes succumb to the temptation to support their positions on questions of usage by citing what they suppose to be historical facts. And when they do, they sometimes get those facts wrong, and thus give the descriptivists the chance to triumphantly point out their errors, and make them look silly. The prescriptivist arguing for the preservation of the distinction most good writers of today observe between *disinterested* and *uninterested* may, for example, carelessly claim that the distinction has always been observed by good writers; at this, the descriptivist dives into his *OED*, and emerges to announce gleefully that the prescriptivist is wrong, as indeed he is. The prescriptivists whose pretensions are thus exposed deserve the embarrassment they suffer on such occasions, but that exposure does not refute their position on usage, since that position is not based on linguistic history. In short, being able to write "*OED*" at the end of one's argument is not like being able to write "*QED*."

A step toward rescuing the dictionary

It would be unrealistic to expect dictionary makers to abjure their sins, even if they come to recognize them, in one bound; if they are to recover, a gentle and gradual path of redemption must be found for them. And a new (2004) dictionary, *Chambers Concise Dictionary*, has found such a way. The review[66] from which I draw my information about it is valuable not just for introducing this new reference book, but for the reviewer's own remarks. Discussing a new slang term ("milkshake") whose meaning is a subject of disagreement even among those few who use it, he writes:

> The problem for dictionary-makers is what to do with such intractable, and possibly ephemeral, material. In the past, "ignore it" would probably have been the answer, but today, all major dictionaries are sold on the basis of the up-to-date vocabulary they contain.

And later:

> Modern dictionary-makers find themselves in something of a paradoxical position. As good linguists, they approach language descriptively: a new way of using "grimy" is an interesting development, not an incorrect corruption. Dictionaries, however, are inherently prescriptive, and to some extent, it is their job to misdescribe the true state of the language to us. ... Something of this paradox comes across when the publishers tell us that the new *Chambers Concise* is "backed by the authority of the British National Corpus®". This is a curious use of the term "authority", since the

British National Corpus was an ambitious attempt to construct a representative sample of spoken and written[67] English: it sought to show us what people actually do, and such a descriptive tool can only have "authority" if we revise our definition of that term to mean the will of the majority, or what everyone does. It is a safe bet that people who buy dictionaries want "authority" in the sense of "correct" spellings, "real" meanings and clear distinctions.

Dictionary-makers are therefore caught between the economic imperative to offer people what they think they want, and the linguistic imperative to describe a language. Clear distinctions are something dictionary-makers impose on their material; not something they discover in the data. There is no absolute solution to this, but *Chambers Concise* comes up with an interesting way of having and eating its linguistic cake in a series of usage boxes which highlight issues likely to cause confusion: effect/affect, libel/slander, flaunt/flout, the use of "literally". Each case is discussed in impeccably descriptive terms, then readers are given clear warnings and sensible advice. After all, who wants to pay good money for a book which simply tells you what all the other fools do?

There are a few points in his review at which Hope gets a little mischievous or careless, and by doing so gives his opponents a talking point: if the dictionary's proper job is to be prescriptive, than in no sense does it "misdescribe" the language, because it is not, in the descriptivist sense, 'describing it' at all. Again, why does he say that a properly prescriptive dictionary gives the people "what they *think* they want" (emphasis supplied); does he really mean to imply that if they knew their own minds better, they wouldn't want the guidance he elsewhere says they do? And it would have been useful and interesting to explore the difference between the "economic imperative" that all who work for a living understand, and the "linguistic imperative" that Hope refers to as if it were equally common and understandable, but is in reality an "imperative" only for lexicographers who aspire to the status of linguists. But these, I think, are just minor deviations from his theme; Hope is clearly on the side of the angels, and it is good to see a dictionary reviewed by someone who knows what a dictionary should be.

The most encouraging part of the review is the news it brings about the practical solution that *Chambers Concise* has adopted: it give the linguists the "descriptive" treatment they demand, while with its left hand it gives the dictionary user the guidance *he* wants (not just *thinks* he wants). This solution to the problem will not make either party totally happy, but as a first step in the liberation of dictionaries and their users from the suffocating grasp of the academic linguists, it may be a sign of happier days ahead.

The attack on Roget's *Thesaurus*

Another example of the damage that has been done to clear thinking about words and their use by the doctrines of linguistics, with their effective decoupling of words and meanings, may be seen in the attacks recently mounted on Roget's *Thesaurus*. I had supposed the first such attack on the man and his book, that by Simon Winchester (Winchester 2001), was a freak, the momentary aberration of a journalist desperate for something to write about. But then Lawrence Norfolk, a novelist, joined Winchester in attacking the man and the book. In a review (Norfolk 2002) of a new edition of the *Thesaurus*, he wrote what would seem to be a warmed-over version of Winchester's piece, but one that was, amazingly, less rational than Winchester's. And most recently, in a review (Whale 2004) of a new history of the *Thesaurus* (Hüllen 2004), John Whale was even more contemptuously dismissive of Roget and his work than his two predecessors.

I have written a full-scale review of Winchester's piece elsewhere (Halpern 2001b); here I limit myself to examining his misunderstandings of Roget. His thesis is that Roget's *Thesaurus* has outlived its usefulness, is now for the most part being used wrongly, and should be abolished. It is, he says, "a crucial part of the engine work that has transported us to our current state of linguistic and intellectual mediocrity." Its misuse is at the hands of people who imagine that its lists of words will supply the inspiration or ideas or polish they lack; if it were abolished, these people would somehow do better (it is not quite clear whether they would start writing better, or stop writing at all).

Winchester's opening words are: "The writing world may at last be having second thoughts about Peter Mark Roget, Esquire — ... ." These second thoughts are ones that demote Roget from his formerly exalted position, and Winchester's two pieces of evidence that such a development is taking place are:

1. The latest version of the *Encyclopedia Britannica* gives Roget only twenty lines, and forces him to share the pages his entry occurs on with some people of whom you will not have heard — or at least, of whom Winchester has not heard, or supposes you will not have heard.

   Comment: what we miss here is some indication of how many pages previous editions gave him, so that we might measure precisely how much Roget has fallen in the writing world's estimation. If, for example, the preceding edition had given him forty lines, we could conclude that he had lost half his reputation since then; but Winchester gives us no baseline from which to measure his decline, so we cannot reach a scientific conclusion. Even more disturbing, the great eleventh edition gave Roget no mention at all, suggesting that his star has risen rather than fallen in recent years.

2. An even more damning indication: the on-line dictionary integrated into Microsoft's *Word*, the best-known word-processing computer program, does not recognize "Roget"; if it finds that name in a file, the spelling-checker will suggest that you mean "rogue"!

   Comment: my own copy of *Word 97* suggests, less amusingly, that "Roget" is a misspelling of either "Roger" or "rote," but Winchester may have a wittier copy.

These two points constitute the entire body of evidence Winchester offers for his assertion that Roget is no longer the admired figure he used to be: the *Encyclopedia Britannica* gives him only twenty lines, and Bill Gates has apparently never heard of him. There is no sign that Winchester is trying to be funny.

Winchester then offers us a very hasty and confusing account of the publishing history of the *Thesaurus*, winding up by asking "And what did [Roget] in fact achieve?" His answer is that *"Roget's Thesaurus* is a stylish and comprehensive list of synonyms." This characterization of Roget, which forms the basis for virtually everything Winchester says of the book, is utterly false. Much of Winchester's essay is unclear, but it is quite clear what he means in calling *Roget* a list of synonyms, and equally clear that on this fundamental point he is wrong. Roget explicitly recognizes that there are virtually no exact synonyms in the English language; he states in the Introduction that "it is hardly possible to find two words having in all respects the same meaning, and being therefore interchangeable...."[68] If in fact synonyms were common in English, we would hardly need the *Thesaurus*; a writer would need only to think of any one of the synonymous terms for the idea he was trying to express, and he'd be done — any one of them would be as good as any other. On the contrary, the book is founded on exactly the opposite (and correct) observation — that *no* two terms in the English language mean exactly the same thing — and on the further (and again correct) assumption that a careful writer will want to find the perfect one, but may be unable to remember it at the moment of need.[69]

Roget is meant for the writer who knows that there's a word that has exactly the meaning he wants, but who can't think of it at the moment. He turns to the *Thesaurus*, finds via the index the section that contains words close in meaning to the one he's trying to think of, and there, usually, finds the unique term he's seeking. He doesn't use *Roget* to find an elegant replacement for a term that's correct, but which he's grown tired of, or fears is not fancy enough, but for exactly the opposite reason: because he wants the one right word, not some loose pseudo-synonym. (If you have to use a dictionary in conjunction with a thesaurus, you're probably misusing the thesaurus; you should already know the *meaning* of the word you're trying to find — it is just the word's *name,* or *form,* that you can't think of for the moment.)

To put it formally, the thesaurus, or converse dictionary, is for the writer who already knows the definiens, but needs to be reminded of the definiendum. This isn't just the way *I* think the *Thesaurus* is to be used, it is the way *Roget* intended it to be used: the first paragraph of his Introduction states that "The object aimed at in the present undertaking is exactly the converse of [the dictionary's]: namely, — The idea being given, to find the word, or words, by which that idea may be most fitly and aptly expressed."

Winchester's next misconception is that Roget had the "naïve" notion that since all users of his book would be as sensitive to language as he was, he needn't define the terms listed in it. But as my last quotation from him shows, Roget meant his book for those who already know the meaning of the word they seek, so definitions would be otiose. And although Winchester is the author of a book on the making of the *OED,* he has apparently forgotten that there existed even in Roget's day reference books called dictionaries, which provide just such helps, and that even if Roget had ever thought of offering definitions, he might have considered that adding to his already large thesaurus the contents of a dictionary would produce a work that was unwieldy, and needlessly reduplicative of a resource already available elsewhere.

To examine all of Winchester's incidental blunders would be tiresome and unprofitable; I will content myself with noting just two, selected for their amenability to quick handling. Discussing Roget's attempt, where possible, to put words of opposite meanings in adjacent columns, he observes that "Agent and Workshop ... do not have obvious opposites, of course." Wrong — *principal* is generally taken as the opposite of *agent.* But if *agent* really had no opposite, how would that discredit Roget's scheme? Still on the subject of antonyms, and dealing specifically with Roget's handling of the term *haste,* he tells us that "So set against Haste is (no, not Less Speed; there is precious little wit in Roget) Leisure." Winchester is even more confused here than usual; "Less Speed" is in no sense, witty or otherwise, the *antonym* of "Haste"; it is, if the proverb is to be trusted, the *consequence* of haste.

Winchester generously recognizes that he is not the very first to criticize Roget on these grounds, and treats us to a couple of paragraphs from one Edwin P. Whipple, who also considers *Roget* a book that tries to spare writers the work of hard thought by putting unearned words at their disposal. Whipple writes, "In our opinion, the work mistakes the whole process by which living thought makes its way into living words, and it might be thoroughly mastered without conveying any real power or facility of expression." But *Roget* makes no assumptions whatever about "the whole process"; it simply observes that we sometimes forget the word we want and that we know exists, and need to be helped to find it. If Whipple's charge against *Roget* were sound, how much more culpable the dictionary would be, which not only gives the lazy writer all the words in the language, but actually provides him, without effort on his part, with their meanings.

Winchester then tells us that when he began composing his piece, he considered writing or phoning some well-known writers to see how they used *Roget,* if at all. He offers us a list of a dozen or more potential respondents, sketches the questions he was planning to ask them — and then tells us that he didn't bother to get in touch with any of them, since he already knew what they would say. This is too bad; it would have been interesting to see the answers he got from Anthony Burgess, Cole Porter, and Robert Lowell, all on his list — it is hard enough to get living writers to answer questionnaires; it would be truly sensational to collect answers by séance. (This may be unfair; perhaps Winchester wrote his piece in 1964, the last year all three men were alive.)

But although he does not bring us messages from the beyond, he at least tells us the truths he would have heard if he'd taken his poll: "Everyone has the book. Occasionally one makes use of it. But one never, never relies on it to help with the making of good writing. It may be used once in a while, to jog the memory, to unstall a synaptic moment. But it should never be trawled through or mined; its offerings should never be taken and transfused into a paragraph as relief for emptiness of thought." To which one can only say, "Right! And never try to eat a fire hydrant, or arm-wrestle with a grizzly bear." It was for talking as Winchester does here that Polonius came to a bad end; one begins to sympathize with Hamlet's impetuous thrust.

The one role that Winchester is prepared to allow the *Thesaurus* is that "It may be used once in a while, to jog the memory…" How often it may in good conscience be so used Winchester does not say; nor does he explain just how one avoids using it "to help with the making of good writing," or what objective one *should* have in using it. But if used as Winchester is prepared to see it used — to jog the memory — why should there be any limit to the number of times a writer may have recourse to it? Winchester is unwilling to conclude by acknowledging that there is a use for *Roget* that is entirely helpful and proper, and his refusal puts him in the silly position of proposing something like a quota system for consulting the book — and then failing to specify the quota.

In the end, it is clear that Winchester is not really interested in the contents of Roget's *Thesaurus* That book's real offense in Winchester's eyes seems to be that it is a resource that, like almost all the resources of high culture, is of help chiefly to the educated and already cultivated, and for that reason may even be harmful to those who are neither. Like all advanced tools, it multiplies both the advantages of the skilled and the disadvantages of the others, just as power tools let a good carpenter be even more productive, and a clumsy one ruin even more wood. This makes *Roget* wicked in the eyes of strict egalitarians, who would sooner that a resource not exist at all than possibly widen the gap between the favored and the non-favored. And the offense, if real, cannot be mitigated by combining the thesaurus with a dictionary, as Winchester seems to imply; if *Roget* is guilty as charged, is not the dictionary itself just another instrument of the elite, whereby they seek to impose their hegemonic authority on us? Aren't all reference books, including the *Encyclopedia Britannica* that Winchester relies on for much of the information in his piece, just more tools that they use to keep us in bondage?

Norfolk follows in Winchester's footsteps — and gets lost

Like Winchester, Lawrence Norfolk loses no time in walloping Roget with a bladder of nonsense; his opening words are:

> Roget's Thesaurus stands somewhere between pornography and Brodie's Notes on the embarrassment scale. Use implies need. Need implies deficiency, whether of sexual partners, revision time or words. In the case of Roget, no one wants to admit to being dumb.

He follows this initial blast with a potted portrait of Roget the man, much of it irrelevant (in this, too, following Winchester), and then offers a couple of very brief and tendentious quotations from Roget's introduction to the *Thesaurus:*

> Roget compiled his Thesaurus for "those who are unpractised in the art of composition, or unused to extempore speaking." "It is to those who are thus painfully groping their way and struggling with the difficulties of composition, that this Work professes to hold out a helping hand."

Norfolk presents these two excerpts in a way that is technically correct — he encloses each in its own pair of quotation marks — but misleading. He implies, by juxtaposing these two fragments as if they occurred as one continuous passage in the original, that Roget created the *Thesaurus* only for the semiliterate, so that those of us who use it today are, in his words, admitting to being dumb. But Norfolk is mistaken. Roget does not say that he created the *Thesaurus* for the simpleminded or semiliterate; he discusses the difficulties *all* writers experience in finding the *mot juste,* then remarks that "To those who are unpractised in the art of composition, or unused to extempore speaking, these difficulties present themselves in their most formidable aspect." This is followed by several more sentences, about the way no one can force his memory to come up with the word he wants when he wants it — and only then, starting a new paragraph, comes the second sentence quoted by Norfolk, the one that begins "It is to those … ."

The preceding paragraph, the one that Norfolk got his first fragmentary quotation from, makes it quite clear that even the most experienced writers suffer from this infirmity:

> Some, indeed, there are more highly gifted than others with a facility of expression, and naturally endowed with the power of eloquence; but to none is it at all times an easy process to embody, in exact and appropriate language, the various trains of ideas that are passing through the mind, or to depict in their true colors and proportions, the diversified and nicer shades of feeling which accompany them.[70]

And indeed Norfolk implicitly concedes the point when he says, "Roget himself was the first of the painful gropers his book was designed to help." Roget was a widely experienced professional writer and lecturer, and hardly at a loss for words or ideas; if he wrote the book to help himself, it was hardly written for dummies.

And what exactly is it that the "painful gropers" are seeking? Not, as Norfolk implies, the meanings that their own wits cannot supply, but the very opposite: if they are using the *Thesaurus* as Roget intended, they already know the meaning they are trying to express, and they already know that there is a word that precisely meets their need — but they cannot for the moment think of that word, and turn to Roget to find it. Roget's own clear statement to this effect, already quoted here, bears repetition: "The object aimed at in the present undertaking is exactly the converse of [the dictionary's]: namely, — The idea being given, to find the word, or words, by which that idea may be most fitly and aptly expressed."

Again like Winchester, Norfolk[71] confesses that he himself has used and profited from Roget, but warns us that "Roget also lends itself to misuse." Waiving the question that naturally arises here — what does *not* lend itself to misuse? — we read on to find two anecdotes supposedly illustrative of Roget's harmfulness.

In the one story, the novelist Jim Crace, looking in Roget for a particular word, found an entirely different word that he decided to use — a crime, apparently, and one for which Roget is to be held responsible. In the other, Norfolk himself was looking for a word meaning violin-shaped, and instead found — and apparently used — a word meaning fan-shaped. Why he accepted that word rather than continue his search for the one he originally wanted he doesn't say; perhaps he decided that the one he found was actually better or just as good, or perhaps he just got tired of looking. In any case, why is Roget to blame for either Crace's experience or Norfolk's — assuming that their experiences were unhappy, and need to be blamed on someone?

Summing up this mess of irrationality and irrelevance, Norfolk says, "The right word can sometimes stop a thought dead rather than usher it forward, and Roget has always had a lot of right words." Norfolk's argument is very loose here, but what he presumably means — like Winchester — is that Roget, by supplying people with so many words to choose from, enables them to shirk thinking their ideas through. Whether this claim makes any sense or not, the two anecdotes Norfolk has just told us are about writers freely choosing to accept words that are *not* "right" — not the ones, that is, they set out to find. Did they sin in using words other than the ones they originally sought? Might it not be that the ones they found were better than the ones they set out to find? And if it *is* a sin to accept a word that hadn't occurred to you before you found it in Roget, whose sin is it? Finally, how does the right word — whatever "right" means here — stop thought? Should Roget, in order not to stop thought, have offered a lot of *wrong* words? I agree with Norfolk and Winchester on one point at least: Roget can be dangerous in the wrong hands, like theirs.

John Whale contemplates the *Thesaurus*, sees danger everywhere

The piece by John Whale (Whale 2004) outdoes even those by Winchester and Norfolk in its contempt for Roget and his book. After describing the general structure of the original *Thesaurus,* Whale notes that it persists in the newest edition of the book, that published by Penguin in 2002, and quotes Hüllen, the author under review, as remarking on such unusual durability. In doing so, he uses a most unexpected and revealing word:

> "The history of the Thesaurus as a book," Hüllen *concedes* [emphasis supplied] in a footnote, "is marked by its incredible stability of form and content over many decades."

What a topsy-turvy world Whale gives us a glimpse of here, where a structure that has needed no major revision for 150 years is considered something of a failure, and where the historian of the book so structured may be said to be *conceding* something when he mentions the fact. Like Winchester and Norfolk, Whale believes that Roget thought there were a lot of synonyms in English, and that his *Thesaurus* is a collection of them. Laboring under this misconception, Whale then wastes space by quoting several presumptive authorities to support his contention that there really aren't any true synonyms in English — something Roget was quite aware of. Then, having decided, against all the evidence, that the *Thesaurus* is merely a collection of supposed synonyms, Whale goes on to point to the dangers such a collection presents, and to attack the book that he thinks exposes us to those dangers.

In doing so, he assumes further that the user of the *Thesaurus* is looking for an elegant variation on some word he is afraid is low, or that he has used too often already; his head is essentially empty, and he is looking to the *Thesaurus* to supply the matter he cannot come up with. Whale lists several difficulties into which an unwary user of Roget can fall, without showing how the use of Roget in any sense causes any of them. You may, he tells us, light on a word you are not sure how to use. So you may, and if you are a fool, you may decide to use that word without checking on its meaning — but how is Roget responsible for your foolishness?

In his last paragraph, Whale notes, as a kind of afterthought, that Roget can also be used to help a failing memory recall an elusive word

— that is, to remind one of what one already knew, but had trouble remembering. This is a use that Whale is ready, somewhat grudgingly, to allow, but even that use poses a problem: "reliance on a thesaurus could end in making more and more words elusive." Yes, ever since Plato, we have been warned that using aids of any kind — clay tablet and stylus, papyrus and brush, paper and pencil, the computer and mouse— can weaken our internal memory, but mankind has decided to take advantage of any aid it can find — we recognize that the number of ideas and words and facts we need to have at our command vastly exceeds the capacity of even the best unaided memory. "The safest storehouse for writers to fetch words from is their own head," Whale tells us sententiously, echoing Winchester. Exactly; and the value of Roget is that it helps us find the word that is in our head, but temporarily misplaced.

CHAPTER 4

Descriptivist, Prescriptivist, and Linguistic Activist

The descriptivist claims summarized, with a Linguistic Activist's replies

For a great many years — a handy
starting point might be 1906, when H. W. and F. G. Fowler's *The King's English* first appeared — a battle has been going on in the English-speaking world between those interested in guiding language usage and those interested in recording it. The former have come to be called the *prescriptivists*, the latter the *descriptivists*. The prescriptivists are usually highly educated and literate, trained in the humanities, and often temperamentally conservative; the descriptivists are usually academic linguists and lexicographers, trained in linguistics or one of the social sciences, and temperamentally "progressive." Both parties, of course, are small minorities; the great majority of the public is very little interested in thinking about language, whether in order to improve it as an instrument of communication or investigate it as a scientific subject. The conflict between the two parties has nevertheless almost always taken the form of appeals to that largely uncaring public rather than direct confrontation between the combatants: the prescriptivists write letters to the editors of the more serious newspapers and magazines, lamenting the latest evidence of illiteracy, and pointing to failures in our education system; the descriptivists write pieces for the same periodicals pointing out the mistakes in linguistic history committed by the prescriptivists in their letters, and lamenting their general ignorance of linguistic science.

These forays into print seem to have had little effect except that of relieving the feelings of the writers; I know of no case in which any prescriptivist or descriptivist has been convinced of the error of his ways, nor of any member of the general public who has been persuaded by either party to regard the issues as critical and deserving of much of his attention. Nevertheless, I propose now to join the battle, and hope to achieve a little more than just the relieving of my personal anxieties (when I feel violated by some abuse of language, I just lie back and think of English). I begin by declaring where my sympathies lie: I am by temperament and training a writer and editor; my interest in language is that of a user, and I feel much closer to the prescriptivists than the descriptivists. But I do not identify completely with the prescriptivists; I find that in too many cases their initial reaction, at least, to any neologism makes them seem as blindly opposed to change as the descriptivists are in favor of it, and they do not always take the trouble to think through their opposition to various *bêtes noires*, or check their remarks about literary and linguistic history for accuracy. These failures of the prescriptivists have sometimes exasperated me; as so many engaged in struggles of one kind or another have said, "I can deal with my enemies, but God save me from my friends."

Again and again, my prescriptivist brethren have attempted to buttress their judgments with what they suppose to be linguistic facts — and again and again the descriptivists show their facts to be wrong, and proclaim triumphantly that this error discredits the prescriptivist position finally and absolutely. In this carnival of error and dishonesty, everyone comes out badly. The prescriptivists are shown to be careless and unscholarly, with the result that their general position is dismissed without examination; even worse, they are shown to misunderstand the basis of their own position, which does not depend on linguistic evidence at all. The descriptivists, for their part, display nasty triumphalism, and show themselves ready to take advantage of immaterial errors on their opponents' part in order to evade rational and civil consideration of their arguments.

Despite my fundamental sympathy for them, then, I cannot quite call myself one of the prescriptivists; instead I call myself a *linguistic activist*, a name I borrow from William Safire. For examples of the way I differ from the archetypical prescriptivist, I point to my attitude toward some semantic changes and neologisms. Most prescriptivists were upset, even infuriated, over the sudden pestilence of initial "Hopefully, …", calling it ungrammatical. I too was repelled by it, but not because of its supposed grammatical faultiness; I loathed it simply because it began appearing everywhere, threatening to become a nervous tic on the order of "you know" and "I mean." (It is also open to criticism as being wholly unnecessary — the idea it conveys is easy enough to convey with simple and well-established locutions.)

Again, I differ with Nero Wolfe over his severe condemnation of the use of "contact" as a verb; I think it is useful to have a word meaning "get in touch with by one means or another," and I see nothing objectionable in it, except for those for whom novelty itself is a transgression. I have even differed with Jacques Barzun, for once, in welcoming the verb "address" for use in contexts other than golf; I think it conveys a shade of meaning ("to turn one's attention to in a purposeful way; to prepare to deal with") that is not quite that of any other term for an attempt to confront an issue or solve a problem, and it has the further merit of brevity, whereas all the near-synonymous expressions are phrases. So when I attempt to list the chief points in the descriptivists' position, and then reply to each of them, those replies will be made from my position as Linguistic Activist, which may not be quite the same as that of the typical prescriptivist — although I hope that most prescriptivists would recognize a close ally in those replies.

The descriptivist position is nowhere, so far as I'm aware, set out explicitly and systematically by those who hold it. Whether this is because linguists feel that their position is so clearly the only acceptable one that it is unnecessary to set it out for examination, or that they suspect there are weaknesses in that position that might be too easy to see if it were so displayed, I can't say. Insofar as anyone in the descriptivist party has tried to give a full exposition of his side's position, it would be Geoffrey Nunberg in (Nunberg 1983), the classic article we have already examined. (In a much shorter article [Halpern 1997] I replied to Nunberg, and that rebuttal has now been paired with Nunberg's in a number of college-course reading lists as the *faut de mieux* standard pro- and anti-descriptivist statements.)

Nunberg's article, as well as being the closest thing I know of to a definitive statement of the descriptivist position, is remarkable for its civility, as only someone who has been participating in the debate between the prescriptive and the descriptive grammarians can fully appreciate. It exhibits relatively little of the bad temper, personal scorn, and hauteur that nearly always characterize the tone of the professional linguist addressing those who lack professional credentials but persist in trying to propose rules for language usage. It is witty, good-humored, and almost always fair, and Nunberg appears to have actually read some of his adversaries' writings, and even to have found some occasional merit in them. And most remarkable of all, Nunberg recommends visitors to his personal Web site to read my rebuttal, although it is highly critical of his position. All this is refreshing and encouraging, and before taking issue with him, I want to salute him as an adversary with whom it is a pleasure to do battle, and hope that in contesting his views I can leave the reader in as sunny a mood as he does.

In his article Nunberg, although holding a professorial title in Stanford University's department of linguistics, presents himself not as the usual hard-shelled descriptivist, but as a moderate and a seeker after compromise or synthesis (the subtitle of his piece, which I would guess was supplied by an editor without his knowledge, is "An Argument for a middle way between permissiveness and traditionalism"). And he almost succeeds in this imposture, claiming with some plausibility to be sympathetic in some ways to prescriptivism: he charmingly 'confesses' that he "can't overcome the feeling that it is wrong for me to use [*gift* and *impact* as verbs]," even while knowing that they may in future come into general use as verbs despite his feelings, just as *contact* has already done. Then he quotes a famous passage of Fowler's, and not only praises it, but tells us that it caused him to modify one of his own writings.[72] In short, Nunberg very nearly disarms us by showing that he appreciates fine distinctions, and shares the literary tastes underlying the prescriptive position.

But his display of neutrality or even collegiality is misleading; Nunberg is indeed not the run-of-the-mill academic descriptivist, but something much more dangerous, a Trojan horse from the descriptivist camp. His demonstration by means of well-chosen quotations and discriminating name dropping that he is as alive to the finest literary nuances and logical distinctions as any admirer of Beerbohm or Fowler is only a diversionary tactic. In taking issue with us prescriptivists and near-prescriptivists, he is gentler than are most descriptivists, and readier to grant some of our minor points, but in all doctrinal essentials Nunberg is the classic academic linguist, chastising us in the joint names of science and democracy.

He makes the two standard objections against prescriptivism. The first is the scientific objection: laws of nature are involved here, and those trying to influence linguistic events without knowledge of linguistic laws are simply demonstrating their ignorance, and making public fools of themselves — he likens them to landscape gardeners trying to stop or modify the processes of plate tectonics. The second is the democratic objection: the prescriptivists are attempting to foist their own linguistic practices, which are usually the practices of the educated, affluent, fortunate members of society, on the less educated and affluent members — and since there is a strong positive correlation between these two classes and the white and non-white portions of the population, respectively, there is some suspicion of racism at work here as well.[73]

One of the points that Nunberg, like all his school, is most eager to make is that the 'rules' of grammar, and of good usage generally, have no scientific basis; they are just someone's idea of what is proper, and that idea changes from generation to generation. The descriptivists are so eager, indeed, to make sure this point has registered that they seldom stop making it long enough to hear the reply: "Yes, we know this; we do not contend that the rules we would like to see observed were handed down from on high. They are ordinary man-made rules, and neither divine commandments nor scientific laws (although they have some claim to a rational basis), and we agree that they, like all man-made things, will need continual inspection and maintenance.

But these facts are no more arguments against rules governing language usage than they are against rules governing vehicular traffic. Arbitrary rules — conventions — are just the ones that need enforcement, not the natural laws; the law of gravity can take care of itself, the law that you go on green and stop on red needs all the help it can get."

Nunberg objects to rules about grammar because, among other things, they interfere with our "working [grammatical issues] out" for ourselves. One wonders what population Nunberg has in mind here; is he imagining that American high school or college students, or many people anywhere, would be puzzling out grammatical issues for themselves if prescriptive grammarians like John Simon had not, by laying down the law to them, stifled their healthy curiosity and hunger for learning? He also objects to the right wing ideology that he sees behind the grammatical strictures of people like Simon, William Safire, and William F. Buckley, telling us that earlier grammarians like Samuel Johnson would "probably be distressed to learn that their standard had been taken up by the right." (This is interesting as evidence that the current non-specialists' misconception about Johnson is that he was a liberal; the traditional error was to think him merely a curmudgeonly Tory). But he can be pretty insulting to the common people himself when he gets his dander up: we are told that Safire brings a certain class of readers "out of the woodwork," whereupon they exchange with him "schoolmarm maxims and scraps of linguistic folklore."

Linguistic science is not the basis of Nunberg's views

There are two great flaws in Nunberg's position, either of them sufficient to destroy it completely. The first is his claim that linguistics is a science, and a science relevant to usage issues, so that those versed in it must have the last word — if not the only word — about such matters.

If one had to select a single sentence of Nunberg's to serve as a *précis* of his paper, it would be this: "But it is impossible to talk intelligently about the language nowadays without having an idea of what the program of modern linguistics is all about…" — and this key statement is false. I contend — and I believe I have some idea of "the program of modern linguistics" — that what linguistic scientists have done in the 20th century, whatever value it may have for other purposes, has absolutely no relevance to the constellation of literary-philosophical-social-moral issues that we are talking about when we discuss usage. And Nunberg, in his own practice, confirms my point: he gives reasons throughout the paper for his own specific judgments in matters of usage, and nowhere are the findings of linguistic science among them.

Nunberg wants us to understand that the study of language is "complex and technically demanding," and that many questions that seem simple to the "pop grammarians" like Simon and Safire can really be handled intelligently only by the professional linguists. As I noted earlier, he gives as an instance the fact that it is acceptable to say *Everyone has taken his coat* but not *Everyone left, didn't he?*, and tells us that "Linguists have puzzled a great deal over examples like these, in an effort to understand the basic workings of English syntax; it is small wonder that they should have little patience with popular grammarians who blithely proclaim that the whole problem is simple…." I think Nunberg does his party a disservice in offering such an example without showing how it relates to some larger issues that his readers might understand; in itself, his example may well seem to those readers final proof that linguists concern themselves with trivia and the inconsequential. But more important for present purposes, Nunberg makes no attempt to show the *relevance* of such puzzlings, or any other aspect of linguistic science, to the issues that concern prescriptivists.

Linguists profess to be practicing a scientific discipline whose object is to learn the laws that govern a department of nature, linguistic behavior. An example (to call it an anomaly, as Nunberg does, is to beg the question of whether there exist laws to be broken, but this point can be waived here) such as that just quoted from Nunberg is their meat and drink; to them, it is like the anomaly in the orbit of Mercury whose discovery and study led to such great advances in physics. But even if the linguists were right in thinking themselves scientists, and in thinking that anomalies such as this are opportunities for the discovery of real linguistic laws, the phenomena they are studying have nothing to do with the interests of the prescriptivists. Nunberg, speaking for "most of my fellow linguists," ridicules prescriptivists as landscape gardeners setting their faces against continental drift, and the analogy is better than Nunberg knows — the relationship between the linguistic scientists and the prescriptivists is indeed very like that between geologists and landscape gardeners, and can profitably be extended beyond Nunberg's use of it. If the "frantic efforts" of the gardeners "to keep Alaska from bumping into Asia" are ridiculous, is it not equally silly for geologists to tell landscape gardeners that they must not presume to pollard a lime tree, or put in a fishpond, without deferring to the experts on plate tectonics?

It is in fact the most striking feature of Nunberg's paper that he makes no use of the "findings" of linguistic science at any critical point, and little use anywhere. After telling us emphatically and at length that only those versed in the mysteries of the science he professes are really qualified to pronounce on issues of language usage, he nowhere calls on his own esoteric learning; his views on specific issues are based simply on his conception of manners, decency, courage, clarity, and other virtues with which one is often glad to agree, but which do not seem to be the product of linguistic science. Many of Nunberg's specific judgments on points of usage are so tactful and sensible that we may easily, in our pleasure at being able to agree with him, overlook the fact that he makes them simply as a tactful, cultivated and sensible fellow, not as a scientist. So Nunberg, in this paper, is not a scientist; but what if he were?

Language is not part of nature, hence has no laws or natural destiny

Here enters his second great error: to suppose, like all the descriptive grammarians, that language is an entity with its own laws of development, or natural destiny, and that prescriptive grammarians are trying to interfere with the course of that natural destiny. I argued earlier that no such laws are known, and that even if we knew of any, there is no reason to think that we would be doing anything wrong by attempting to transcend them, and make our own wishes prevail. We have in the past made many attempts to encourage or defeat some particular usage, and have sometimes succeeded, sometimes failed. Are we to suppose that we succeeded only when the usage we proposed was in consonance with language's rules or destiny, and failed whenever we proposed one that contravened those laws or destiny? In fact, that is just what Edward Sapir, one of the greatest figures in 20th century linguistics, claimed. In a chapter of (Sapir 1921) titled "Language as a Historical Product: Drift," he wrote:

If the historical changes that take place in a language, if the vast accumulation of minute modifications which in time results in the complete remodeling of the language, are not in essence identical with the individual variations that we note on every hand about us, if these variations are born only to die without a trace, while the equally minute, or even minuter, changes that make up the drift are forever imprinted on the history of the language, are we not imputing to this history a certain mystical quality? Are we not giving language a power to change of its own accord over and above the involuntary tendency of individuals to vary the norm? And if this drift of language is not merely the familiar set of individual variations seen in vertical perspective, that is historically, instead of horizontally, that is in daily experience, what is it? Language exists only in so far as it is actually used — spoken and heard, written and read. What significant changes take place in it must exist, to begin with, as individual variations. This is perfectly true, and yet it by no means follows that the general drift of language can be understood from an exhaustive descriptive study of these variations alone. They themselves are random phenomena, like the waves of the sea, moving backward and forward in meaningless flux. The linguistic drift has direction. In other words, only those individual variations embody it or carry it which move in a certain direction, just as only certain wave movements in the bay outline the tide. The drift of a language is constituted by the unconscious selection on the part of its speakers of those individual variations that are cumulative in some special direction.[74]

The meaning — the "drift" — of this passage may be a little obscured by its wordiness and extended marine analogy. What Sapir is saying is that all the changes that are introduced into a language originate the same way, in the utterances of individual speakers, but that their conequences are not all the same: some will become part of the language, others be forgotten and allowed to disappear. Those that survive do so, he assures us, because they are consistent with the

"drift" of the language, which is a force quite apart, he claims, from that which prompts any individual speaker to introduce a change; an individual speaker's innovation is "random," the drift "has direction." How can we judge whether a newly-introduced change is part of the drift? We wait. If the change survives for some unspecified period of time, we know it must be part of the drift; if not, not.

This is simply Darwinian evolution by natural selection applied to language, except that in the biological realm, unlike the linguistic, we know something about the 'drift.' We know that in living creatures those random genetic mutations that favor the survival of the individual at least up to the age of procreation, and hence the propagation of the species, themselves tend to survive, and we can often predict just which mutations will meet that criterion. In the linguistic realm we have no such criterion; changes that are damaging to a language's expressive power somtimes survive, and some that would seem useful perish. All Sapir, like other linguists, can do is assure us that in some mysterious way the language is evolving as it should, and we are not to worry.

A few pages earlier than the passage just quoted, Sapir makes it clear that he sees language as fundamentally autonomous by saying, in words that are often quoted by linguists and their sympathizers, that "Language moves down time in a current of its own making. It has a drift."[75] Sapir's "drift" is more commonly called the "Genius of the language," and the answer to his rhetorical question, "are we not imputing to this history a certain mystical quality?" is Yes. To say that every change that becomes a permanent part of the language does so because it agrees with some otherwise undefined "drift" is no more useful, or scientific, than to say that everything that happens does so because it is in accord with God's will. Both assertions may be true, but they cannot be tested, nor help us learn other truths.

On what grounds do descriptivists rule out prescriptivism — or any other data?

To return to our examination of Nunberg's paper: he and his allies have no *scientific* standing in their quarrel with a Simon or a Safire; if they disagree with such prescriptivists, they do so not as scientists observing from above the fray, distinguished by superior knowledge and disinterestedness, but simply as fellow gladiators down in the arena, as partisan and opinionated as their adversaries. How the battle will turn out, how it *should* turn out, no one can say with any authority; and since there is no natural course with which to interfere, there is nothing that can properly be called an interference; 'interferences' are simply what linguistic scientists call those events of linguistic history that they cannot accept.

The title 'descriptivist' raises a problem that has been often noted, but to which the people who so describe themselves have never offered a reasoned reply: descriptivists, as their name indicates, profess simply to be describing the language and the various forces acting upon it, and prescriptivism is one of those forces — so why is it, and it alone, to be disallowed? The practitioners of linguistic science cannot reasonably quarrel with prescriptivists any more than they do with ghetto youths; like those youths, *we are their data*. The explanation of this anomaly is that linguists are in the grip of a delusion: they think, as aspirants to the title of 'scientist' must, that they are investigating a branch of nature rather than an artifact. Given this false premise, it follows that prescriptivists, in trying to guide language usage, are interfering with a phenomenon under scientific investigation, just as someone secretly slipping peanuts to laboratory chimps would be compromising an investigation into their metabolism.

It is instructive to observe that those who pride themselves on being pure descriptivists, standing neutral above all usage battles, recording the facts they find without bias, and searching for the laws of linguistic nature, should take issue with the prescriptivists when they do so with no one else. Why do the grossest offenses against cultivated speech or writing arouse in the linguists no emotion, but only scientific interest, when other linguistic phenomena — the strictures of a John Simon, for example — arouse their passions to the point where even so civilized a man as Nunberg sounds as if he'd like to have Simon whipped? Nunberg's view, I think, is this (what follows are my words, not his):

> Simon is sophisticated, and a man who has thought long and hard (however mistakenly) about language usage; the uneducated offender against traditional correctness has given such matters no thought whatever. Hence Simon is interfering with nature, where the ignorant offender is simply exemplifying it. If Simon is allowed to influence matters, the natural laws of linguistic development will be obscured or distorted; he is interfering with the experimental animals and corrupting the experimental results.

The linguists have not absorbed Burke's dictum: *Art is Man's Nature.* And the nature under investigation by linguistic science is man's nature, of which a desire to erect standards, and use them to correct practice, is an essential element, not an aberration.

Perhaps because he thinks of himself as a scientist, and listens to ordinary speech as if observing the curious behavior of some primitive tribe, Nunberg's comments and questions on specific points of usage are sometimes thuddingly unperceptive. Thinking that he has spied another of those contradictions in the views of "modern critics" that a scientist can use against them, he asks, "Why is it all right for a politician to use *capital-intensive,* once a technical term of economics, but not *revenue enhancement?*" One has to think of oneself as a scientist, perhaps, to miss the simple answer that the former is merely a neutral technical term now found useful by non-economists, while the latter is an attempt at deception; at concealing a tax increase from the public. He defends borrowings from technical usage against the charge of barbarism, saying, "For the most part, the borrowing is natural and inevitable — what else would you call a minicomputer or a quasar?" Again, only an expert could fail to see the answer: one would call them nothing else, because those are their proper and only names. Technical terms are perfectly in place when applied to technical matters; it is only when they are borrowed (actually, *stolen;* they are never returned) to inflate some triviality or mask some mendacity that we "modern critics" get riled.

After expressing admiration for Fowler's little gem[76] on using quote marks to show one's superiority to slang even while availing oneself of it, Nunberg says "It obviously has done little to stem the mania for quotation marks (**We are "closed,"** I saw in the window of a shoe-repair shop the other day)...". No, Fowler's discussion of quote marks as devices for simultaneously using slang and showing oneself superior to it did nothing to prevent the ignorant of a later day from misusing quote marks as general intensifiers, and for the excellent reason that it did not address that problem.

Nunberg's observation, although a digression from the argument in which it occurs, was nevertheless an important one for him to make and for us to notice. He has caught himself praising an effort made by an educated man to influence usage, and fears he may in doing so have conceded an important point to the opposition. So despite its strictly logical irrelevance, he hastens to repair the damage with an anecdote that is supposed to show that individual effort, even that of a Fowler, must be futile in matters linguistic. The laws of that realm, he implies in pointing to the shoemaker's sign, will work their will, whatever we may do or say.

Discussing the conflation in popular speech of *disinterested* and *uninterested,* he says:

But there is no point making a fuss about [it], because it was forgone that *disinterested* would lose its older sense once *interested* lost
the sense of "having a stake in," which we retain only in the fixed
phrase *interested party*. Even if disinterested had survived intact,
therefore, it would eventually have become one of those curious
asymmetric negatives like *untoward* and *disgrace*, whose senses are
not recoverable as the sum of their parts.

Nunberg's reasoning is faulty in several respects here.[77] First, he
contradicts himself in telling us that the disappearance of *disinterested* in the sense under discussion became inevitable once *interested*
had ceased, for most purposes, to carry the opposite meaning; in the
very next sentence he describes a whole class of terms — "those curi-

ous asymmetric negatives" — that have suffered the same loss, but
survived very nicely. Second, he makes a question-begging assumption in stating that *disinterested* must lose the sense he mentions —
notice that he speaks of it in the past tense to convince us that it has
already done so. Finally, he suffers from the erroneous notion that
disgrace is "one of those curious asymmetric negatives ... whose
senses are not recoverable as the sum of their parts"; apparently the
word has fallen from grace in linguists' eyes.

But as to Nunberg's main point — his claim that *disinterested,*
if it had survived intact, would have joined the (presumably disrep-
utable) company of *untoward* and its kin — its definitive, conclusive
refutation is, So what? What is undesirable about such "curious
asymmetric negatives"? Their lack of a positive form presents no
difficulty to anyone, and they positively increase the gaiety of nations.
They lend themselves to a form of verbal playfulness based on writing and talking as if they *do* have such forms: there are those
who derive harmless amusement from using the officially non-existent *ept, *choate, *kempt, *sheveled, *trepid, and the like;
Nunberg may have misgivings, even be nonplussed by the practice,
but most of us have ample *givings, and remain coolly *plussed. To
such considerations Nunberg may be indifferent, but we linguistic
activists are quite *different.

And so susceptible is the language to unsanctioned amateur initiatives that such simple joking may eventually bring some or all of those non-words into general use and respectability (as with *burgle*, for example), whereupon Nunberg and his colleagues will write heavily footnoted papers explaining how *symmetrising back-formation* is part of the ineluctable march of linguistic laws, and further evidence that amateurs are out of their depth in talking about usage.

The other side of Geoffrey Nunberg, the one that shows him to be a far more perceptive observer than most linguists of the issues involved in this debate, may be seen in an ingratiating piece (Nunberg 1995) that makes it even clearer than his old *Atlantic* article did that his views can on occasion differ significantly from those of standard academic descriptivism; for example, he says:

> And I think the public resistance to some of the things that linguists are saying grows out of an intuitive sense that our point of view is not so much incompatible with their interests as irrelevant to them. (page 175)

and:

> When ordinary people do talk about the language, ... what they're thinking of is all those lexical niceties and fine distinctions that language critics get themselves worked up about. Linguists tend to see these as trivial matters, and can get pretty indignant at the thought that people should take them (or more to the point, the critics who write about them) so seriously... But of course ... it is a bit dismissive to suggest that the critical issues that people attach so much importance to are merely aesthetic matters that have no moral weight. In fact, there's a liberal helping of condescension (and vice versa) running through most of the linguistic critique of prescriptivism. (page 177)

I'm not certain what the parenthetical "and vice versa" means in this passage — that there's also a liberal helping of condescension in prescriptivists' critique of linguists? or that there's a condescending helping of liberalism in the linguistic critique of prescriptivism? There's some truth in both; perhaps Nunberg intends both. In any case, he goes on:

> Like most linguists, [Steven] Pinker has a high time pointing out mistakes and inconsistencies in the syntactic and morphological principles that prescriptivists offer to justify their judgments.... But all that his observations really show is that the critics haven't been very skillful in explaining their judgments, not that the objections themselves are unfounded. (page 178)

These are all admirable sentiments to which I gladly subscribe — so much so that if I hadn't written very similar things before Nunberg published this paper, I'd suspect myself of unconscious plagiarism. But for all the common sense and modesty of these observations, Nunberg still reacts to many skirmishes between prescriptivists and descriptivists with (kindly) condescension for the former, and support for the latter — if war were to break out he would, I think, however reluctantly, join the descriptivist army rather than that of prescriptivism. (I have some sympathy for his loyalty problem; my own views, as I noted earlier, differ somewhat from those of most prescriptivists.)

If the points Nunberg makes in the passages just quoted were to be generally accepted by his fellow linguists, the great prescriptivist-descriptivist controversy would be over, and both sides could pursue their own interests in peace. But if Nunberg himself finds it hard, in the heat of battle, to remember these truths, what can we expect from most of his colleagues, who have not evolved to anywhere near his stage of understanding?

As noted earlier, after all Nunberg says about the death of *disinterested* in the sense 'having no personal stake in the matter,' that's exactly how he uses it himself. And he is in error in saying of *interested* that the sense of "having a stake in" is one "we retain only in the fixed phrase *interested party*"; surely he has heard such phrases as *conflict of interests* and *in the interest of economy* and *declaring one's interest* and *the*

Interests (as rapacious business combines used to be called by reformers and muckrakers), to name just the first few that occurred to me? But the comment of his that most amazes me is:

> Even if *disinterested* had survived intact, therefore, it would eventually have become one of those curious asymmetric negatives like *untoward* and *disgrace*, whose senses are not recoverable as the sum of their parts.

Coming from a linguist, this is truly remarkable. If there is any practice that linguists are as one in ridiculing, it is the layman's habit of trying to infer what a word means from its parts. Along with its double, *folk etymology, folk definition* is the very mark of the rank amateur and the linguistic naïf, and has been almost laughed out of existence by the academic linguists. To hear a professor of linguistics appeal to that officially discredited practice is like hearing a professor of physics claim to have invented a perpetual motion machine, or an astronomer wonder if the sun doesn't go around the earth after all.

The reason why linguists deride the practice is that it is so frequently misleading, often producing truly bizarre results. Consider the word *cowboy*. Its first part denotes an animal noted for placidity and passivity; applied to a human female, it is an insult. And its second denotes an immature human male — a term that, applied to any grown male is an insult; to a Black male, a deadly insult. Put the two together, however, and we get a word that denotes a bold, daring, self-reliant, even slightly wild and heroic figure, one that every American male has played at being — and sometimes even after growing up. No wonder linguists ridicule folk etymology!

A few comments on Steven Pinker's
The Language Instinct

A more recent presentation of the descriptivist position comes from Steven Pinker, now professor of psychology at Harvard. Although not officially a linguist, he is one in everything but title; his special interest in psychology is language, and in particular the mental mechanisms that underlie language acquisition by children, and his *The Language Instinct* (Pinker 1994) is for the most part a popular report on the findings of cognitive psychologists and other investigators into those mechanisms. The novelty and main value of the book lies in his weaving together the recent findings of brain researchers, geneticists, and developmental psychologists to formulate an admittedly primitive but suggestive picture of how humans learn to speak. It includes a presentation of some of the work of Noam Chomsky that is one of the clearest I have yet seen; a balanced and sober analysis of the efforts over the last decade or two to get chimpanzees and gorillas to use language as humans do; and an interesting attempt to show that the development of language can be accounted for by standard Darwinian natural selection, despite Chomsky's doubts.

On the subject of language usage and the prescriptivist-descriptivist debate, however, he is on the side of the descriptivists and the academic linguists — a most surprising position for him, since other writings of his, particularly his later *The Blank Slate* (Pinker 2002), show him to be ordinarily immune to the academically orthodox and the politically correct. But he has succumbed to the descriptivist position on questions of correct usage; he even tells with delight (pages 64–65) the story of how Pullum and Martin shot down the Eskimo canard, or Canada goose: "No discussion of language and thought would be complete without the Great Eskimo Vocabulary Hoax. Contrary to popular belief, the Eskimos do not have more words for snow than do speakers of English." And so on for a page and a half, unwittingly showing by example how silly stories get transmitted from book to book.[78]

But it is in the twelfth of his thirteen chapters, "The Language Mavens," that Pinker takes a complete holiday from science, and attempts to show how ridiculous most non-linguist writers on language usage are — his chief target is William Safire, although glancing blows are aimed at John Simon and Jacques Barzun in passing. He wastes little time with either of the last two: Simon is simply a "malicious know-nothing," while Barzun "earned an 'F' when he called a possessive noun like *Wellington's* an adjective" — if we wonder where Barzun did this, and what he meant by it, we are referred in the endnotes to an entire book by Dwight Bolinger; Pinker offers no further explanation for Barzun's failing grade.

Most of the chapter consists of analyses by Pinker of specific usage arguments offered by the 'mavens' — sometimes attributed to a specific maven (usually Safire), sometimes to unnamed "defenders of the standard" (Pinker nowhere mentions Fowler). And in most of these encounters Pinker, I think, comes out ahead. He wins partly because he has carefully hand-picked the battles he fights, and has little trouble finding cases in which various mavens have taken indefensible positions; partly because he has chosen straw men to attack — is anyone of substance still worrying about *ain't,* or the splitting of infinitives? But the chief reason for his triumphs is that many of the mavens make the fatal mistake of trying to justify what I earlier called their literary-philosophical-social-moral views with historical facts, or supposed facts, about the development of the language — in short, with citations and arguments about which the professional linguist will usually be better informed, or at least able to sound more authoritative.

In acting as amateur linguists, the mavens not only commit the tactical error of playing their adversary's game, but profoundly falsify their own position; they often become so engrossed in finding what they suppose to be good logical or historical reasons for their preferences that they forget that they are not linguists, but moralists and literary critics. There seems a kind of poetic justice in the mavens' losing so many of their battles this way; if it is ignorant and silly of the linguists to pretend to occupy the scientific high ground, it is unforgivable in the mavens — they should know better. They are as much to blame here as are the linguists when *they* try to defend some ephemeral and witless new usage, professing to be speaking for science.

The difference between the linguists and the mavens — or the descriptivists and prescriptivists, to use the more usual terms — is captured neatly in the dual meaning that "grammar" bears in such books as Pinker's. To the descriptivist, "grammar" is usually short for "generative grammar": the hypothetical mechanism, embodied in the brain, that produces sentences. To call any recorded utterance ungrammatical, given this sense of the term, is to make a strange, almost meaningless statement; as some linguist has observed, it is like criticizing the way the stomach produces digestive juices. To the prescriptivist — and the majority of the educated public — grammar means the set of standards and rules, embodied in books and teachers, that decides whether what you've said was well said, and the charge of being ungrammatical is one that we often find justified. Now Pinker is well aware of the dual meaning of "grammar" and its derivative forms — he spends the first pages of chapter twelve in making the distinction I have just summarized — and he draws a correct conclusion: "They [the descriptive and prescriptive meaning of rules, grammar, etc.] are completely different things.... One can choose to obsess over prescriptive rules, but they have no more to do with human language than the criteria for judging cats at a cat show have to do with mammalian biology."

Pinker's phrase "obsess over" does not sound like the language of a scientist (unless he is seriously asserting that prescriptivists suffer from a clinically recognized variety of psychopathology), and his statement that rules have nothing to do with language needs qualification — he means that they have nothing to do with those aspects of language he is professionally interested in — but apart from these characteristic descriptivist blemishes, his statement is unexceptionable. But one wonders why Pinker is unable to proceed to the next step in the argument: if the two viewpoints are so radically different, on what grounds does the descriptivist criticize the prescriptivist? Pinker provides in his biologist-versus-cat fancier analogy another argument, like Nunberg's analogy of geologists-versus-landscape gardeners, that deserves to be pushed a step beyond where its author leaves it. Cat fanciers clearly have no grounds for telling mammalian biologists how to go about their business; have the biologists any more grounds for telling the fanciers that this shorthair is too cobby, or that Siamese's points too dark?

This radical difference in interests and goals makes it impossible

114

for the descriptivists to criticize the prescriptivists with scientific authority; surely they may comment, but when they do, they do so merely as rival prescriptivists. Pinker quotes from someone he identifies only as "a poet" (why he is reluctant to say "Auden" isn't clear) this dictum: "when [language] is corrupted, people lose faith in what they hear, and that leads to violence,"[79] then remarks:

> The linguist Dwight Bolinger, gently urging this man to get a grip, had to point out that "the same number of muggers would leap out of the dark if everyone conformed overnight to every prescriptive rule ever written."

One wants to ask Bolinger, with equal gentleness, "How do you know?" Does an academic post in linguistics qualify one to make dogmatic statements about the incidence of crime in a hypothetical world? A world in which all usage rules were followed would certainly be very different from the present one; perhaps the crime rate in so rule-respecting a polity *would* be lower. And Bollinger's unwarranted assumption of authority is made even more ridiculous by the fact that he hasn't the slightest idea of what Auden was talking about in the dictum he quoted. In talking about the corruption of language, Auden meant not simple grammatical solecisms and illiteracies, but the deep and systematic perversions of language that such critics as Karl Kraus, George Orwell, and Jacques Barzun have fought in their various ways — perversions such as the attempt by ideologues to build their notions directly into the language so that criticism is inhibited or suppressed entirely (a stratagem to which I gave the name mindshunt in Halpern 2001).[80] Auden's biographer remarks:

> ... he began to come to the conclusion that the chief 'political duty' of a writer in the 1960s was to defend the language against the inroads of the modern world, arguing that if the language was allowed to decay then the consequences would be disastrous for everyone. "Today', he wrote in 1967, 'nine-tenths of the population use twice as many words as they understand ... So befuddled,

how can the man-in-the-street be expected to resist the black magic of the propagandists, commercial and political?"[81]

If Auden also took the trouble to oppose such innocent errors as a reviewer's calling a book "enervating" to praise it for being stimulating, or using "nauseous" to mean "nauseated," he did so for the same reason that the police attempt to enforce even relatively trivial laws if they would keep the streets safe. Like the authors of the 'broken window' school of thought on crime control, they know that a failure to enforce the law in minor matters leads to a breakdown of respect for law in general, and encourages the commission of more serious offenses.[82] The corollary strategy has proved successful in crime control, and it seems reasonable to apply it to deviations from good language usage. Making people sensitive to mere solecisms increases their sensitivity to language in general, and is a big step toward getting them to detect and reject dishonest and tendentious usages. This is what Auden had in mind, and Bollinger's riposte is not merely offensively condescending, but quite uncomprehending.

Again, Pinker examines an analysis by Safire of an utterance of Barbra Streisand's, and defends Streisand against Safire's charges of bad usage. But at one point in his defense he says "Now, I cannot be sure that this is what Streisand had in mind…," which rather gives the game away; if we assume that Streisand wanted to be understood, then her utterance has failed — even her defender cannot be sure he knows what she meant. Pinker's usual defense of vogue words, solecisms, and other problematic examples of language usage is just the opposite, though. In examining an assortment of utterances that have been attacked by prescriptivists, he defends them by saying in effect what every English teacher hears every day from students shocked at the grades their compositions have received: "You knew what I meant!"

To which the proper answer (but one which the teacher seldom gives, out of the kindness of his heart) is, "Of course I knew what you meant — but not because of what you said; rather, in spite of what you said. I understand only because I'm older and wiser, and have a great deal of experience in reading students' compositions. What I'm trying to do in this class is to teach you to write so as to be understood even by those who *aren't* that much more experienced than you are, and who *aren't* already aware of what you're trying to say, and who may *not* be ready to make the many accommodations and imaginative leaps I'm ready to make in reading your work." In virtually every case that Pinker examines, the utterance under examination can be understood, at any rate by a reader who's willing to meet the author at least half way. But equally, in virtually every case the impropriety the prescriptivist has complained of is one that will prevent understanding on another occasion, or allow the reader to think he has understood when he has not.

Another fallacy that is a standard part of the descriptivist campaign against the prescriptivists is the Irrelevant Historical Fact, and Pinker does not neglect it. Talking about *disinterested,* he reveals that in the eighteenth century it had just the meaning that today's prescriptivists reject: uninterested, uncaring. And this he seems to regard as a decisive consideration, rather than the antiquarian curiosity that it really is. Careful writers today use *disinterested* to mean "having no personal stake in the matter"; what it meant in the eighteenth century is neither here nor there. But Pinker builds another fallacy atop this one; the fact that the word meant one thing then and another now leads him into the "language is always changing, so there's no point in resisting any particular change" fallacy. And in support of this fallacy he thinks he can enlist no less an authority than Samuel Johnson.

His chapter on "The Language Mavens" ends with what Pinker must consider a masterstroke: a quotation from the preface to Johnson's *Dictionary* that he evidently thinks a thorough vindication of his own position, all the more imposing for being from a great writer, lexicographer, and moralist:

Those who have been persuaded to think well of my design, require that it should fix our language, and put a stop to those alterations which time and chance have hitherto been suffered to make in it without opposition. With this consequence I will confess that I have flattered myself for a while; but now begin to fear that I have indulged expectations which neither reason nor experience can justify. When we see men grow old and die at a certain time one after another, from century to century, we laugh at the elixir that promises to prolong life to a thousand years; and with equal justice may the lexicographer be derided, who being able to produce no example of a nation that has preserved their words and phrases from mutability, shall imagine that his dictionary can embalm his language, and secure it from corruption and decay, that it is in his power to change sublunary nature, and clear the world at once from folly, vanity, and affectation. With this hope, however, academies have been instituted, to guard the avenues of their languages, to retain fugitives, and to repulse intruders; but their vigilance and activity have hitherto been vain; sounds are too volatile and subtle for legal restraints; to enchain syllables, and to lash the wind, are equally the undertakings of pride, unwilling to measure its desires by its strength.

Only a linguistic scientist, perhaps, could read this as meaning "Isn't it just great that language changes! And aren't people who dream of controlling it foolish!" What, one wonders, does Pinker make of Johnson's statement that he *did* originally hope that his *Dictionary* might have the effect of fixing the language? What of Johnson's using the aging and death of men as a parallel to the processes by which languages change? And what of his using terms like *folly, vanity, affectation, corruption,* and *decay* in surveying the causes and consequences of those processes?

So Pinker closes his campaign against the prescriptivists by quoting at length from perhaps the greatest and wisest of prescriptivists, and utterly mistaking the man. And in thus demonstrating an inability to grasp the tenor of a great piece of rhetorical prose, he gives us further reason to distrust linguists when they try to legislate on matters beyond their professional competence, such as how language should be used. Had he read a little further in Johnson's preface, Pinker would have come across words that he could not have misunderstood:

...tongues, like governments, have a natural tendency to degeneration; we have long preserved our constitution, let us make some struggle for our language.

As for Pinker's award of an 'F' to Jacques Barzun, here is what Mr Barzun himself has to say:

> Since you quote Mr. Pinker's award to me of a failing grade, you may be interested to know the occasion — indeed, you ask for the context. I don't remember where I made the stupendous error, but the point of it was that a proper name in the possessive should not be referred to later by a pronoun. Perhaps I should have said "Wellington's" has the force of an adjective, is adjectival, as indeed it is, since if we start with *Wellington's boots,* we go on with *his* hat and *his* gloves — possessive adjectives having the same function and meaning.
>
> Mr. Pinker is naughty to jump on me for not using "possessive noun," when he knows what chaos the scientists have created in grammatical nomenclature. One grammar for schools insists on *head word* for *subject.* Another says that in the dialogue "Are you coming home soon? — I'll be there in half an hour," *there* is a pronoun, because it stands for the preceding home. If the Pinker system is to show the noun quality in "Wellington's," how does it handle [the first word in each of the phrases] *house guest, drama critic, office furniture,* and the like? They are adjectives, as the very meaning of that term implies: a word "thrown at" another to qualify it.[83]

On Debating With Linguists Generally

After several years of debating with various linguists, what I find most striking is their silences. They jump on every point in my papers that they think they can refute or ridicule, however trivial — one well-known British linguist[84] declared an essay of mine (Halpern 2001) entirely discredited because of the way I used the word "it" in the first sentence of that paper — while simply ignoring any point that they find they cannot refute. (I am happy to be able to name one exception, John McWhorter, formerly of the University of California at Berkeley, who has shown himself ready to acknowledge a good point make by an opponent, even while arguing forcefully for his own point of view.)

It is clear from the quickness with which they pounce on what they suppose to be errors in my work that they are reading it with close attention, so they cannot be excused on the grounds that they are unaware of my arguments or too busy to engage me, nor are they at all loath to attack me anywhere they think they find a weak spot in my argument, so it is not unwillingness to engage in controversy. If they are silent, then, on all my major points, I conclude that that is because they have no answer to them; one needn't be the world's greatest consulting detective to understand that sometimes it is the fact that the dog did nothing in the nighttime that tells the story. As I said in the Preface, it would be gratifying and a contribution to the quest for truth if linguists learned to concede with grace what they cannot contest. It would also have the effect of increasing one's respect for them.

Nunberg and Pinker, between them, introduce virtually all the ideas and beliefs that underlie descriptivism, but neither presents them systematically and explicitly. So I have tried to do that myself in the following table, based on years of reading in the linguistic literature and of arguing with linguists.

Descriptivist Claim	The Linguistic Activist's Replies
Language is a fit subject for scientific study.	For reasons given in Chapter 2, this claim is unacceptable. To summarize them: language is an inseparable aspect of virtually all human activities; to study language in general is to take all of human life as one's subject. In short, it is not an isolable part of human behavior, intelligible apart from context and circumstances of use.
The scientific study of language has made steady progress since it began in the 19th century.	What was achieved by linguistics in the 19th century was the discovery of some striking regularities in some sound changes in Indo-European languages. That early success was taken as evidence that all of language could be so studied, and that the study would soon yield other such findings. No further findings of that caliber have been produced.

continued from previous page

Descriptivist Claim	The Linguistic Activist's Replies
All languages are in continual change, and such change is a healthy sign that a language is alive and serving the needs of its speakers.	Changes have indeed been observed in every language in active use, but many such changes do nothing to increase language's power, and some clearly diminish it. For example, the replacement of *reluctance* by *reticence,* with all its potential for confusion, and the resulting need for a replacement for *reticence.*
A languages changes in answer to the needs of its users, who are seldom conscious of causing the needed changes — they are caused by some mysterious force called, inter alia, "the genius of the language" or its "drift."	It is true — almost tautologically so — that all lexical changes come about for human reasons. But only a small number of new words or new senses for old words are coined in response to a felt *linguistic* need, such as the need for a name for a new phenomenon. The great majority of changes are introduced for non-linguistic reasons; six of the most common are discussed in Chapter 1, and among them they probably account for 98% of all lexical changes. The human traits and motives behind such changes explain why few of them improve the language, and many positively hurt it.
Fear of change, and resistance to it, is a sign of ignorance of the nature of language.	There may be a few prescriptivists who are as much against all change as descriptivists are in favor of it, but these extremists, if they exist at all, are few, unorganized, and without influence — their activity is limited to writing indignant letters to the editor, most of them so angry and ill-considered as to harm their cause. Most prescriptivists agree that some changes are desirable, and have even proposed and promoted some changes — they just don't agree that *all* change is good, or that resistance to any change is futile.
The history of language shows innumerable cases in which neologisms were rejected strenuously by critics at the time, but have since become fully accepted parts of the language.	True — and likewise there have been innumerable cases in which such rejection was effective, and nothing more has been heard of the neologisms in question. But even if every neologism ever introduced had been successful in becoming part of the language, what would that prove other than that error is often successful? The question is whether those neologisms made the language more expressive, more capable of nice distinctions, more responsive to the permanent needs of their speakers and writers.

121

continued from previous page

Descriptivist Claim	The Linguistic Activist's Replies
Usage is the only judge of changes; if everyone adopts a new term or construction, then it is part of the language.	True — but how should we regard a change that *not* everyone has accepted? At what point is a solecism committed by a single person transformed into a change in language that it is futile to resist?
The idea that any human language or dialect is better or more correct than any other is mere superstition, refuted by the findings of linguistic science.	When one language or dialect has a much larger general vocabulary than another, along with a richer literature and a much wider array of syntactic resources, it is better — if *better* has any meaning at all — than that other as a medium of communication. What linguists offer as proof of the essential equality of all languages is their finding that all of them are regular — a fact that was never in doubt, since only a language with that property would be usable at all, but one that proves nothing so far as relative merit goes. Linguists are unwilling to concede this common-sense point out of fear that the people who speak the less developed language will be judged to be inferior themselves.
The claim that Standard English (for example) is better than other dialects is false — it is merely the dialect of the ruling class — and is founded on elitism and, often, racism.	There is, as linguists are always pointing out, a strong positive correlation between a purportedly superior language and that spoken by the ruling or upper class — which they take to mean that it is called superior only *because* it is the dialect of the upper class. It seems not to occur to them that the cause-effect relationship may run the other way: perhaps one reason among others for the ascendancy of the ruling class is that they have a better language. The rich also have nicer homes and cars, and access to better education and health care than the poor, and it is not just because the rich have them that they're considered better.

continued from previous page

Descriptivist Claim	The Linguistic Activist's Replies
Discussions of language usage, as of all aspects of language, carried on in the absence of the expertise possessed by linguists is very likely to be unsound.	In many years of reading the linguistic literature I have yet to see a single case in which linguistic science has been able to settle or even help settle a usage question — that is, a question of the form "How should we …"). As an example, look at Nunberg 1983, an extended argument for linguistic knowledge as a contributor, at least, to the settling of usage questions, and note that not one of Nunberg's many judgments on usage appeals to the findings of linguistics. The only cases in which linguistics impinges at all on usage questions are those in which prescriptivists or usage mavens (to borrow Pinker's term) have attempted to buttress their positions with supposed language-historical facts, and blundered in doing so.

123

Descriptivists may object to the way I have presented the issues (so, for that matter, may some prescriptivists) or think that I have omitted some important arguments for their position. If so, and if my short-comings make them organize and present those ideas and arguments themselves, I will be greatly pleased. I ought not to have to represent both sides of this dispute, and formulate arguments for both of them.

When linguists consent to argue: the descriptivist/prescriptivist war

When linguists argue with their critics, it is not often that they deal with the concrete arguments put forward by actual contemporary spokesmen for good writing, or put forth positive arguments of their own. Professor Tom Shippey, concluding a review[85] of David Crystal's *The Stories of English*, writes "Crystal's sentiments are perfectly sound. But they are sentiments, not arguments, not analyses. Maybe that, sadly, is where we are at as regards both the historical and the contemporary study of the English language." What linguists much prefer when they do argue with contemporaries at all is to direct their attack at people who write letters to the editor warning that if we split infinitives we will go to hell in a handbasket, embark on crusades against usages that are neither shockingly novel nor dangerous to clarity, and generally make themselves and their cause look silly. These straw-man prescriptivists (a remarkable number of whom turn out to be long dead), the linguists claim, are trying to become dictators in matters of language usage, whereas they, the linguists — for these purposes dubbed the descriptivists — want merely to record what people actually say, what is really happening in language.

And linguists are not only, if they are to be believed, pure descriptivists, with no agenda other than that of recording and making sense of what they hear, but also, as the servants of linguistic law, on the side of the future, of the inevitable. When they're asked why, if their triumph is inevitable, and their critics are just the dogs who bark as the caravan moves on, they become so furious at those critics, they are reduced to claiming that they just don't want to see those critics waste their own time. Such is the pass to which we are brought when we undertake to defend the indefensible, and brazen our way through predicaments that our errors have landed us in.

In reality, our language, like any communal artifact, is something whose design anyone is free to push in any direction he likes, his success limited only by the inertia of the mass he is attempting to move, and by those pushing it in other directions. (I'm speaking here, as throughout, about semantics primarily, and perhaps in small part about syntax. Phonology and other aspects of language that are in part determined by the physical apparatus of speech production do to that extent obey natural laws, but are not my concern here.) In this free-for-all there is no referee, like the French Academy, to pass judgment on any attempt to shape this artifact, nor does the language have an intrinsic nature, as a living organism would, that might operate to divert or resist any attempt to push it around — if it seems to resist certain efforts, that is because it has, as just noted, enormous mass, and the difficulty of moving such mass may well seem to be positive resistance. In so wide open an arena, to rule out as somehow illegitimate the efforts of one group — the prescriptivists — to influence language is not to let the general public set the standards (they have no interest in the matter) nor to let the Genius of the Language express itself (there is no such thing), but simply to free other factions to determine the course the language will take: litigators, politicians, bureaucrats, marketing men — in the worst case, the villain of Orwell's *1984*, O'Brien. If we will not honor the King's or Queen's English, we will find ourselves in thrall to Knave's English.

We descriptivists will do all the thinking about language, thank you!

What linguists find unacceptable in prescriptivism is the conscious, planned nature of its influence on language. When television teaches us to say "No problem [or even better, *problemo*]" rather than "You're welcome," it does so without forethought, plan, or theory, but when a prescriptivist tries to encourage the use of *disinterested* in the sense "having no personal stake in the matter," he is doing so on the basis of a principle — the principle that a word that has a distinctive and useful sense, one not conveyed by any other word, should be reserved for use in that sense. Television and other popular media, having no designs on language, but simply using it (however poorly or meretriciously), are for the linguist part of nature, hence unobjectionable; the grammarian, by contrast, is trying to impose something artificial on that unspoiled child of nature, language, and is thereby interfering with its natural development.

What the descriptivist attitude amounts to, in practice, is the welcoming of all the forces that affect language except for that which springs from rational thought, explicit choice, and defensible principles; the motto of the linguists might well be "Where ego was, there id shall be!"[86] Their battle is not against good English *per se;* as noted repeatedly, the same linguist who will resort to every sophism in the book to argue against the use of *disinterested* in the sense just noted, or in favor of using *imply* and *infer* interchangeably, will himself use those terms just as correctly as the most rigorous prescriptivist. It is not so much the specific recommendations of prescriptivism that he rejects as it is the idea that usage should be guided by conscious thought — and most particularly, by the conscious thought of those who make no claim to be students of linguistic science, but are simply caring users of language, trying to make that tool more graceful, efficient, and expressive. And when he argues for some particular usage that prescriptivists deplore, it is almost never for himself that he wants it, but for The People; what he insists on is that the ordinary man should not be urged (*compelled* is the word he will use) to do likewise. In writing correctly even while encouraging the ordinary man to write in his own way, regardless of what it may cost him in respect and effectiveness, the linguist reveals that it is he, not the prescriptivist, who is the elitist, the expert condescending to the masses.

The general educated public would find it bizarre if historians of the industrial revolution, for example, should angrily oppose the efforts of engineers to improve automobiles, insisting that such efforts were impositions on ordinary drivers, interferences with the natural evolution of vehicles, and obstacles to the historians' effort to discover the laws behind natural vehicular evolution. But just such a position is taken by historians and chroniclers of language usage with respect to efforts to improve language, and their arguments have prevailed at least since the mid-20th century, much to the detriment of public education, publishing and editing standards and practices, and lexicography — and hence to the clarity and soundness of public discourse and debate on many issues.

Descriptivists ignore critics whenever possible, but when they are cornered, or think they can score some easy points against their critics, they fight back. When they do, they start by telling us that prescriptivism is an attempt at some kind of tyranny, an attempt by a small elite group (the word *cabal* is often heard when such charges are made) to impose their ways on The People (an unusually mild example of this is to be seen in a message from one Tom Collins quoted in Chapter 6). Then, no anti-prescriptivist argument is complete without reference to the ignominious failure of the French Academy to control the French language, and to the putative attempts of 17th- and 18th-century English writers, grammarians, and divines to impose Latinate grammar (at this point, expect heavy usage of *harsh, rigid,* and *strait-jacket*) on the natural, freedom-loving English language. To these charges is added the implication, if not explicit assertion, that prescriptivists are mindless reactionaries, inflexibly opposed to all change, and dedicated to returning the language to the perfect state they suppose it enjoyed at some earlier time. And finally, it is often hinted or plainly stated that prescriptivism is racist in effect or even in intent, because it would deny to various minorities the right to speak as they wish, or at least make them uncomfortable in speaking as they wish.

None of the descriptivist's points is valid. The notion that prescriptivists seek to have people observe certain conventions in diction is true; the notion that they would *impose* these conventions on the unwilling is so absurd that to call it false would be to pay it too much honor. Even assuming that prescriptivists were as unenlightened, despotic, and bigoted as they are often portrayed by their adversaries, how would they go about imposing their views on anyone? What authority or power do they possess or seek? All prescriptivists can do is argue for their views, and hope to convince readers that they're right — is this tyranny in the making?[87]

Linguists triumph easily over the dead

The references to the French Academy and the supposedly Latin-fixated grammarians of three and four hundred years ago are simply red herrings. It is centuries since anyone has called for a revival of these institutions or practices; they are dragged into current debates by descriptivists simply to suggest that any attempt to influence the course of language development in a purposeful, deliberate way is silly and doomed to failure. A particular favorite among the straw men set up by descriptivists is Bishop Robert Lowth (1710–1787), since he is the last person of consequence they can name who has, at least reputedly, taken a hard prescriptivist position. A typical and recent example of this is noted by Professor Tom Shippey in the review (aptly titled "We're still at it") cited earlier of David Crystal's history of the English language:

> The villains of the piece in this account are, first, the seventeenth- and eighteenth-century imposers of "polite English", or "correct English", from Dryden through to the grammarians Robert Lowth and Lindley Murray; and second, and even more culpable, those poor souls who still write to the newspapers protesting about double negatives, split infinitives and the abandonment of "grammar" in education.[88]

If even a fellow linguist cannot help observing that, after dealing with Lowth and the less-known Lindley Murray (whose chief gram-matical work was published in 1795), Crystal has to turn to plaintive letters to the editor to find further villains, the game is up. That linguists have to resort to such anachronisms and desperate measures in arguing against today's prescriptivists is further evidence that they are bereft of respectable arguments for their views, and have to use whatever they can scrape up if they're not to be altogether silent in the face of criticism. Apart from the silliness of attempting to discredit today's prescriptivism by attacking a position held by a man dead over two hundred years, it is not even true that Lowth, descriptivist's stan-dard punching bag, took a really hard position. Here is a sample of his thinking — an example selected by Professor Aitchison to show how reactionary and harsh he is:

> The Preposition is often separated from the Relative which it gov-erns, and is joined to the verb at the end of the Sentence ... as 'Horace is an author, whom I am much delighted with' ... This is an Idiom which our language is strongly inclined to; it prevails in common conversation, and suits very well with the familiar style

of writing; but the placing of the Preposition before the Relative is more graceful, as well as more perspicuous; and agrees much better with the solemn and elevated style.

So in this passage selected by Aitchison as a horrible example, Lowth finds ending a sentence with a preposition quite acceptable not only in speech but even in writing "of the familiar style"; only in what he calls "the solemn and elevated style" does he find it inappropriate, and even there he hardly calls down hellfire on anyone who disagrees. If this is the worst that the narrow, bigoted pedants of the 18th century could do, I'd say that the language would have been quite safe in their hands.

Even John McWhorter, one of the most enlightened and fair-minded of contemporary academic linguists, has descended to attacking Lowth. In fact, he has chosen the very passage quoted by Aitchison for evidence of Lowth's fatuity, and in doing so both misreads him and suppresses a vital part of his statement. McWhorter writes:[89]

> Lowth neatly undercut his case [against ending a sentence with a preposition] by committing the very "error" while warning against it: "This is an idiom, which our language is strongly inclined to."!

But the words McWhorter quotes, despite the terminal period that he supplies for them, are not the final words of Lowth's sentence. In Lowth's actual text, as shown in the fuller quotation of the same passage by Aitchison, they are followed by a semi-colon, and the sentence goes on for another forty-two words. So it is only a clause, not a sentence, that Lowth ended with a preposition. But more important than this, McWhorter misses Lowth's liberality in explicitly allowing the ending of a sentence with a preposition, not only in speech, but in the "familiar style" of writing — which is what he was himself practicing in the passage in question. Even if Lowth *had* ended the sentence with a preposition, then, he would not have been breaking the "rule" — more accurately, the recommendation — he was offering writers.

The claim that prescriptivists want to return to some imaginary Golden Age of Language, in which everyone spoke correctly and the language was perfect, and the claim that prescriptivists are opposed to any change in language are, like references to the French Academy and to putting a Latin straitjacket on English, simply false. The descriptivists cannot name one modern prescriptivist — anyone since Fowler, say — who ever supposed that there was such a Golden Age of Language, nor one who ever cried "Freeze the language! All change is forbidden!" And even if they could name any such figures, and give supporting quotations, what bearing would that have on the arguments offered by the critics of today? The refusal of the descriptivists to engage the arguments of their current opponents is a glaring sign of their inability to do so.

Prescriptivists & descriptivists: which are the elitists?

Prescriptivists frequently have it thrown in their face that they are assuming an authority to which they have no right; "Who made you the arbiter of … ?" is the question they are always hearing. There are good answers to this charge, or question, if only the descriptivists would listen. Prescriptivists have no personal authority in matters of usage, nor do they seek any. They seek to persuade, not to dictate; on the question of linguistic change, they argue that no change should be accepted until the educated public is aware of the issues it raises. For example, since about 1980, some people have been using *reticent* to mean *reluctant*. They do so not because they have made a conscious decision to drop the latter word and adopt the former in its place, but out of sheer ignorance or carelessness. No one claims that anything is gained for the language by such a change; indeed, it is clear that all that it will accomplish if it prevails is to create confusion, make it harder to understand some English literature, and make us search for a new word that will mean what *reluctant* meant.

There is no rational reason, then, to accept this incipient change, and every reason to abort it while we can. But one supposed authority on usage, R. W. Burchfield, in the new usage guide[90] that Oxford University Press disgracefully calls the "third edition of Fowler," has already yielded to this change, evincing all the reluctance (not, unfortunately, the *reticence*) of an eager virgin pretending to spurn the advances of a handsome rake. In his entry for *reticent,* he describes the new usage, and concludes that "The new use is non-standard at present, but has an air of inevitability about it." It seems not to occur to Burchfield that in a book that purports to guide usage — not just record it — and one bearing, however undeservedly, the name *Fowler,* the author is expected to give us not his vague and unsubstantiated intuitions about the 'air' some recent departure from standard usage has about it, but a judgment founded on such considerations as a refusal to bow to mere ignorance, at least while it is still vulnerable. Nor does it occur to him, apparently, that in suggesting that the change is inevitable, he is in fact coming down in its favor, and helping to make his prediction come true. In short, even though there is nothing to be said in favor of this change, and much to be said against it, still it is a change — and as such, near-sacrosanct to descriptive linguists.[91] Portraying himself as a mere observer of usage, Burchfield in fact passes judgment — poor judgment — on this issue; he is not a descriptivist or linguistic scientist, he is a prescriptivist — an incompetent one.

CHAPTER 5

The Eskimo Snow Vocabulary Controversy– A Case Study

The background of the case

The topics that linguists usually occupy themselves with depend on such specialized knowledge, and are written about in such specialized terminology, that outsiders are not in a position to follow their arguments and form independent judgments. But occasionally an issue arises that permits the intelligent and educated layman to understand and criticize the linguists' position. One such occasion arose in 1989, when Geoffrey Pullum, professor of linguistics at the University of California at Santa Cruz, published an essay announcing that the popular view that Eskimos had a great many more terms for varieties and conditions of snow and ice than others did was simply a myth. His claim was a factual one, subject to checking, but it appears that very little checking was done by anyone; journalists who pride themselves on their hard-nosed skepticism and immunity to being fooled happily repeated Pullum's claim, and it was accepted uncritically even by other linguists and language specialists, like Steven Pinker, Geoffrey Nunberg, and John McWhorter.

I too began by accepting Pullum's claim, assuming that a reputable linguist would hardly be making so bold an assertion unless he had evidence to back it up, but I was troubled by both the tone in which he made it, and by some questionable arguments and observations I found in the essay announcing it. At first I had reservations only about these side issues, but a little investigation made me wonder if Pullum was right even on his central factual claim about the size of the Eskimo snow vocabulary. Eventually I found that he was almost certainly wrong, and wrote an essay[92] in which I did challenge and, I believe, refuted his claim. I have drawn heavily on that essay for this chapter, but also added much new matter.

A linguist punctures a myth, at some cost in facts and logic

The Eskimo Snow Vocabulary (ESV) controversy concerns the number of words Eskimo languages have for snow and ice in their various forms and situations, as compared with other languages. The debate was set off several years ago by Pullum's essay, "The Great Eskimo Vocabulary Hoax," (Pullum 1989, 1990, 1991). Pullum there ridiculed the idea that the Eskimos had significantly more words for various types and conditions of snow than did English, for example. He was motivated to do so, he explained, partly by a wish to correct this particular popular misconception, but much more by a wish to use this canard as a cautionary lesson on human gullibility, shoddy scholarship, and even latent racism.

His essay attracted a good deal of attention, and has even, according to his friend and ally Geoffrey Nunberg, gone a long way toward correcting the error in question, if not the underlying faults in human nature or society that Pullum tells us are his real targets. After reviewing the history of Pullum's attempt at straightening us all out on the ESV question, Nunberg writes, "But has the world paid any heed? Amazingly, it has,"[93] and reports that many stories in the press and periodicals have picked up Pullum's thesis and joined him in laughing at or scolding the sillies or miscreants who still languish in a state of error. It is not clear whether these journalistic sallies really represent a paying of heed by the world, or just the casual exploitation of a very minor item of intellectual froth by journalists always desperate for something to talk about, but Pullum's piece does seem to have had an unusually successful career as such things go. It is taken as authoritative, for example, by Steven Pinker, who says, "no discussion of language and thought would be complete without the Great Eskimo Vocabulary Hoax,"[94] and goes on to summarize, with glee, Pullum's supposed final settling of the matter. It was similarly accepted by John McWhorter,[95] although that former U. C. Berkeley linguist has since indicated that my counter-arguments have some weight with him. And in a *reductio ad absurdam* that would seem to be unsurpassable, one author[96] opens his discussion of the "myth" in the standard manner:

> The myth is that the Eskimos have a large number (50, 100, 500; it varies with the telling) of words for snow.

and goes on to tell the traditional story, with approving nods to Pullum and Pinker, and side glances at Boas, Sapir, and Whorf — but winds up his hard-hitting, fearless exposé by saying:

> The conclusion is that yes, even though the details are exaggerated and confused, the legend about Eskimo words for snow is basically true. ... The fact is utterly unremarkable. If the Yup'ik and Inuit peoples did not have a large number of ways to express different types of arctic weather conditions, we should be surprised.

The notion that Eskimos have an exceptionally rich snow vocabulary has apparently achieved a state in which, transcending mere sublunary logic, it remains mythical even though true. And the myth-buster informs those of us who always believed that Eskimos have such a vocabulary that there is nothing remarkable about the fact, as if we ever thought there was.

To the best of my knowledge, my own essay on the subject (Halpern 2000 and 2004) remains the only attempt to critically analyze Pullum's thesis. Even that essay, though, as its name indicates, did not take that thesis as its main target, but simply used Pullum's failings, as I see them, to introduce and illustrate my own concerns about linguistics and usage, just as Pullum had used the ESV issue to lead into the larger questions of concern to him. And both he and I have been at some pains to emphasize that the ESV, as such, is of only secondary interest to us, compared with the larger social and intellectual issues that we see involved. But while all parties seem to agree on the relative unimportance of the ESV question, it keeps coming up, and keeps generating heat. And whatever the intrinsic interest of the ESV question, the answer to it proposed by one linguist, and the uncritical acceptance of that answer by so many others (despite the faults that raised a red flag immediately for me), can tell us something about linguistics' claim to scientific status. So this chapter attempts to clear away some confusions and fallacies — not all of them Pullum's — that continue to impede the settling of this troublesome if incidental question. I have not forced myself to stay strictly within the linguistic arena while discussing the ESV — I'm not sure it is possible to say much about it without glancing at broader issues of scholarly practice and social outlook — but I have tried to keep myself from roaming beyond the purely linguistic any further than is necessary to present a coherent argument.

Metic terms: not all words are created equal

Some claim that the Eskimos have words for many more varieties and conditions of snow and ice than do the languages of the temperate zone; others say they have no more. The evidence usually offered consists of lexical counts, with each side in the debate claiming authority for its own list of such words gathered from native informants, or from dictionaries compiled earlier from such interviews. But besides all the difficulties regularly associated with the compilation of word lists for a language that until recently was purely a spoken language, and whose present-day written form is largely the work of non-natives, there is in this case a special problem: these lexical counts seldom if ever distinguish between words in common use and those never used by, or even known to, ordinary users of the language in question. This failure vitiates virtually all attempts made so far to settle the matter.

Those who reject the notion that Eskimos have a significantly richer snow-and-ice vocabulary, for example, often compile lists of English snow-related words in order to show that there are roughly as many such words in English as in Yup'ik or Iñupiaq; what they fail to note is that most of those English words are far from being in common use among English-speaking people. Most English speakers live their entire lives without once using such words as *rime* and *glare;* these words are in the English language, for the majority of its speakers, only in the sense that they're in English-language dictionaries. They are not, for that majority, even in their passive vocabularies — most have never seen or heard such words used, and could not define them. I think that a label is required for words that are part of the language only in so tenuous a sense, and I propose *metic* for that role — a term used to describe resident aliens in ancient Athens, who were allowed to live in the city, but severely restricted in their legal rights, and sharply distinguished from Athenian citizens.[97] It is particularly important to make such a distinction when considering English, because that language is so acquisitive, so omnivorous, so ready to assimilate words from any source — the metic contributions to English from the languages of the Indian sub-continent alone have been collected in a book that runs to just short of 1,000 pages (Yule 1886) — that otherwise, we'll soon have to conclude that English subsumes every known language, including the Eskimo languages. That would settle the debate about whether Eskimo languages have more snow-related words than English, but not in a useful way.

By contrast, the many words that appear on Eskimo-language lists of snow and ice terms are very much native words, and in common use among all speakers of the language in question. The Public Information Officer for the North Slope Borough, Barrow, Alaska, has said, "... the Inupiats have more than 30 words for snow, and more than 70 words for ice. In the Arctic, the specific conditions of snow and ice are critical to hunting and survival ..." (Patkotak 1994). And again, "Ice is very important here because of whaling and hunting done on the pack ice. Each word denotes ice in a very specific place or condition. Use the wrong word when you go hunting on the ice and you are apt never to be seen again" (Patkotak 1996). If we exclude the metics, and compare lists of just those snow-related words *that are in common use* among speakers of English with corresponding lists from Eskimo languages, it is obvious that the Eskimo snow vocabulary is many times greater than the English (and, presumably, other temperate-zone languages), just as one would expect.

What is a 'word'? Does it matter?

The suggestion has been made that the very term *word* is out of place in discussions of polysynthetic languages such as the various Eskimo languages; these, it is claimed, are largely made up of free-floating segments that can be combined freely at need, making their semantic units incommensurate with those of English, which for the most part is a corpus of fixed terms that have to be used as given, or not at all. This claim is a red herring. Whether the snow-related terms of the Eskimo languages are words in the same sense as the words of English is not to the point; what matters is that those Eskimo-language features — call them *standard locutions* or *standard constructs,* if you like, to avoid the controversial word *word* — are recognized and commonly used features of their languages. What the debate is about is whether there are significantly more such *constructs* or *locutions* for snow-related phenomena in the Eskimo languages than there are in the languages of the temperate and equatorial zones.

(When the debate gets down to specifics, the comparison is usually between one of the Eskimo languages and English, but of course this is far from satisfactory: first, the Eskimo languages should be compared to *all* non-Eskimo languages to eliminate the possibility that, for example, Swahili might contain just as many snow-related terms; second, if just one language is to be chosen to represent the non-Eskimo languages, English is a bad choice, because of that omnivorous appetite mentioned earlier.)

Of course any urgent warning about ice or snow conditions that the Eskimo languages can convey could also be conveyed in English — but it would take in general many more English words than Eskimo-language constructs; it would take the English-language speaker much longer to frame his utterance, since he would have to improvise; and he could not be certain that his improvised utterance would be understood in time — or ever — by those he was addressing. In contrast, the Eskimo wishing to convey the same warning would be able to reach for a ready-made tool, immediately comprehensible to his countrymen. And the Eskimos' need for such a tool is readily understandable, I think; it is rather more important for an Eskimo to be able to say quickly "That ice you're standing on is the kind that splits suddenly when the tide turns, as it is doing right now" than it is for the typical Alabaman. As has often been noted, when excited or in trouble, we fall back on clichés — and when it comes to trouble on ice, the Eskimos have many clichés, and we do not.

Need a snow-related term be exclusively snow-related to count?

Another frequently heard claim is that only those words or phrases of which all parts are exclusively snow-related are to count when we're enumerating snow-related terms. According to this notion, *powder* as a descriptor of a type of snow is not to count, since it is a term originating outside the snow context, and used only figuratively of snow. That this proposed rule is wholly arbitrary and invalid may be seen by applying it to words on other topics: would we deny that *strawberry roan*, for example, is a horse-breeding term because *strawberry* originates, and is used, in other contexts? Isn't *donkey engine* a mechanical term, even though a donkey is an animal, not a machine?

What matters for this kind of investigation is the number of distinct objects of interest within the subject area the linguistic community under examination has identified, and for whose expression they have standard, recognized constructs — constructs, that is, that can be used without improvisation, and with assurance that any member of that community will understand them clearly and immediately. For these purposes there is no reason to distinguish between simple words and more elaborate verbal constructs, or between those constructs of which every part is peculiar to its subject area, and those that draw on the vocabulary of other subject areas for analogies and metaphors.[98]

Need a rich snow vocabulary subject Eskimos to Sapir-Whorf ignominy?

Yet another red herring is the claim that one's position on the Eskimo snow-vocabulary question is in effect one's position on the Sapir-Whorf hypothesis[99] about the role that language has in shaping and constraining its speakers' worldview. But this claim simply has no merit; one can hold any imaginable position on the Sapir-Whorf hypothesis, or even never have heard of that hypothesis, without reference to the number of snow-related constructs one finds in Eskimo speakers' live vocabularies. The one point of interest offered by this particular red herring is that it may explain the heat and rancor that have attended many debates on the snow-vocabulary question. If one imagines that the attribution to Eskimos of a large snow-related vocabulary necessarily, or even probably, entails supposing that Eskimos are limited to a very narrow, primitive worldview, and hence may be treated as our inferiors, even as less than human, than one might well strongly oppose such an attribution, and even bring charges of racism against those who find that Eskimos do have such a vocabulary. But why one should imagine any such thing is a mystery. In the minds of most observers, it is perfectly natural, and fully human, to possess and use a large vocabulary for the most prominent concerns in one's daily life — so much so that we would be likely to doubt the humanity of any group that did *not* do so.

Should Eskimos be called 'Eskimos'?

A point that is raised often enough in debates about the ESV to need putting to rest is that it is insulting to indigenous Arctic and Sub-Arctic peoples to call them *Eskimos*. This notion seems to rest — insofar as it can be said to rest on any clearly expressed reasons — on the facts or supposed facts that, first, the peoples concerned do not call themselves by that name, and second, the name is a Cree Indian word meaning 'eater of raw meat,' or 'eater of fish,' or even 'eater of rotten fish,' and hence an insult.[100]

The response to the first point is that while the Eskimos do not, in their own languages, call themselves by that name, that is because *Eskimo* is an English word, and they are not speaking that language. The Eskimos, more tolerant than their self-appointed champions, not only do not require English-speakers to use Eskimo names, but often call themselves *Eskimos* when speaking English. The claim that one must call each people by the name they call themselves in their own language is in effect the claim that there must be no English-language name for any foreign group. The right principle is that stated by C. S. Lewis when, anticipating rebuke for using 'Scotch' as the term for those Britons who come from north of the Tweed, he simply pointed out that he was writing in English, not Scots.[101]

The response to the second is that no insult is intended, nor felt by the Eskimos, when they are called *Eskimo*. The origin of the name is unclear, and it may in fact mean 'eater of *fermented* [not *rotten*] fish,' but there is no reason in any case to regard it as derogatory — see the discussion by Damas in the Introduction to (Woodbury 1984). And how, one wonders, can the politically correct defend their rejection of a term coined by the Cree, another indigenous people; is that not insulting to the Cree? And is it not insulting to the Eskimos to assume that a bunch of Cheechakos can detect insult to Eskimos where the Eskimos themselves cannot, and to assume that the Eskimos must be protected as if they were children or mentally deficient? Hard is the path of the politically correct — and may it remain so.[102]

The facts retaliate by puncturing the linguist

I found Pullum's claim that Eskimo languages had no more elaborate a vocabulary for describing forms and conditions of snow and ice than did English starkly contrary to common sense, and additionally suspect for being embedded in dubious argumentation and casual charges of racism. In the hope of determining for myself the trustworthiness of his claims, I started reading some of the work of linguists and others concerned with Eskimo languages, and seeking information from various people who speak those languages or are at least deeply involved in Eskimo culture. Among those I have to thank for useful information are Dee Longenbaugh of Juneau, Elise Sereni Patkotak of Barrow, and Harley Sundown of Scammon Bay; several members of the staff of the Alaska Native Language Center, University of Alaska, Fairbanks: Professors Anna Berge, Steven Jacobson, Lawrence Kaplan, John Ritter, and Siri Tuttle, and Ms Kathy Sikorski; and at the Technical University of Berlin, Professor Elke Nowak.

None of these informants is responsible for any errors in my account of the matter, nor necessarily in agreement with all my conclusions, but I can say that the communications I've received from them are overwhelmingly supportive of my account of the Eskimo snow vocabulary. One of the most senior of the experts just listed wrote: "I have read the essay you sent me as an attachment and the list of snow terms,[103] and I agree with almost everything you say. ... The only place where I have to disagree with what you have written is concerning the word "Eskimo" itself, and actually any discussion of the acceptability of that word is not too very relevant to your essay."

Their responses confirmed my own conclusion: Pullum is wrong, and the popular idea is right; Eskimo languages do indeed offer a much larger and richer vocabulary than does English (for example) for describing conditions of snow and ice, just as common sense would suggest. And since Pullum and others have charged that the popular view is tainted by racist attitudes toward the Eskimos, it is important to note that other, non-Eskimo dwellers in the extreme north have similarly enriched vocabularies; see Tim Bayliss-Smith, letter to the editor, *Times Literary Supplement* (October 18, 2002), who points out that the Lapps of northern Finland also have such extensive vocabularies. And more recently I learned from Professor Owen Gingerich that Russian, too, is far richer in snow-and-ice terms than English.

CHAPTER 6

A **P**eople's Linguistics

A
People's
Linguistics

It is an article of faith — or perhaps better, a plank of the political platform — of most academic linguists that The People and their Right to Speak as They Wish are under attack, and that they, the linguists, are the People's main line of defense against those who would bully them into False Correctness — sheepdogs bravely protecting their sheepish flock against the wolves of prescriptivism. It must be greatly troubling to the linguists, then, to find themselves so unappreciated by those they are so gallantly guarding; people *will* turn to usage guides like Fowler, Follett, Garner, Safire, and Bernstein in their pitiful quest for Correctness, despite the efforts of their protectors to assure them that there is nothing wrong with their language usage — certainly not with their speech, and perhaps not even with their writing.

On becoming a spokesman for The People

I write "people" at some places and "The People" at others to denote very different things. The uncapitalized form stands for you and me and the man who comes to read the gas meter; capitalized and with the definite article, for something from a different realm altogether. "The People" is a mystical emanation from you and me and the meter reader; it represents all that is best in us, and wants what we would want if only our eyes were wide open. As such, it carries far greater moral weight than we do, and should a conflict seem to exist between it and the people, it must and should prevail (Rousseau provides a rationale if one is needed).

The People, as a mystical emanation, does suffer from one disadvantage: it cannot speak for itself, but needs to be represented by spokesmen. Luckily, there are some willing to take on that role, even though the rewards they get for their services are meager. Those who speak for The People *politically* get a considerable license; once it is accepted that you are The People's political spokesman, you can do anything you like to people; acts that would be highly reprehensible, even criminal, if you committed them acting *in propria persona* are sacrosanct if you commit them in the role of Spokesman for The People. Whatever Rousseau's intentions, the effect, as the entire twentieth century tried to teach us, is that The People is a concept ideally formed to give despots a pretext for doing whatever they wish. The consequences brought about by those who claim to speak for The People in matters linguistic are hardly so horrific (nor the rewards anywhere near so great), but they are, in their own way, harmful.

Just two steps must be taken by a linguist wishing to become a spokesman for The People: First, claim that language has a nature, or destiny, or Genius, which expresses itself through The People — or at least so expresses itself whenever those fools, the prescriptivists, cease to torment and mislead the people with their antiquated, discredited, elitist ideas of 'correctness' and similar superstitions. Then, make it clear that you yourself have no personal stake in the matter; you simply want to see The People liberated to speak as they wish (but beware of expressing this by claiming to be *disinterested,* forgetting that you have elsewhere railed against the prescriptivist insistence on using that word in that false, outmoded, elitist sense); you are simply acting as the Good Shepherd, protecting your flock from the predations of the prescriptive wolves. (And your analogy is not altogether unsound; shepherds do protect their flocks from wolves — because they want to reserve shearling coats and lamb chops for themselves.)

If real people seem to care little or nothing about language, The People, linguists contend, do care, and have appointed the linguists their spokesmen (though people seem not to realize this), and what the linguists want for their ungrateful charges is that they should be set free in matters of usage from the strictures of grammarians and prescriptivists. Linguists believe, or speak as if they believe, that if the last traditional grammarian were strangled with the bowels of the last prescriptivist, the genius of the language, expressing itself through the usage of The People, would be liberated; everyone would speak vividly and effectively (yet inoffensively to anyone), and all manner of things would be well. This may be what The People want, but flesh and blood people, knowing little and caring less about language, do not wish to be thus "set free" or otherwise troubled; they wish to be let alone, except when drafting things like job and college applications, and résumés. Then they *do* want some outside aid — they want to be helped to write with reasonable correctness; the last thing they want at such times is to be told that they're fine as they are, and shouldn't worry about silly, elitist ideas of "correctness." They know perfectly well that their writing isn't very good, and that those to whom they are submitting their applications and résumés will be judging them at least in part on how they write.

The linguists are to their flock what Communist Party cadres are with respect to the American working class: in both cases the intended protégés suffer from false consciousness, persist in refusing to recognize that they are victims of the System or the Bosses, and utterly fail to see where their true interests lie. Maddeningly, ordinary people don't care one way or another about language; for them, language is to be used, not analyzed or worried about. They think no more about what they do when they talk than what they do when they walk. (Why does everyone groan when a pun is made, even a good one? Because it shows that someone — some *pervert* — is *thinking* about language, rather than just using it.)

Is anyone in charge here? Need anyone be?

What the linguists seem constitutionally unable or unwilling to grasp is that in matters on which the people have no strong opinions of their own, such as language usage, *some* outside influence is going to determine how they behave; *some* authority figure's practice will prevail — it will not be one generated by the ordinary people themselves, because they aren't much interested. (To demand, as linguists do, that The People be left alone to make their own decisions about language usage is to demand that other parties — especially prescriptivists — shut up so that one's own views can prevail.) The most difficult point to make, as it is the most important, is that all of us have to accept someone's lead, someone's rules; the only question is, *whose?* Linguists, like anarchists, argue as if the abolition of all man-made rules would solve the problem of power and free us, when in fact rules are the only thing that can moderate power, and give freedom a chance. Language is a communal, social possession, and only the acceptance of rules, in one form or another, makes such a thing possible, just as only traffic regulations make mass automobile use possible.

So when linguistic freedom fighters declare that no one is going to tell good Americans how to speak or write their own language, they don't really mean it. What they mean is that they're not going to be told what to do by pedants, highbrows, bookworms, and snobbish intellectuals — and indeed they are not; which means they get told what to do by television gag men, advertising copywriters, political flacks, and aluminum-siding salesmen. Here is one of my critics, Tom Collins, inadvertently providing a beautiful example of such a rebel digging his own pit, and then gladly jumping into it:

> Mr. Halpern has missed the real point ... that is, that people, not "experts" will decide what is right and wrong [in English usage]. Mr. Halpern says that prescriptivists depend on "books and teachers" for providing guidance on "correct grammar." But our society today is driven so much more by television, radio, movies, and popular music, that this is laughable by its irrelevancy.[104]

So the public, having sung its traditional last-day-of-school song, "Good-bye schoolroom, good-bye books, good-bye teacher's dirty looks!", is condemned instead to parrot the latest catchphrase of some late-night television performer, thereby demonstrating its independence of authority, just as its sons show *their* independence by all wearing their caps backwards. (Harold Rosenberg's wonderful phrase, "the herd of independent minds," covers the case nicely.) Their transference of fealty to television personalities and the rest of the entertainment and opinion-manipulating world would seem to leave the public at least as far from independence as when it was under the thumbs of the grammarians, but the new fealty has one saving grace: the television personality does not threaten his audience's dignity and *amour propre;* he never lectures, never corrects, never reveals by the flick of an eyebrow that he thinks himself better than they are — so if *he* determines what they are to say, they don't resent it, don't feel talked down to.[105]

The position of the linguists with respect to the people is like that of Party cadres in another way too; the grievances against which they would protect their involuntary wards are, to the extent that they really are grievances, mostly ended or so ameliorated as to be little more than minor nuisances by now. Just as the real horrors of 19th-century "capitalism" — actually, of early industrialization under any known system or regime — have by now, at least in the Western world, been almost entirely eliminated, just so the attempts of 16th- and 17th-century grammarians to reform English grammar on the model of Latin, and of 18th century prescriptivists to found an English Academy analogous to the French Academy, have been by now almost utterly forgotten. But just as today's Party cadres thunder on as if ten-year old children were still being worked twelve hours a day in dark and dirty Birmingham workshops, so today's linguists still thunder on as if hordes of uninformed schoolmarms were still cracking children's knuckles with hickory sticks for splitting infinitives, and continue to attack the prescriptivism of Bishop Lowth, dead these two hundred years and more, as if he were still a power in the land (and as if he had been when alive a martinet and harsh reactionary, which he was not).

The analogy is so close that it is fitting to call descriptivism People's Linguistics, bearing the same relation to genuine philology that People's Democracies do to real, law-respecting polities. And the ultimate outcome of the People's Linguistics would no more be the liberation of language users than the ultimate outcome of People's Democracies is the freedom and prosperity of the working class; in both cases, the result is the acquisition and retention of power by the cadres, and the perpetuation and aggravation of the problems the cadres supposedly exist to solve. But wait — is this (gasp! choke!) *McCarthyism?* Am I accusing linguists of being members of a subversive conspiracy, agents of a foreign power, traitors? In a word, no; linguists are no more conspirators than a flock of pigeons or a school of sardines are conspirators when they all wheel in the same direction, nor are they trying to impose a new system upon us; each of them is simply doing what the exigencies of his situation impels him to do, with no plan, pre-arrangement, or leadership. To the extent that sincerity is a virtue, they are virtuous; and if their pursuit of their truth incidentally coincides with their own interests, and confirms their position as authorities on language usage, they can hardly be blamed for reaping the rewards that naturally fall to those who defend the truth.

The language gang flaunts its colors and fights for its turf

This doesn't mean that they are without fault, only that they are individual combatants fighting to remain kings of the language hill, rather than organized ones working, knowingly or not, on behalf of hidden objectives. First, they are academics, and academics whose department is generally regarded, despite their claims to being tough-minded scientists, as a humanities or at best a social sciences department, which means that they are largely bored with their nominal duties, envious of the respect that people in the Physics Department enjoy, and seeking restlessly for some more exciting and prestigious role to play. Their colleagues in the English Department have cornered the political and social radical role (Chomsky himself has refused to recognize the proprietary rights of the English professors to that role, but celebrities of his magnitude are above the ordinary rules); those in the Philosophy Department have gone the postmodern route, claiming to have discovered that there is no Truth; members of the Linguistics Department, with exemplary modesty, are asking only that their claim to be scientists be honored.

Second, linguists are supposedly professional experts on one aspect of human behavior, the linguistic aspect, who are half frightened, half outraged by finding themselves challenged, on matters that they regard as within their professional purview, by amateurs. The refusal of so many English-language speakers to play the role of native informants, to remain passive and naive while their linguistic behavior is studied,[106] would in itself be quite enough to depress the linguists; the impudence of people like Safire in trying to usurp what little authority the linguists might still hope to enjoy must be — and evidently is — quite intolerable. *Here I am,* the linguist must *think, having spent years studying Old English and Romance Philology, having memorized tables of sound changes and the phonetic alphabet, and having ruined my eyes reading closely-printed books by obscure Germans and Scandinavians while my contemporaries were building careers in law and medicine, or making fortunes in business and the stock market — and now I can't get people to show me due respect even in that narrow sector where my expertise would seem relevant!*

153

So linguists must be exonerated of the charge of being members of a large, well-organized conspiracy; instead they are simply a collection of nervous academics who feel themselves dissed and threatened with loss of turf, and react as any aggrieved small property owners would.

Racism, sexism, and other isms: the fight gets ugly

Disputes between the linguists and their critics, or what is nearly the same thing, between the descriptivists and prescriptivists, rarely proceed very far before the former charge the latter with some form of bigotry, usually racial or sexual.

The notion that Geoffrey Pullum has tried to establish, that Eskimos have no more words for snow and ice than do those who live in the temperate zone, was put into his head, he tells us, by a paper delivered by Professor Laura Martin, a linguist and anthropologist, at a meeting of the American Anthropological Association in 1982, and published in 1986.[107] In that paper, Professor Martin was not content to refute the popular fallacy (as she thought it) with facts and reasoning, she added some gratuitous comments about our readiness to embrace such errors. Pullum quotes her and adds his own approving comment:

> "We are prepared to believe almost anything about such an unfamiliar and peculiar group," says Martin, in a gentle reminder of our buried racist tendencies.[108]

It was good of Professor Martin to be gentle, and to say "we" when she clearly meant "you fools" or worse. But she, like Pullum, failed to explain why it is racist of us to credit the Eskimos with words for many varieties of snow. Speaking for my possibly bigoted self, I felt closer to the Eskimos when I supposed them to be walking Rogets on the subject of frozen water — that's just what I would be, I think, if I lived near the Arctic Circle. But it may be that to understand my feelings, Professor Martin would have to learn something of the ways of my unfamiliar and peculiar group, the non-academics.

The accusations of racism made against prescriptivists, made even by so normally sensible and fair-minded linguists as Nunberg, as well as the more pugnacious ones like Pullum, are not merely false, but deeply ugly and offensive. (And the readiness of linguists to sink to such *ad hominem* arguments is yet another sign of their inability to mount a respectable defense against their critics.) Pullum, as we have seen, wants us to think that in crediting Eskimos with an unusually rich snow vocabulary, we are insulting them — we are implying that they think so much about snow that they cannot think of much else, and are therefore our intellectual inferiors. His claim derives such support as it has from the Sapir-Whorf Hypothesis, that rather nebulous notion that the structure and vocabulary of a language limits the mental horizons of its speakers.[109] It is not much referred to these days — and it is not really a hypothesis, since it cannot be tested — but is occasionally taken out of storage and dusted off when needed to discredit some critics. (How the Sapir-Whorf Hypothesis, which sees one's language as a constraint on one's thought, can be squared with the dogma of orthodox linguistics that holds that language is ever changing in response to the needs of its speakers, is hard to see. Are we to suppose that the speakers of such constraining languages do not notice, or do not mind, being so constrained? Linguists are not troubled by this difficulty; they ignore it.)

The other Geoffrey, Professor Nunberg, directs his charge of racism against those who would have the schools teach Standard English (SE) to all students, whatever their race, and require its use while they're in school. This attitude, he half says, half implies, is the result of racial arrogance on the part of whites, who think their own dialect is best simply because it is theirs, and of linguistic ignorance, which fails to understand that the dialect spoken in the "inner city," as poor Black neighborhoods are euphemistically called, is just as logically structured and expressive as that of the dominant race and class. He writes:

> First, every language is a complex system with an internal logic, the full understanding of which requires scientific investigation. And second, since nonstandard forms of English possess internal logic just as standard English does, they are not inherently inferior; rather, the doctrines of prescriptive grammar reflect covert class prejudice and racism.[110]

Several dubious assumptions are packed into these two sentences. There are many aspects to a language or dialect, and the possession of an "internal logic" is just one of them; to declare two of them equal because they both possess such a "logic" is to ignore many other bases for comparison. In particular, the possession of an "internal logic" would seem to be an absolute necessity for any language or indeed any "complex system" — how could it function at all without that quality? — which makes it particularly useless as a basis for comparing any two of them. Then, it is not clear that a "complex system" needs to be scientifically investigated in order to be understood, unless

Nunberg is using *scientific* here just to mean *scholarly* or *critical*. And after defending a minority dialect as being a system, and a complex one to boot, Nunberg doesn't seem to have grasped fully just what a system is; later in the same piece he writes:

> Two negatives do not make a positive in French or Italian, for example, nor does French use the nominative case after *to be*. Would we really want to argue that these languages are less logical than English? And if not, why do we insist that there is something illogical about the English sentences *It is me,* or *I didn't see None?*

The reason is that French and English are two different systems, and you cannot arbitrarily transplant an element of one to another, as anyone so keen on the notion of system might be expected to realize. When a French general decorates a soldier, he gives him the formal accolade that Americans call "kissing on both cheeks." If an American general did that, spectators would wonder if he had lost his mind; if a French general failed to do that, the person being decorated would feel insulted. Our language, like our military etiquette, is a "system" that differs from theirs; what makes perfect sense in one would be an aberration in another.

But to return to the linguistic arena: whether the dialect of the inner city is as linguistically respectable as the mainstream one is not to the point; most of us who want African-Americans, like all Americans, to be taught SE in school, and required to use it there, do so not because we find inner-city dialect syntactically faulty or morphophonemically deprived, but because it prevents Blacks from escaping the inner city. One of the greatest obstacles faced by racial and ethnic minorities in their quest for advancement is lack of ease with SE. Employers and others in a position to award good things discriminate against those without a good command of SE not merely because they themselves usually speak SE, and are most comfortable when surrounded by others who do so too, but because a lack of fluency in SE often causes serious communication problems, and makes employees and associates suffering from that deficiency useless or worse. This does not mean, as should be needless to say, that racial, ethnic, or religious minority groups should not speak as they please among themselves; only that they must be able to use SE when dealing with the general public. Those who call this effort to help minorities get ahead "racism" never offer a reasoned explanation of their charge; as someone has bitterly observed, such a charge is too serious to require evidence.

When faced with the argument just made, their reply, when they stay to make one at all, is that employers *shouldn't* require employees to speak SE — they should simply learn to be more respectful of minority dialects. And if employers are right in thinking that most of their customers would rather shop and conduct business where the employees spoke SE, then the answer is that the customers, too, must reform, and learn to accept the dialects spoken by others. And if getting the entire population to drop its prejudices (assuming for argument's sake that that's all they are) takes a few centuries or so to accomplish, with Blacks and other linguistic minorities in the meantime remaining highly disadvantaged, why that is just the price that has to be paid for progress (luckily for the linguists, paid by someone else), the eggs that must be broken so that the politically correct can enjoy an omelet.

The charge of sexism is not as frequently made as that of racism, because men and women of a given race at least seem to be speaking the same dialect; members of different races, such as a great many Caucasians on the one hand, and African Americans on the other, often do not. But it crops up whenever, for example, the question arises, as it keeps doing, of whether *he* is acceptable as the neuter pronoun, or the similar question of whether *man* should be taken as a synonym for *homo sapiens* rather than the name of the males of our species. When those questions arise, the discussions that follow are almost always marked by bitterness, sarcasm, and general animosity, to the detriment of clear thinking about what one is saying. One recent critic, Miriam Watkins Meyers, writes:

> In the good old days — between the mid-eighteenth century and the late 1960s; specifically, before women insisted on being

included in the human race — writers employed the allegedly generic *he* to fill the void. In the name of "correct" grammar and without so much as a murmur of rebellion, we embraced the idea that *he* meant *she* as well as *he* and rejected the notion that feminine gender mattered. Thus embracing the ideal of genderless *he*, we didn't even smile at the absurdity of a sentence such as, "No person shall be forced to have an abortion against his will" or "Man, being a mammal, breast-feeds his young"[111]

The internal quotations in this passage are offered as examples of the absurdities we're led to by supposing that *man* refers to a species, not a sex. But the writer misses the point of her own examples; the sentences she quotes were written not as jokes or insults, but as serious statements, and were by her own admission taken as such by their readers — which means that for both writer and readers, there was no absurdity in using *man* to mean just *homo sapiens*, not *males*. So the use of *man* for *human being* was not meant to exclude or belittle women, and was not, apparently, taken as doing so by either sex — and the interesting question it raises is when, how, and why it has come to be taken as such today. This misunderstanding of her own example by the quoted writer does not settle the question whether *man* should be so used now; it merely provides an illustration of the way charges of bigotry are made so carelessly today that the plaintiffs, in their confusion, often offer arguments that work against their own thesis.

Finally in this chamber of horrors, the charge that the dialect of the upper or ruling class is favored simply because it is theirs is similarly ridiculous. That dialect, known less tendentiously as Standard English, has many attributes besides its association with the top dogs of our society: it is the dialect in which almost all literature, from the most ephemeral to the most permanent, is written; it is the dialect of the law courts, of academia, of mainstream religion; it is the dialect studied by millions of foreigners who want to do business with us; it is the international language of science; it is even, for the most part, the dialect that popular culture, including television and the movies, speaks. It is the dialect in which scholarship writes, even in the act of trying to protect and promote other dialects, as Nunberg is in the cited article. (It would be interesting to see Nunberg try to rewrite that article in the language of the inner city, that perfectly equal dialect.) In making it possible for speakers of minority dialects to avoid acquiring the mastery of SE that yields these overwhelming advantages, while winning diplomas and other marks of achievement in education, the linguists and their allies are costing their protégés a heavy price, as I noted earlier.[112]

But that price seems to the linguists quite reasonable (particularly because they are not the ones paying it) if that's what it takes to make the point that all dialects are equally good from the linguistic point of view, and hence should be accepted as equal in all ways, and by everyone. Just one linguist that I know of, the late James Sledd, took a perfectly consistent position on this matter: he conceded that in opposing what he called "bi-dialectalism" (speaking SE in the great world, one's mother tongue at home and with friends) he was making it harder for ethnic minorities to "get ahead" — but getting ahead, he asserted, was an ignoble thing compared with supporting one's people and one's ethnic pride by speaking their private dialect exclusively.[113]

In all this we have supposed for argument's sake that SE, the dialect of the masters, has no practical superiority, but is merely the dialect the masters happen to speak, and is promoted by those masters and their prescriptivist toadies for no better reason than that. But members of the upper class have a habit of providing themselves with the best of everything; is it not possible that they use SE because they find it serves them best? The upper class also, generally speaking, gets the best education and drives the best cars; is Princeton more prestigious than some backwoods diploma mill only because the upper class sends its offspring there? Is a Bentley better than a Ford Pinto only because the rich drive the former and not the latter? In short, is it not possible that one reason among others why the upper class rules is that it has provided itself with the best dialect, just as it provides itself with the best in every other line of goods, and that SE is valued not simply because the rich use it, but because it is the best dialect on offer?[114]

This suggestion may or may not turn out to be true; what matters for present purposes is that it is a possibility that no linguist I know of has ever entertained, even to scoff at. Here as elsewhere, linguists look at language as fundamentally a matter of syntax and other formal aspects, with little regard for its communicative and other functions. They think that all human languages are on a par because they all have regularity or "inner logic" — which is simply to say, because they are languages, as opposed to animal-like streams of grunts and squeals. By the same logic, all humans are physically equal because they all have skeletons.

CHAPTER 7

Restoring Rhetoric to Its Throne

If it's not hard to read, it can't be important: an apologia for bad writing

The generally wrong-headed approach to language of the academic linguists has helped perpetuate a similarly wrong-headed view of rhetoric, the art of using language effectively. Rhetoric, founded on a true understanding of the relation of thought to language, was once one of the foundation stones of liberal education; today it is virtually unknown as a subject of study, and its name has become a term of abuse, almost always used in such contexts as "My opponent has attempted to deceive you with inflated [or *fancy* or *empty*] rhetoric," and the like. In some quarters, to use words well is to give grounds for suspicion; is the speaker or writer who does so casting a spell over us with those words?[115] And if I can grasp his idea without pain (without pain on my part, that is; making it painless for me may have cost him great pains) can they be very important ideas? Mustn't medicine be bitter? And if an idea is presented lucidly, must it not be the case that it is an *old* idea, when we advanced thinkers want new ones? This last question is, in a way, a good one, and if the questioner stayed for an answer, he would learn something. Yes, a well-expressed idea is always, in a sense, old — old, that is, to the writer, who has long wrestled with it in order to clarify it. The clarification is first for himself and then for his readers — although it may be, and often is, new to those readers.

But Professor Judith Butler of the University of California at Berkeley, who has won a mock prize for bad writing, has explained to us that a thinker who is trying to convey very original and unorthodox thoughts cannot be expected to do so gracefully; the deeps are necessarily turbid.[116] (It is almost too rich that her academic title begins "Professor of Rhetoric ..." — reality sometimes has no shame.) The most revealing part of Butler's defense of her own writing, and by extension much academic writing, was that in which she demonstrated inadvertently that the gnarled and cryptic utterances of her intellectual masters, men like Theodor Adorno and Herbert Marcuse, could in fact be expressed with reasonable lucidity. She did this by translating their sentences into new ones that, if not models of English prose, are at least much more intelligible than those her masters themselves had produced. She writes:

> The philosopher Theodor W. Adorno, who maintained that nothing radical could come of common sense, wrote sentences that made his readers pause and reflect on the power of language to shape the world. A sentence of his such as "Man is the ideology of dehumanization" is hardly transparent in its meaning. Adorno maintained that the way the word "man" was used by some of his contemporaries was dehumanizing.
>
> Taken out of context, the sentence may seem vainly paradoxical. But it becomes clear when we recognize that in Adorno's time the word "man" was used by humanists to regard the individual in isolation from his or her social context. For Adorno, to be deprived of one's social context was precisely to suffer dehumanization. Thus, "man" is the ideology of dehumanization.

So Adorno's thought, complex and profound though Butler thinks it, *can* be expressed in clearer terms, as she herself has just shown. Why didn't Adorno himself do so, then? But when one reflects on the quality of the thought so expressed, one has to wonder if Adorno may not have been prudent to express it in impenetrable language. The thought of Adorno's that Butler chooses to illustrate her thesis that profound thoughts cannot be expressed in a language tainted by common sense casts an interesting sidelight on her notion of profundity. And she fails to note the difference between pausing over a sentence in order to "reflect on the power of language to shape the world," and pausing over it because you can't make head or tail of it.

Is there any merit to Adorno's idea, as he expressed it? One cannot tell. Clarity, the quality it lacks, is an absolute prerequisite to critical judgment. The reader may, at least for a while, be taken in by a plausibly expressed falsehood, but he cannot begin to understand that it is false until he understands what it asserts, cannot exercise critical judgment until the idea is expressed firmly and clearly. To say "Beware of well-expressed arguments — they may be false" is much like saying "Beware of automobiles that can move — they may get involved in collisions."

Academics like Butler and her mentors have apparently never been introduced to the notions of *editing* and *revision;* it may well be true that one's first attempt at expressing a really original idea is very likely to be far from satisfactory — but why must that first attempt be foisted on one's readers? It is really too bad that people blessed with the power of having profound thoughts should have missed the elementary thought that good writing conveys ideas better than bad, as well as making them accessible to greater numbers of readers, and that the more important the idea, the more effort it is worth putting into saying it clearly. Their refusal to invest enough effort in their own writing to achieve that end raises a dark suspicion that they don't *want* their thoughts clearly expressed, because they are really writing for a coterie that prides itself on esoteric knowledge, and would feel diminished if intelligent laymen could understand them. It also suggests that they may know, on some level, that their ideas are neither profound nor original, and that their defects would be all too visible if they were clearly expressed. What other explanations can there be for thinkers who seem to hope that their writings will be taken for plodding translations of works by French deconstructionists or German sociologists?

If these proudly bad writers have really come up with ideas so radical and profound that they cannot be expressed in conventional good prose, we may be faced with an actual example of a theoretical phenomenon introduced by the post-modernists: a set of ideas, a paradigm, or even a *weltanschauung* that is totally incommensurable with traditional ideas; ideas that cannot be well expressed in what is in effect the enemy's language, since the very attempt to do so would necessarily falsify them. This would be a startling, even an unprecedented state of affairs, but perhaps a happy one for those who have trouble reading such writers: if what they're saying is truly inexpressible in our language, then there is no point in our trying to understand it — profound it may be, but since it is by hypothesis forever unintelligible to us, we can ignore it without loss. But in fact the difficulties posed by postmodernist writings can for the most part be overcome; those writings can, as Butler demonstrates, be translated into conventional language by anyone who cares to take the trouble — it is just that in much postmodernist writing, the trouble is left to the reader.

Our doubts about the incommensurable-paradigm thesis are best expressed as a question: How does a new paradigm come into being, if not as the brainchild of someone raised under an earlier paradigm? How did Einstein, trained in classical pre-relativistic physics, come up with a concept of space-time utterly incommensurable, under your hypothesis, with that of Newton — and remain capable of reasoning within that older paradigm, as well as in the newer? (Of course the way of the man who bridges the gap between the old and the new can be hard; one thinks of the anecdote told of Enrico Fermi, who was discussing some advanced physics with a group of much younger men. When they showed some impatience with his failure to grasp their arguments instantly, he said, "Gentlemen, you must excuse me; remember that I was trained in pre-Fermian physics")

Worst of all, the writer who claims that his thought is too profound to be expressed clearly raises the suspicion in some readers' minds that he himself doesn't fully understand what he's trying to say. One of the greatest of all mathematical physicists, James Clerk Maxwell, has told us that until an idea is fully captured in words, it is not fully understood:

> Mathematicians may flatter themselves that they possess new ideas which mere human language is as yet unable to express. Let them make the effort to express these ideas in appropriate words

without the aid of symbols, and if they succeed, they will not only lay us laymen under a lasting obligation, but, we venture to say, they will find themselves very much enlightened during the process, and will even be doubtful whether the ideas as expressed in symbols had ever quite found their way out of the equations into their minds.[117]

Curiously, while the great mathematical physicist urges that even mathematical ideas be expressed in words as the only guarantor of understanding, modern linguists, as shown in an earlier chapter, denigrate the subdiscipline of semantics, and regard meaning as a kind of awkward supercargo that gets in the way of a truly scientific understanding of language. The idea that thought and words can be so decoupled is at least in part a consequence of modern linguistics, which has convinced many that language usage has at last been put on a scientific footing, and that the study called rhetoric is as outmoded and irrational as astrology or alchemy. Like so many of the impressions that linguistics has spun off, this one is false. The notion that linguistics is a science has already been dealt with; what remains is to show what the proper study of language once was, and may be again — that is, to reintroduce rhetoric.

Rhetoric and the relation of thought to language

The fall of rhetoric in the estimation of teachers, or at least of "educators," is like that of Lucifer in *Paradise Lost,* a fall from a height all but supreme to the lowest depths. In antiquity those who taught rhetoric or grammar — the language arts in general — were taken because of their skills in language and particularly in written language to be knowledgeable about everything. A leading expert in the subject says:

Moreover, reading — or grammar to give it its classical name — was comprehensive rather than exclusive in its interests. Since the

grammarians were expected to lecture on all the topics treated by
their authors, they were bound within the compass of a reasonably
wide course of reading to cover nearly everything that an educated
man might need to know.[118]

And another eminent authority on education in classical antiquity,
Robert A. Kaster, adds to that:

> From about age seven or eight ... the student's experience was
> governed by three goals, pursued first in the grammarian's school,
> then in the rhetorician's mastery of correct language, command of
> a fairly small number of classical texts, and an ability to turn the
> knowledge of language and literature to a facility in composition
> and speech.[119]

Since that day the discipline which was for long the keystone of
education has fallen in intellectual esteem to the point where the task
of rehabilitating the name *rhetoric*, in any except a few small scholarly circles, may be a hopeless one. But whether under that name or
another, the discipline it denotes must be rehabilitated, because the
health of language, and with it intellectual coherence, requires it.

A few defenses of the discipline itself have been attempted in recent
years, of which that by Brian Vickers[120] is the latest and most substantial. But even a sympathetic reader must admit that it doesn't work,
because it doesn't even attempt the bold strategy that must be adopted
if success is to be achieved; Vickers argues like a defense attorney
who hopes to get his client off on a technicality, perhaps claiming that
the evidence against him, however damning, was obtained improp-
erly. Rather than a forthright assertion of rhetoric's innocence of all
charges, and indeed of its sterling character in general, it is little more
than a collection of materials for such a defense — a solicitor's brief
rather than a barrister's plea. It comprises a history of rhetoric and
its reputation; a sustained account of Plato's attack on rhetoric; a
catalogue of rhetorical devices; and a number of other interesting
things that will be of great value to the writer who will someday

undertake a full rehabilitation of rhetoric. One thing such a writer will have to do is to recognize that he is not fighting for a verdict of "Not Proven" nor even of "Not Guilty"; he needs to carry the fight to the enemy, put *them* on trial, and, like a defense attorney on television, vindicate his client by unmasking the actual perpetrator in the courtroom. Nothing less will restore rhetoric's reputation.

And such a radical rehabilitation of rhetoric must be made if the campaign against the academic linguists' usurpation of language-usage authority is to be successful. What must be overturned is a view of the relationship of language to thought that is so widely accepted today that it is difficult for even an adversary to escape it whenever he is not actively opposing it. In this prevalent view, language is the sauce that is ladled over the meat of thought. The quality of the sauce and the quality of the meat are completely independent; they are not necessarily prepared by the same cook, or even in the same kitchen. It is just as easy (and more tempting) to ladle good sauce over bad meat as over good. (As a corollary, it is also possible to put bad sauce on good meat, giving us the modern phenomenon of the important thinker who doesn't write so good.) At best, sauce may somewhat enhance the flavor of good meat, but is never really needed if the meat is good; at the all too frequent worst, it is used to cover the smell of rotten meat. The rhetorician is the dishonest cook who covers his bad meat with good — in this context, usually called "fancy" — sauce to disguise the rottenness of the dish.[121]

169

Fixing on the right metaphor

The meat-and-sauce metaphor is very popular, because every man who can read a little believes that he has thoughts much like those printed in books, but which he cannot put into words. He believes this particularly when presented with a striking piece of evidence to the contrary. When given an outstandingly lucid argument, analysis, or proof, whose formulation has cost its author more pains than he will ever know, this reader finds that he understands just what is meant, and assimilates his new understanding so thoroughly and quickly that he soon enjoys the illusion that he's always so understood the matter — no credit to the rhetorical power of the writer.[122] On the other hand, he has sometimes believed statements he has read, only to discover later that they were false; this he thinks is usually due to his having been taken in by the attractive way they were presented — by rhetoric.

A widely used alternative metaphor has it that words "clothe" thoughts; if I had to choose between them, I'd prefer the culinary metaphor because it is more fruitful, more suggestive, to talk about the meat of thought not needing sauce than about the body of thought not needing clothes. But the entire family of metaphors is unsound, and with it all its corollaries and implications.[123] A better one can be created, however, from its wreckage: language is the meat in which an idea is incarnated, thought is the nutritive content of the meat. The idea of eschewing the meat (but without giving up chewing the fat), and ingesting the nutrients directly, as if through an IV line, is as futile in discourse as in nutrition; as meat (in the older sense of the term) is the only form in which man can regularly ingest the nutrients he needs, words are the only form in which he can apprehend thought. (Yet another family of fruitful metaphors is suggested by Karl Kraus's "Speech is the mother, not the handmaid of thought."[124]) There are better and worse cuts of meat, there are good cooks and bad; but meat there must be, and someone must cook it.[125]

Thinking without words

The delusion of the common reader that he is, but for one or two minor accidents, a writer himself is based on the popular notion that many people think important and interesting thoughts, but just "can't find the right words." The picture that lies behind this and similar formulations is that of thinking as an activity quite distinct from the embodying and articulation of thoughts in words, and really far more important than the latter activities, which are almost tricks — thought is a

Cinderella who doesn't get to go to the ball merely because she doesn't have the right dress, even though she is of far more worth than her older, ugly sisters. Writers, in this view, are just lucky people who have the knack of finding the words; almost anyone could do what they do, given the leisure and a copy of *Roget*. A consequence of this belief is that published authors are regularly approached by people who have important books "in their heads" which they propose to have the published author — the "wordsmith" — put onto paper for them. In return for this simple service, they generously offer to split the profits fifty-fifty.[126]

The notion that I'm making fun of is a very widespread one, and has more serious consequences than that of causing a nuisance to published writers. It is responsible for bad judgments and policies in education, lexicography, literary criticism and history, linguistic scholarship — all the language-related disciplines and projects. In relegating language usage to the minor role of covering the cake of thought with a thin frosting of words, it conceals the fact that all *sustained* and *communicable* thought is utterly dependent on words. Of course "ideas" or "notions" or "thoughts" come to us in a pre-verbal form, but our ability to capture those thoughts, let alone connect them to other thoughts or communicate them to others, is completely dependent on our finding words for them. We must find appropriate words just to accomplish the simple task of *remembering* the idea or notion in question; we must put the notion into words in order to examine it critically, to see if it connects to any other notion we may have, to determine its value. Some intellectual life exists, of course, even in the pre-verbal mind, but it must remain a rudimentary kind, in which only those connections and consequences of a thought that are immediately apparent are available; connections not so apparent are lost unless the thought can be given verbal, and especially written, form.

When a writer searches for the right words, he is not trying to find a suitable wrapper for an already-realized idea; he is trying to capture, complete, and build on a notion that is so far just the germ of an idea — a mere glimmer of an analogy, an antithesis, a distinction, a similarity. And he must find the right words in good time; the notion cannot be put on a "Pending" shelf, where it remains in good condition, awaiting another attempt to wrap it in words; it is a wasting asset that soon fades, decomposes, and is lost, perhaps forever. The writer's *initial* effort at finding words is not so much for the purpose of conveying his idea to others, but rather for his own possession of the idea; he is writing, or talking, to himself. Even if he is in solitary confinement, or marooned alone on a desert island, he will have to find words for his thoughts, or lose them. Of course when the idea has been captured and well expressed, he will want to communicate it to others, but at the outset the writer is a man talking to himself, though perhaps willing to be overheard.

And this is why precision and continuity in language usage is so important; without that we fail not only to communicate our ideas to

others, but to have them, in the full sense, ourselves. The popular view of language as a mere disposable wrapper of ideas is a profoundly dangerous one; in robbing language, and particularly stable language, of any serious role in ideation, it deprives thinking of its indispensable medium. Thought may be the spirit where language is the body, as the conventional view often has it — but if so, the analogy needs to be pressed further; how does the spirit survive if not embodied?

The anti-rhetorical tradition

Plato is the first "enemy of rhetoric" who must be faced — Plato, whom Auden well called "a man of genius who's always wrong."[127] Although Vickers devotes a great many pages to an attempt to refute Plato, he curiously never makes the obvious point that Plato's attack on rhetoric is almost entirely rhetorical, in the bad modern sense of that term. In making such an attack, Plato founded (or perhaps continued) a tradition lasting to our day, in which a rhetorician, fearing he may be losing a debate, plays rhetoric's trump card by charging another rhetorician with using rhetoric. But even Socrates, when he gets down to particulars, charges the Sophists not with using rhetoric (as opposed to rigorous argument), but of telling half-truths or untruths — of being factually or logically wrong.

The closest thing we have today to an adequate defense of rhetoric is that provided by Professor Bernard Knox in a few pages of his "The Walls of Thebes," the inaugural lecture that he gave in 1981 at the opening of Yale's Whitney Humanities Center, and since reprinted in a collection of his essays.[128] It is of course just the merest fragment of a full defense, but it strikes the right note, and shows the direction a full-scale defense should take. In those few pages, Knox observes that Plato succeeded in making *Sophist* (by which he meant the rhetoricians) a word of abuse largely because his dialogues survived when the works of the Sophists themselves almost entirely perished. And he points out that in ancient Greece, the ability to speak persuasively was a necessary art if democracy was to flourish; it was only in autocracies such as Plato's ideal Republic where no one needed to be or could be argued with; there the truth was already known, and had only to be imposed and enforced.

We may well blame Plato for dishonesty in charging his opponents with being rhetoricians, implying that he himself was no such thing, and thereby committing *suggestio falsi*. We cannot fairly blame him, though, for being a rhetorician, since a philosopher cannot and should not avoid that role; it is only for being a *poor* or *dishonest* rhetorician that he may be blamed. Rhetoric, besides being in general effective speech, is known for use of a battery of standard "rhetorical devices" or "figures" or "tropes"; that is, of well-known succinct relationship templates that can be applied in any discourse in order to set up quickly in a listener's or reader's mind the wanted view of a subject. It plays much the same role in ordinary-language discourse that standard transformations and identities do in mathematics and logic; it implicitly likens the situation in question to another that the listener or reader already understands. The use of such templates or ready-made analogies is unavoidable; the alternative would be to be absolutely and flatfootedly explicit on every minute point of a exposition or debate, starting from first principles (if such things can be found); it would render sustained discourse impossible.

It is observed by very austere thinkers that such devices can deceive, and are even sometimes used with *intent* to deceive. Indeed they can, and are; what follows? Swift has given us a picture of how we might avoid the dangers implicit in the condensed speech we call rhetoric: we might, like the philosophers of Laputa, carry about with us examples of the objects we might wish to discuss, and avoid all language problems by brandishing the actual object of interest at the moment, rather than "getting into semantics" by using a word for it.[129] Even the sternest enemies of rhetoric seem to find this radical solution unworkable, though, and acknowledge that resort to language is unavoidable. And if communication is to be verbal, how can rhetoric be avoided? Rhetoric is simply language condensed to an intensity that makes extended argumentation possible, that makes it possible to get to the point before we forget what we were trying to argue for, and our audience forgets why they cared.

We may be uncertain about how long thought can exist without words, or to what extent thought can even occur without words; what is clear is that thought cannot be *communicated* and *preserved* without words (and communication is necessary even to the recluse; we need internal dialogue to develop our own thought). When Yeats says "The rhetorician would deceive his neighbor, the sentimentalist himself; while art is but a vision of reality," our reply is, "A very pretty piece of rhetoric, Mr Yeats — so much so that we absolve you of trying to deceive us."

The decline of rhetoric and the decline of fiction

Rhetoric is a vital partner of literary fiction, and the decline of one is closely linked to that of the other. Since every right-thinking person claims to eschew rhetoric, it should not be surprising that many writers of recent times, who would a generation or two ago have aspired to write the Great American Novel, now more or less happily settle for writing the Readable American Essay or Magazine Piece. These two phenomena have a common root: authors' loss of confidence in the Great American Reader. Neither good rhetoric nor good fiction can be written when writers cannot be sure that their readers will understand the devices and conventions and allusions that both modes depend on. The novel and other forms of fiction, like eloquent speech and great oratory, depend on an audience that is prepared — and *uniformly* prepared — for the highly developed verbal structures we call literature, just as brilliant improvisation and spinning of variations at the keyboard depends for its effect on an audience that is thoroughly familiar with the fundamental theme. We laugh at Macaulay's "as every schoolboy knows" because nowadays nothing can be taken for granted as universally known; but the joke is very much on us.

The essay or magazine piece has gone far to replace the novel and fiction in general because it takes little or nothing for granted; it introduces its subject as if to a visitor just arrived from the next galaxy — an intelligent visitor, but one little acquainted with earthly events or the thinking of the last few decades. A common device among the writers of such pieces is an opening along the lines of "For the benefit of those who have spent the last twenty years on a desert island, Wittgenstein was a philosopher who ..."; they make a little joke of saying this, but in fact many of their readers might as well have been on that island for the last twenty years, and the writers know it — again, the joke's on its maker. By the time the writer has prepared his audience to receive whatever is presumably new in his message, teaching them everything they ought to have been taught in school or learned later by reading canonical literature on their own, both he and they are near exhaustion; he has to rush to make his point, usually in a fairly rough-and-ready way, before he loses his audience's attention or his editor's patience. It is not only the disgrace that rhetoric has suffered, of course, that is responsible for this sad state; as just implied, the rejection of canonical literature is a major contributor — but both are in turn derivatives of that false view of thought and language that we have been looking at, and the rehabilitation of rhetoric may be the most practical first step toward restoring both to their rightful places.

CHAPTER 8

Decadence and Diseases of Language

Two
flavors of decadence:
hothouses
and
means-become-ends

Jacques Barzun has described decadence as a condition in which people accept the futile and bizarre as things that cannot be resisted, and see no clear path ahead of them, even a dauntingly hard one.[130] Barzun was speaking of the *effect* decadence has on us; I want to complement his observation with a sketch of the *forms* decadence takes. There are two chief forms: one is the transformation of means into ends, the other dependence on luxuries and artificial aids, "hothouses," even when such dependence threatens one's very survival. (Note that what is being called decadent here is not the enjoyment of luxuries, but helpless dependence on them.)

The supplanting of ends by means may be illustrated by male bodybuilding. As recently as the middle of the 20th century, most men worked hard physically; in particular, a great many of them had to work the land to keep us fed, and that hard work made them muscular. Today very few work the land, and those few have a much easier time of it, physically at least, than our grandfathers did. But the muscular physique that used to be men's normal condition is still admired, so millions of men join gymnasiums and health clubs, and spend much money and expend much energy to look as if they still did regular hard physical labor. A few go further, and jeopardize their health by "pumping iron" and taking anabolic steroids in order to look not like a healthy outdoorsman, but like a Baroque sculpture of Hercules strangling a centaur.

Relying on hothouses for our very survival may be illustrated by the many vitally necessary systems we have built or allowed to evolve that are dangerously vulnerable and fragile: for example, our jerry-built electricity grid and water supply system, our dependence on foreign oil, our need of cheap labor from Mexico and Asia, our reliance on monoculture and artificial fertilizer and insecticides for our food crops. Other examples are our deep reluctance to give up the conveniences and amenities — usually known to us as our "rights" — that were practical when the Atlantic and Pacific oceans protected us from attack by foreign enemies, but may be no longer; I mean such things as traveling freely around our country without "papers" or leaving any trail behind us, and leaving our borders effectively unguarded.

Some of the practices I call decadent are no one's business but their practitioners'; if urban men of sedentary occupation want to spend their time, money, and sweat in an effort to look like mountaineers, stevedores, or farm laborers, that's of no concern to any but themselves and their families. But others of the practices that I've labeled "hothouse" are of concern to all of us, because they affect the survival of all of us as individuals and as a nation. And in some cases it is not easy to decide along which path decadence lies: for example, automotive engineers long ago refined automatic transmissions to the point where they are quiet, reliable, and efficient, and do the job of shifting gears better than all but a tiny minority of drivers. This development may be considered a form of "hothouse" decadence, in that it accepts a good deal of complexity and expense in our cars just to let us avoid manual shifting. But if that is decadence, what shall we say of the enthusiasts who pay extra, sometimes a good deal extra, to have their cars equipped with manual transmissions, on the grounds that they are expert drivers who can shift better than automatic transmissions, and that it is fun to shift manually? Here we have a perfect example of the means-become-ends variety of decadence. Perhaps what is truly decadent is a culture in which all one's choices are decadent ones, the only difference among them being one's personal preference as to the form of decadence to adopt — a situation that results in the feeling of futility that Barzun described.

Because I will be talking here almost exclusively of decadent practices that are clearly undesirable and even highly dangerous, it may be inferred that I think all such practices are bad, and always were. That is not the case. A few of them are certainly bad: for example, ruining one's health, and thereby harming one's family, in order to resemble a mythical hero of antiquity. But most of them, if reprehensible at all, are so simply because they are inappropriate in present circumstances. When we were effectively invulnerable to attack by foreign enemies, an easy-going attitude toward security was perfectly in order; when there were few fanatics resolved either to convert or to kill us, complete tolerance toward all creeds and cults was the right position to take. If that attitude and that position are no longer appropriate, it is not morality or ethics that have changed, just practical circumstances. But when we cannot change the practices we followed in one set of circumstances to those called for by another, even when the perils of the new era demand it, we have decadence, and dangerous decadence. And language too can become decadent, for reasons much like those just examined.

When language is no longer a tool for dealing with reality, but an alternative to it

Decadence in language is chiefly a means-become-ends phenomenon, and, because language is so much a part of all human life, a highly dangerous one: a disease of language is like blood poisoning, affecting every organ of the body. Normally, the use of language is to deal with extra-linguistic reality; language is principally a window through which one looks out at the world.[131] It may not be a perfectly clear window, nor is it altogether passive, but for most people, most of the time, it is a means to an end, not a subject of interest in its own right. In particular, it does not constitute for most an alternative world, much less a preferable alternative world. For the decadent-language user, however, language is primary, and the world of common experience secondary, if not wholly negligible; the window becomes a mirror.

It is hard to make such observations without seeming to utterly condemn the phenomenon being observed. To contrast one thing with another that has been called "normal" is inevitably to suggest that the first must be abnormal, pathological. But the two things being so sharply contrasted here are the extreme endpoints of a continuum, not the two states of a binary switch. The great majority of human beings live well away from either endpoint, although much closer to the language-as-means endpoint than the language-as-world-in-itself endpoint — hence my calling the former *normal*. And each of us moves back and forth along that continuum as we go about our business; we all become somewhat "decadent" when we read fiction, and even more so if we write it. We owe all literary art to those for whom words are especially substantial and immediate, and the material out of which they build the alternate realities we call novels and poems. Within limits, the taking of language as primary is the source of much of the pleasure and instruction afforded by civilized and cultivated life.

So the liberation of words from their original humble task of reflecting reality has effects both good and bad. The good is the creation of some fascinating works in both prose and poetry. To this liberation we owe, for example, *The Importance of Being Earnest* and the poetry of Wallace Stevens, along with puns, word games, and Modernist literature in general. The bad is the way this verbal autonomy makes writers forget that the words they use for esthetic and expressive purposes still have important effects in the primary world when read by ordinary philistines (that is, the vast majority of the human race, for whom words are not chiefly, if at all, esthetic devices) — and its corollary or reverse face, the way it makes many readers forget that when reading most literature, particularly modern literature, they are not reading a commentary on life, but experiencing what is, for its authors, life itself.[132]

In examining in earlier chapters the ideology of modern linguistics, I identified as its root fallacy the notion that language is essentially autonomous, obeying its own laws, and following its own course as inexorably as the drifting of the continental plates. (A favorite expression of this notion, quoted frequently by linguists and their followers — and quoted earlier here — is Sapir's dictum that language "moves down time in a current of its own making.") Decadence in language is a variant on the same theme of language as a world in its own right, and a rather more interesting one than the everyday world we all share. And those in thrall to language to the point where facts and common experience become intrusions to be evaded so that they can return to what is now their natural element quickly become carriers of a form of social pathology. Despite their lack of real interest in the world of fact, they refuse to disqualify themselves from acting in that world, or recuse themselves from passing judgments on men and events in that world. On the contrary, they often flatter themselves that their literacy and fluency with language constitutes evidence of their special competence in worldly matters, and want not only to be heard on such topics, but to assume leadership positions in the bodies that deal with them. The result is that horror of modern times, the intellectual and artist in politics.

Language decadence engenders a strange muse

You think it horrible that lust and rage
Should dance attention on my old age;
...
What else have I to spur me into song?
        – Yeats, *The Spur*[133]

Among the uglier features of our world for which language decadence is partly responsible is anti-Semitism. The history of anti-Semitism is marked by one paradox so familiar that without ceasing to be paradoxical, it is also a cliché: we find in that history so many anti-Semites with Jewish friends, agents, lawyers, doctors, lovers, and spouses that when we find one without such an 'exceptional' Jew in his life, we almost feel a glimmer of respect for him. (Some anti-Semites, exasperated by having their inconsistency pointed out to them, have told us, like Mayor Lueger of Vienna, "I'll decide who's a Jew!") An exploration of this paradox, as of paradoxes in mathematics or logic, can yield insight into matters that are otherwise obscure.

And the resolution of this particular paradox, I suggest, comes with the realization that for a great many intellectuals and writers, anti-Semitism, like many other of their views and passions, is far more a matter of reacting to words than to people.

The case of T. S. Eliot will serve nicely as illustration, since his life, and the place of anti-Semitism in it, is exceptionally well documented, Anthony Julius's book[134] being only the latest in a growing literature on the subject. But Julius' study of the role of anti-Semitism in Eliot's life and writing seems not to have been properly read by some critics; he was not, as they thought, mainly engaged in charging Eliot's verse with anti-Semitism — that case was tried and decided long ago, with a clear verdict of guilty — but pointing out that anti-Semitism seems to have been the fuel, or the catalyst, driving some of Eliot's best poetry. Julius was right, and his analysis of the role Jews and hatred of them played in Eliot's life and work applies well beyond his case; it can lead to an understanding of how the replacement of common reality by words gives rise to both good poetry and monstrous opinions.

As Julius shows, the literate public's way of dealing with the blatantly anti-Semitic passages in Eliot (a way practiced even by Jewish critics and readers), was to ignore them. It was the easier to ignore them because a syllogism accepted by all right-thinking critics proved that they could not exist: "Art is wonderful; anti-Semitism is not wonderful; therefore no art can be anti-Semitic." Apart from its defects in logical rigor, this syllogism is contradicted by masses of experience. After the revelations in every modern literary biography showing that virtually every writer whose work we ever revered was a drunk or a drug addict or a misogynistic womanizer or a wife-beater or a deadbeat or a disloyal friend or a family tyrant who drove a child to suicide or, often, some combination of these, it is a wonder that anyone could have failed to note that art does not necessarily — to put it as mildly as possible — derive from pure and high-minded sources; roses are not fertilized by roses, but by dung.

One would have supposed this a commonplace by now, but when Julius pointed out that anti-Semitism was not incidental to Eliot's poetry but of its essence, and sometimes the motive force driving it, many readers seemed appalled, incredulous, indignant. Their reaction to Julius' point is strange; had they not read the lines of Yeats' quoted above? And if lust and rage, why not hatred of Jews as a spur into song? Poets don't need noble emotions to recollect in tranquility, just strong ones. Poor Eliot — one is almost sorry for him — found that loathing of Jews was one of the few strong emotions he could call upon, and that he needed it in order to produce.

It is often urged in defense of Eliot and others of similar bent that they were unfailingly courteous to actual Jews, even had some Jewish friends.[135] *Of course* they were; literary anti-Semitism, like other literary emotions, has little bearing on a writer's sublunary life; the anti-Semitism of writers, like other writers' attitudes, is mainly a matter of verbal symbols rather than people, and does not preclude their having Jewish business associates, friends, or even spouses. (Indeed, the discovery of Jewish ancestors by apparently plain-vanilla gentiles is now so common — think of Christopher Hitchens, General Wesley Clark, Madeleine Albright, John Kerry — that I expect that when Valerie Eliot finally releases all the material about him to which she now refuses access, it will be discovered that Eliot was partly Jewish himself; some remote ancestor will turn out to have been a cattle feed merchant from Odessa or *mohel* from Vilna.)

What Eliot and other writers hated was not actual Jews, but the word *Jew* and all that it brings to mind, as it must for someone steeped in English literature — and in Eliot's case, Anglican churchiness, and some shards of the literature of classical antiquity. After a lifetime of hearing the Jews routinely reviled in religious services and traditional prayers, and depicted as Christ-killers and poisonous vermin by some of the greatest writers of one's own language, and of getting one's loathing further ratified by the echoes of it to be found in works surviving from classical antiquity, one would have to be something more or less than human not to be deeply affected by that exposure. Education and cultivation are not safeguards against anti-Semitism, they are among the vectors — for the highly literate, the chief vector — by which the pathogen infects its hosts. The more literate and sensitive to language, the more susceptible one is to that disorder;

it is a *déformation professionelle* that strikes just those who live primarily in the world of words.

It can be seen everywhere in modern English-language fiction: from the quiet leafy London squares and country houses of cultivated Bloomsbury to the bleak plains and arid towns of the American Midwest, this level of verbal anti-Semitism is endemic; it is in the letters and diaries of Virginia Woolf and John Maynard Keynes (and his wife Lydia Lopokova) and Harold Nicolson as it is in the writings of Henry Ford, Charles Lindbergh, H. G. Wells, Henry James, Ezra Pound, George Santayana, James Gould Cozzens, H. L. Mencken, Wallace Stevens, and Theodore Dreiser. It is found, perhaps even more strangely, in Gottlob Frege, the greatest logician between Aristotle and Gödel. It is to be seen in the private remarks of such American presidents as Franklin D. Roosevelt and Richard Nixon — remarks that did not preclude their surrounding themselves with Jewish advisers and aides, like Felix Frankfurter and Henry Kissinger. And Jews themselves, when of similar temperament and education, can find themselves reacting the same way. (It is not only anti-Semitism, of course, that is aroused in those for whom words are more real than people: Auden noted that "Words so affect me that a pornographic story, for example, excites me sexually more than a living person can do."[136])

But writers are so accustomed to living in the world of words that they are puzzled and sometimes wounded when held accountable for the real-world consequences of their utterances, as if they inhabited and were responsible to that world. Eliot, who apparently enjoyed lunches with Groucho Marx and S. J. Perelman, seems to have been so puzzled and wounded, and made one of the silliest remarks ever recorded of a major writer when he claimed that he could not be an anti-Semite, because anti-Semitism was in the church's eyes a sin. We are told that he was properly horrified when he learned of the Holocaust, but he never gave any sign of recognizing that there could be a connection between the dehumanizing treatment of Jews in his poetry (and in *After Strange Gods*) and what happened to real Jews in the real world. The critic failed to note even long after the event that while he was expressing his loathing of Rachel née Rabinovitch and Sir Ferdinand Klein in his poetry, the objective correlatives of these poetic tropes were being murdered in the death camps.

Marrying Ms. Cthulhu

Eliot's case is not uncommon among writers; it is better documented and more widely discussed than most not because there is anything intrinsically special about it, but simply because Eliot is Eliot — the preeminent literary critic in English for much of the 20th century, and one of its major poets. There are other cases from which we can learn as much as from Eliot's, even though the writers involved are very far from him in literary distinction. One in particular, that of the fantasist H. P. Lovecraft, is particularly valuable for present purposes. Lovecraft was, like Eliot, a New England Protestant by heritage, an anglophile, and a horrified observer of what he saw as the progressive contamination and mongrelization of America by Jews, Italians, French Canadians, Orientals, and other such non-Nordic peoples. His fiction was strongly influenced by those feelings, although he would probably have denied it vigorously — and denied it quite honestly, being as unaware of the roots of his own work as most writers are.

Lovecraft was a very minor but quite genuine artist who has become something of a cult figure since his death in 1937.[137] There was but one string to his lyre, and he only occasionally struck it squarely, but when he did, he made his reader feel a *frisson* of horror such as very few writers of horror stories or fantasies have achieved. His theme was the ineffable *otherness* of the cosmos, a quality so infinitely alien as to be indistinguishable from malevolence. At his best, he could make readers experience for a moment, as an actual emotion, his vision of a cold, mindless universe inhabited by beings incomprehensible to man, and utterly indifferent to him. He embodied this alien power and utter inhumanity in the form of creatures who visit the earth — his human characters do not need to seek the abyss of which Nietzsche spoke, the abyss comes to them.

Lovecraft achieved his effects, when he did achieve them, by invoking some strange beings — in particular, the being called *Cthulhu* — who are the incarnation of that utter callousness to man and all that man cares for, beings who existed long before man appeared, and presumably will exist long after he is gone. So long as he hinted obliquely at the precise nature of Cthulhu and other such beings, he had a fair chance of touching his reader in a delicate place in the mind, but he too often succumbed to the temptation to describe and elaborate instead of giving hints and oblique glances; when he so succumbed, he often became ridiculous, creating conventional monsters with slimy tentacles, eye-stalks, and all the other apparatus of Hollywood special-effect extravaganzas. When over-described, such creatures, whatever other properties they might have, are utterly lacking in the *eldritch* — Lovecraft's favorite word for the hair-raisingly uncanny, and the quality he strove for. Nameless, faceless horrors have to remain nameless and faceless if they are to remain horrors; fully named and described, they take their place on our list of nasty problems, those we'll get around to dealing with right after we've fixed that leaky faucet in the laundry room.

(It should be mentioned in fairness to Lovecraft that the use of Cthulhu as the basis of an over-organized and rationalized hierarchy of horrible creatures, with their own history and internal relationships, was almost entirely the work of his epigones; he invented Cthulhu, they are responsible for the 'Cthulhu Mythos,' as the elaborated and formalized structure based on his original vision is called.)

In one of Lovecraft's stories, the author/narrator learns much about this awful being:

> I learned whence Cthulhu *first* came … It was shocking to have the foulest nightmares of secret myth cleared up in concrete terms whose stark, morbid hatefulness exceeded the boldest hints of ancient and medieval mystics.[138]

But, perhaps wisely, he did not see fit to share his shocking knowledge with his readers. Nor can we turn to other witnesses to learn about

Cthulhu, for the powers and malignity of that entity are so great that few who have suffered even the most glancing contact with him have survived to report the experience. All that may be said with certainty about this dread being is that he is one — if not the chief — of the Great Old Ones, a race of beings who ruled the world, if not the universe, before humans appeared. They are not, we are given to understand, divine or even necessarily supernatural, but simply utterly inhuman beings who ruled under an older covenant with the ultimate power than that known to man. And Lovecraft, whose works contain virtually all that is known or conjectured of them, in turn attributes his knowledge to one George Gammell Angell, a professor emeritus of Semitic languages.

Of the other Old Ones, most have names somewhat more pronounceable and familiar-looking than Cthulhu's: typical examples are Yuggoth, Yog-Sothoth, and Azathoth. These names, Lovecraft tells us,

> are designed to suggest — either closely or remotely — certain names in actual history or folklore which have weird or sinister associations connected with them. Thus 'Yuggoth' has a sort of Arabic or Hebraic cast... .[139]

So the source to which Lovecraft attributes his knowledge of Cthulhu and his kind is a professor of Semitic languages, and their names are of an Arabic or Hebrew cast (Lovecraft's first and by far best biographer, L. Sprague de Camp, points out that *–oth* is a common feminine plural ending in Hebrew, as in *Ashteroth.*) It may seem puzzling that unspeakably alien life forms from parts of the universe so remote that they are not merely inconceivably distant, but outside our familiar four-dimensional space-time continuum altogether, should bear vaguely Semitic names — indeed, almost *consist* of their vaguely Semitic names, since little more is known of them (apart from their inexpressible malignity) than those names — but so it is.

The mystery of the Semitic aura surrounding Cthulhu and the other Old Ones may be dispelled by considering Lovecraft's attitude toward Jews: one of shuddering loathing. Sprague de Camp discusses those feelings about Jews (and to a lesser extent the other national and ethnic groups listed earlier) at great length; in particular, he reprints a large part of a long letter Lovecraft wrote in January 1926 to an aunt:

> The mass of contemporary Jews are hopeless as far as America is concerned. They are the product of alien blood, & inherit alien ideals, impulses, & emotions which forever preclude the possibility of wholesale assimilation.... On our side there is a shuddering physical repugnance to most Semitic types ... wherever the Wandering Jew wanders, he will have to content himself with his own society until he disappears or is killed off in some sudden outburst of physical loathing on our part.[140]

This is just a tiny fragment of the letter, and the letter, in turn, is no isolated item among Lovecraft's writings. It should be noted that in his last years, with the rise of the Nazi regime in Germany and the earliest reports of the persecution of the Jews, Lovecraft somewhat moderated his racial feelings. But throughout most of his life, and his most productive years, Lovecraft's racism was a major obsession; a quick way of grasping the extent and depth of it is to note the number of pages Sprague de Camp's index lists under "Jews" and "Judaeophobia": under the former, 110, 201, 249f, and 378f. Under the latter, 5, 9, 93, 101, 110ff, 116, 160f, 222f, 239, 249–54, 289, 291, 308f, 351, 372f, and 377ff.

Since Sprague de Camp's, another full-length biography of Lovecraft has appeared. Why it was needed isn't clear; no important new information about him has emerged since Sprague de Camp wrote his, nor has Lovecraft's place in literature seemed in need of revaluation. But one S. T. Joshi, who has become perhaps the leading specialist on Lovecraft in recent years — not that he has had much competition for the role — has nevertheless given us one.[141] He thinks very little of Sprague de Camp's biography, and in particular, perhaps reflecting a shift in the sympathies of contemporary enlightened and progressive folks, he thinks that Sprague de Camp made far too much of Lovecraft's anti-Semitism and general racial bigotry. "It would,

I suppose, be uncharitable of me to speak ill of [Sprague] de Camp's work," he says, after which he proceeds to savage every aspect of that book, concluding that "[Sprague] de Camp simply did not have the intellectual and personal resources to write a biography of Lovecraft. He was out of his depth..." And he thinks that Sprague de Camp "harps upon Lovecraft's racial views all out of proportion to their significance in his general philosophy, and without even a proper understanding of their origin or purpose."[142]

It cannot be said that Joshi makes the same mistake: he says absolutely nothing on the subject (which is too bad; one would be interested to learn what he thinks the "purpose" of Lovecraft's "racial views" might be). The very full index to his biography has no entries for "Jews," "Racism," "anti-Semitism," "Judaeophobia," or any related term; what was clearly a major passion, even obsession, of Lovecraft's during most of his life simply doesn't interest Joshi. His criticism of Sprague de Camp for spending so many pages on that topic is an amazing exercise in wrong-headedness. The truth is that even Sprague de Camp didn't go far enough in considering that aspect of Lovecraft's life, and in connecting it to his work: it was only his racial feelings, and his anti-Semitism in particular, that gave him both the need and the psychic energy to write, and to create in Cthulhu — a Wandering Jew who has wandered very far indeed — the embodiment of that obsession.[143]

It remains only to add that some of Lovecraft's few close friends were Jewish, and that in 1924 he married Sonia Greene (*née* Shifirkin), a nice Jewish girl. Perhaps it was his way of thanking the Jews for making him an artist.

Subverting the subversives: the unspeakable remarks of Philip Larkin

The English poet Philip Larkin is another victim, though of a very different kind, of the general failure to understand that writers, and perhaps poets most of all, live the better part of their lives among words, not facts or events or deeds. If Larkin's views on England and life in general had to be summarized in a word, it would be *elegiac;* even in his youthful writings, he seemed to be looking back on a long and disappointing life. One of the persistent strains in his poetry is a lament for England's lost greatness, a loss partly linked to the dissolution of the Empire, partly to the blight of commercialism, hooliganism, and slickness spreading over the land, but this was taken by many critics as just a way of sublimating his private troubles; they were sure that no enlightened person — a poet least of all — could actually regret the loss of Empire, actually wish back the days of dominion over palm and pine, and the queen as empress of India.

But after his death, the publication of his letters[144] and of a full biography[145] revealed that, among other things, his views on Britain and the Empire were not very different from Kipling's or even from

those of a retired colonel of the 18th Lancers. Even more horrible, it revealed racist, misogynistic, and sadistic chat among Larkin and two old friends and regular correspondents, the novelist Kingsley Amis and the historian and poet Robert Conquest. And this revelation blinded many to what should have been obvious; words like *bigoted, misogynistic* and *sadistic* are so strongly charged that, dazzled by them, many critics missed the real key word, which is *chat.* The critics, almost all them literary types themselves, waved away Larkin's honorable life of service and kindness to all around him; what counted, what revealed the real Larkin, they contended, was the words he used in his grumpy, jokey, boyish letters to the friends of his youth.

Among the few honorable opponents of the lynch mob that descended on Larkin was Martin Amis, who, in a brave and cogent defense of Larkin,[146] used "correspondence" to mean much what is meant here by "chat": "Words are not deeds. ... In a correspondence, words are hardly even words." I subscribe completely to Amis' defense of Larkin, but my purpose here is somewhat different. The distinction between words and deeds that Amis used to defend Larkin is for present purposes not a weapon of defense, but an object of study in its own right, and if a better understanding of it contributes to the restoration of Larkin to the respect and affection he deserves, that is a very welcome but secondary consequence. Another honorable defender was Christopher Hitchens, who also had some useful points to make,[147] but in whose essay the best thing is a quotation from Robert Conquest: "Anyway, anyone who's a member of the united front against bullshit can see that Philip's foul mouth was a form of subversiveness. Saying the unsayable because it is unsayable."

Among modern progressive people, being subversive is normally just fine — it is understood to mean the undermining of the *others*, the philistines, fascists, and fools — but Larkin had the audacity to subvert the *progressives'* ideology, *their* program, and that was not fine with them at all. (Like another modern shibboleth, *diversity*, subversion is supposed to make *others* uncomfortable.) Modern progressives are also passionately in favor of free speech, very much including words that offend deeply — provided, that is, that they don't offend the progressives themselves. You are free today to curse God, or deny His existence (or, if totally liberated from logic, do both at once); you can describe or depict any act of violence, sexuality, or rage; you can defy Queen Victoria and all her supposed rules — and everyone from kids in school to television personalities take full advantage of that license, and are defended by the ACLU if anyone seeks to silence or otherwise rein them in. But somehow these gestures are seldom fully satisfying; everyone knows that they are simply poking at a toothless old lion who is safely behind bars, perhaps even dead. What good to scream "fuck you!" at someone, when you heard it on a cop show on television last night, and kids in some schools get away with screaming it at their teachers? As Robert Graves put it in his study of swearing, "Any swearing that fails to wound the susceptibility of the person sworn at ... is mere play."[148]

So when you have exhausted the vocabularies of blasphemy, obscenity, and scatology — and they are quickly exhausted these days — you have, if you are truly angry, bought yourself little relief. To really express your anger, you need to offend not Queen Victoria or Mrs Grundy, those caged or dead lionesses, you need to offend those who set the tone *today*. Larkin was really angry; he was defeatist as well, but defeatism doesn't put out the fire of anger, it stokes the fire, and makes it smoky and acrid. He was angry about the end of England, the England of the shires and villages and cricket and good beer, of learning and piety and poetry. And he had to express that anger (there was plenty left over even after he used it to drive his poems) by offending the modern world that was robbing him of England. So, in his correspondence with friends — mainly Amis and Conquest — he let himself go with a torrent of language offensive to that modern world. And the modern world has responded just as Queen Victoria or Mrs Grundy would have to words offensive to *them:* by lifting its skirts and crying "For shame!"

It seems remarkable, at first, that some of the foremost of Larkin's vilifiers were themselves poets, who might have been expected to understand that Larkin's shocking words were his way of raging at the turning of England into a block of ugly offices and housing projects on one hand, and a theme park for tourists on the other. But his poet-detractors (chief among them Tom Paulin, who has since further distinguished himself by an outburst of anti-Semitism so bizarre that his friends and admirers have tacitly agreed to ignore it), are themselves caught in the web of words; for them, too, words are central and primary, deeds just epiphenomena, so Larkin's invariable kindness and courtesy to everyone from his library staff to Barbara Pym count for little or nothing. (His relations with his women friends and lovers were turbulent and complex, but no one is expected to be other than maddened and bewildered when in the grip of Eros.)

Larkin's poetry and reputation — all that matters now for him — will survive, and he needs no further defense against the sort of attacks made on him, which have already begun to seem like pigeon droppings on a stained-glass window. But the insults he had to endure from the high-minded are another sign of the gulf between the real world and those for whom words are reality, and "the world" trivial.

Why Communism, But Not Nazism, Gets a Sigh

"...why are we not offended by ex-Communists, or those who still evince some nostalgic sympathy for the Communist project, whereas we execrate Nazi sympathizers and shun the company of ex-Nazis?

As time moves on, this conundrum and its implications will become, I believe, the most important question to ask about the twentieth century and our relation to it — as writers, as historians, as citizens."

— Tony Judt[149]

An essay by the late Martin Malia, "Judging Nazism and Communism,"[150] is only the latest of numerous published attempts — many of which he cites — to deal with Professor Judt's question, and to try to understand the strange difference in the attitudes of so many educated Western observers toward Nazism on the one hand and Communism on the other. I think that Malia well summarized the main arguments and views that have been expressed on the subject, and that he was dead right in urging that Communism be seen as a movement as loathsome as Nazism. What neither he nor any of the writers he cites does, however, is to pin down the reason why so many of the Western intelligentsia cannot accept this. I think that language decadence has a great deal to do with it.

195

The great difficulty this explanation faces, in this context as in others, is that it violates the Law of Proportionate Profundity, which lays it down that great consequences must be seen to have equally great causes. Since one of the few points that virtually everyone agrees on about Nazism and Communism is that they had the most terrible of consequences, those in thrall to the Law of P.P. will expect that any proposed explanation be complex, portentous, and deep, just as the things it tries to explain are. My proposed explanation fails to meet that expectation, and for that reason the Law's upholders will find it hard to accept. It falls short not in explanatory power, but in *dignity;* it does not satisfy the widely felt human need for explanations that are emotionally commensurate with their explicanda, for tragic grandeur in the cause when there is tragic grandeur in the consequences.[151] In extenuation, I can only repeat what Ludwig Boltzmann said when some work of his was criticized as lacking elegance: "if you want truth, leave elegance to the tailor" — and add, "and leave dignity to the used-car salesman."

As Judt, Malia, and many others have observed, one of the great puzzles of our age — the period, say, from the end of World War I to the present day, early in the 21st century — is the persistent soft spot that so many intellectuals retain for Communism and communist regimes. Even of those who call themselves moderate liberals, and repudiate all desire for revolution, a great many cannot quite bring themselves to condemn Communism without qualification or reservation; even when they criticize it, there is always a sigh and an "and yet…" at the end.

This reluctance persists despite decades of revelations of Communist lies, crimes, and atrocities; it survived the Moscow Trials of the '30s, it survived the Nazi-Soviet Pact, it survived the Katyn Forest Massacre, it survived the publication of *The God That Failed,* *The Gulag Archipelago,* and *The Black Book of Communism;* it survived the work of Boris Souvarine, Franz Borkenau, George Orwell, Arthur Koestler, Friedrich von Hayek, Raymond Aron, Leszek Kolakowsi, Sidney Hook, Bertram Wolfe, Robert Conquest, and François Furet; it looks like surviving anything that may turn up in the future. It is widely agreed that the number of deaths deliberately caused or connived at by communist regimes far outstrips those by Nazi Germany, but any suggestion that Communist Russia was as bad as Nazi Germany is strongly resisted by many Western intellectuals, particularly academic intellectuals.

It is clear that the source of this resistance does not lie in any significant difference between the behavior of the one regime and that of the other. Judged simply by their acts rather than their words, Nazi Germany and Soviet Russia were almost indistinguishable. There were differences, to be sure, between the *leaders* of the two regimes, at least during World War 2: Hitler was more principled and idealistic than Stalin (though not, apparently, than Lenin). He was no mere opportunist, but a sincere believer in the need to rid the world of Jews, and was prepared to weaken Germany, throw away any chance of winning the war, and even abandon hope of surviving personally, in order to pursue his vision of a *Judenfrei* Europe and world. Stalin, on the other hand, seems to have believed in nothing but himself, and to have been interested in little but conserving and expanding his personal power.

But these differences between the two leaders are epiphenomena; in their overt acts and their effect on those subject to them, the two regimes were essentially indistinguishable — Stalin was even exhibiting Hitler's rigid anti-Semitism in his last days. Both were despotisms; both killed, tortured, and imprisoned millions; but Nazism is remembered with universal loathing — we were treated recently to the spectacle of a German government minister[152] condemning the policy of an American president by comparing it to Hitler's — while communism still enjoys a lingering tenderness on the part of millions throughout the Western world. Judged by their acts, the two regimes are Tweedledum and Tweedledee — but judging by acts rather than words, where the two diverge, is precisely what large numbers of Western intellectuals cannot do, and therein lies the root of the problem.

Every intelligent observer feels occasional impatience with representative democracy — its endless bickering and chattering, its indecisiveness, its corruptibility, its almost invariable mediocrity and hypocrisy — and wonders if we wouldn't be better off under a benevolent despot. But although all of us feel the attractions of despotism at one time or another, and may even wander into its showroom to browse and kick the tires, we fall, as potential despotism buyers, into two quite distinct classes, and the salesmen handle the two kinds of potential customer quite differently. The differing requirements of the two markets, though, are satisfied simply by different marketing, merchandizing, and packaging; the goods themselves are the same.

Communism is despotism packaged and marketed for the literate or at least semi-literate — the typical Western intellectual, academic, or journalist — while Nazism is despotism packaged and marketed for the subliterates and anti-literates: Marx's *rural idiots* and *lumpen proletariat*. As the despotism salesmen well understand, these latter want to parade around in snazzy uniforms, and to have concrete targets to vent their fury on: barbarians outside the gates, traitors within — they want someone to hit. The former are very little attracted to uniforms or punch-ups, but are suckers for ringing verbal formulations, striking paradoxes, and grandiose "theory"; it is not, *pace* Auden, Time that "worships language, and forgives everyone by whom it lives," but intellectuals. No matter what was done in the Gulag, they cannot help heaving a soulful sigh when they hear "From each according to his ability ..." and "Workers of the world, unite!" and all the rest of it. The Gulag is merely a historical fact, receding from us at the speed of oblivion and forgetfulness; slogans live forever.

The primacy of words over things, for intellectuals, comes about because language is both a tool and an art medium, both means and end. We use language both to represent the public world and to create private worlds, with one part of the population tending to the practical use, the other — the intellectuals and artists — tending to the imaginative and creative. According to Burke's dictum that "Art is Man's Nature," the intellectual, in responding to words virtually always as an art-medium, and relatively seldom as mere bearers of information about the common world, is Man *par excellence.* But there is a terrible danger in this: if he brings to documents like *The 18th Brumaire of Louis Napoleon* and Mao's little red book the same sensibility he brings to *Within A Budding Grove* and *A Room of One's Own,* he may lend himself to the greatest horrors the human race has so far perpetrated.

He is abetted in his lapse by language's tendency, which it shares with all other human tools, to become an end rather than a mere means; every tool we create to help us do a job goes on to strive for autonomy, to try to become something with a meaning, an aspiration, a purpose all its own. Language, originally meant to refer to a preexisting world, now more and more is used to build imaginary worlds; a tool meant for discussing a given world is now more and more its own subject, and words are increasingly "mentioned" rather than "used." The poet tells us that the poem "should not mean, but be"; he has prevailed beyond his fondest wish — more and more of our written words are now used "creatively," and the symbol of our age is framing quotation marks, used to proclaim "art at work here." So Communism (with all its isotopes and Lite versions — socialism, progressivism, left-liberalism, radicalism, Utopianism, "activism," and so on), as despotism packaged for the word-intoxicated, gets a free ride on the literary wagon; it prevails with those who write and read books, while poor old down-market Fascism and Nazism have to court the unlettered, trying to sell despotism by rousing the rabble with long hypnotic speeches, heavily rhythmic music, mass-formation marching, and street fighting.

The answer, then, to the question "Why are intellectuals so soft on Communism?" is "Because Communism is despotism wrapped in enthralling words, and intellectuals are enthralled by words." The intellectual and political world in which we live is shaped to a great extent by what would seem a mere tautology: books are written by and for the bookish. But like the mere tautologies of mathematics, it unfolds into the most illuminating of revelations for those who can see its implications and corollaries. If books are by and for the bookish, then every book is "prejudiced" in favor of the literate, of those hypersensitive to words, and all the things that come wrapped in pleasing words. They are created by and for people preternaturally disposed to judge men and movements much more by what they say than what they do; people who, to the extent they can, close the door on mere external factuality, and live within their gated community of verbality. And it is quite to be expected that writers and readers — intellectuals, in a word — should be easy prey to the despotism salesman whose marketing and PR staffs are so expert in producing stirring verbal formulations, whether a heavily footnoted treatise on Kojéve's interpretation of Hegel, or a bumper sticker to be hawked on Berkeley's Telegraph Avenue.

In being asked to condemn Communism absolutely, Western intellectuals are being asked to do something far more painful than merely to give up some political and economic doctrines; they are being asked to accept the primacy of fact over "ideas" and "theories" and other imaginative verbal constructs — and this is to ask them to yield on a vital point, to surrender their ultimate citadel. Few if any intellectuals today believe, or even know, what Marx or Engels said about the labor theory of value, or the Asiatic mode of production, or the structure of the primitive family, and very few would say today, with the communist British historian Eric Hobsbawm, that the promise of the Revolution is such that, even if it can be realized only by millions of deaths, the price is still not too high. But what most intellectuals cannot do is to accept that intellectual constructs, their stock in trade, cannot defeat facts — such an admission would cut them to the heart. In a way, then, to bombard the typical Western intellectual with damaging facts about Communism, as *The Black Book of Communism* does, generally has no good effect, and may even had a bad effect; it is merely a compendium of facts, with no wit, style, irony, or any of the other literary properties that really speak to the intellectual's heart. De Gaulle said "Blood dries quickly"; he might have added, "but ink stays bright and clear for a long time."

It was very honest of the archetype of all intellectuals to reply, when asked what he read, "Words, words, words." And equally honest of his modern incarnation, the archetype of intellectuals in our time, to call his autobiography *Les Mots*.[153]

Denial of objectivity: the first refuge of a scoundrel

"We are the first men who do not possess the truth, but only seek it."

– Nietzsche[154]

The gift of language, perhaps the greatest the human race enjoys, carries with it a potential curse of the same magnitude: the risk that we may by misunderstanding that gift define our way into trouble so great as to disable us. A prime example of this curse at work is the way we have framed the notion of *objectivity*. Both as an example of a class, and as a crippling mistake in its own right, it is deserving of extended examination.

The death of God, although widely noted and generally lamented, has brought with it one problem whose severity seems not to be fully appreciated. Although most agree that His death may well have been a mercy — He was very old, and visibly suffering — it is not yet clear to all that when He died, He took with Him absolute certainty, and in doing so left us in difficulties. This concomitant of His death is proving troublesome to us mortals, because we have been accustomed since our own creation to plan and justify our actions by reference to Divine commands and teachings; denied that aegis now, we find ourselves acting, when we do act, without the sanction of higher authority.

We have today far better evidence for many of our beliefs than our predecessors of a hundred and more years ago had, but we are less sure of anything than they were; all we have is weighty evidence, they had the Word of God. And, already uncertain of anything, we are constantly being exhorted to keep an open mind; to respect the opinions and beliefs of others; to realize that different people see things differently; and even to entertain the possibility that there is, at least in the most profound matters, no such thing as *the truth*. For many people, especially the highly educated, this awareness that we are on our own and working without a net, that any of our beliefs may someday be overturned, that apparently intelligent people reject our most deeply-held values, is simply incapacitating. Asked to act in accord with their own beliefs and values, they wail, "But some people disagree with us! New evidence may turn up! Posterity may laugh at us! We may be shown to be wrong! We can't be sure that we're being *objective!*" — and they wring their hands in an ecstasy of self-doubt while fools and thugs have their way.

The tendency of the best and brightest to refuse to decide and lead was noted by Plato (the emphasis is supplied):

> And for this reason, I said, money and honour have no attraction for them; good men do not wish to be openly demanding payment for governing and so to get the name of hirelings, nor by secretly helping themselves out of the public revenues to get the name of thieves. And not being ambitious they do not care about honour. Wherefore necessity must be laid upon them, and they must be induced to serve from the fear of punishment. And this, as I imagine, is the reason why the forwardness to take office, instead of

waiting to be compelled, has been deemed dishonourable. *Now the worst part of the punishment is that he who refuses to rule is liable to be ruled by one who is worse than himself.*[155]

The chief consequence of our loss of divinely sanctioned certitude has not been to make us self-reliant, but to make us timorous and ineffectual; to disable many well-intentioned people, and play into the hands of charlatans. Every modern con man has learned to exploit the worries and inhibitions of the high-minded and those with excessively tender consciences; learned how easy it is, when caught at some wrongdoing, to point out that the law he has been caught breaking contains imperfectly defined terms and unspoken assumptions, that it was framed by fallible people acting in accordance with views that were merely the product of their time, and no longer universally held — we have seen a president of the United States try to defend himself against a charge of perjury by claiming that *is* is ambiguous. (It was not for nothing, apparently, that he attended Oxford, home of linguistic analysis; when we supposed that what he was doing in the Oval Office was copulating with his muse, he was actually musing on the copula.)

We are so vulnerable because our nostalgia for God and the apodictic knowledge He afforded us takes the form, today, of a call for *objectivity;* a yearning for all the assurance of correctness that the devout enjoyed, but without the embarrassment of involvement in religion. But to seek the attributes of divinity in a being other than God is idolatry, and the modern idolaters have been punished for their sin: they have trapped themselves in a definition of objectivity that makes it not only impossible to achieve, but impossible even to recognize. What it means to the idolaters is a view of things exactly as they really are — a view undistorted by the special angle from which the observer happens to see the object; a view that is not partial, in either sense of the term; a view that some philosophers have called the "God's eye view" — the one God would have if He still lived.

But no rule, no intellectual construct of any kind, can meet that standard. Every attempt to claim for a concrete assertion that it does so is promptly assailed by critics, who bring against it the objection, first, that it is merely a product of human judgment; and second, that if pressed to the limit, it depends on concepts that are themselves imperfectly specified. And if we cannot have perfect knowledge, the critics imply, we can have none at all: because we cannot say exactly when life begins, we cannot agree about abortion; because we cannot say exactly when it ends, we cannot agree about when to switch off the respirator; because we cannot measure anything with absolute precision, we cannot say how long the coastline of Britain is.

The notion that because we can have no apodictic knowledge we can know nothing at all is a poison that has infected every corner of the intellectual realm. It is a poison that has been encapsulated in slogan form by Wittgenstein in the words *"Everything that can be said at all, can be said clearly; and about what cannot be said clearly, we must be silent."* But the truth, as we all know and witness in our practice every day of our lives, is that few things worth saying can immediately be said clearly, and what we cannot yet say clearly, we must practice saying. But there are many so trapped by what I will call Wittgenstein's Fallacy that arguing the value of any particular rule with them is futile.

Defining our way into perdition

Since no one can demonstrate to others, or even be sure privately, that his views are objective in the idolatrous sense, it follows that we are all *prejudiced,* and our views are open to the deepest suspicions on the part of everyone else, especially those who hold other views. The one thing that is clear about *objectivity* so defined is that, since it describes a quality that is by definition unobtainable if not nonexistent, it is of no value in characterizing any particular person or view.

But this dilemma springs from faulty definition. Rightly understood, the concept of objectivity is far from useless; it stands for a quality that human thought *can* achieve, and ought always to aspire to. What it properly denotes is a systematic effort to correct for the partiality — again, in both senses — of our vision. We automobile drivers sit to one side or the other of the cars we drive, our picture of the road ahead conditioned by the angle from which we view it. And yet the experienced driver has no trouble staying in his lane and driving straight down the road, or threading his way through a narrow passage with bare inches of space on either side of his car; he has learned to correct for his own visual 'prejudice', and steer 'objectively'.

Similarly, an official whose duty it is to select candidates for some form of preferment, such as admission to an elite school, may be charged with, or suspect himself of, irrational prejudice against some group — Ruritanians, let us say. That official will be practicing objectivity if, whether or not he believes himself to be guilty as charged, he sets up a screening mechanism to remove from every application submitted to him any indication as to whether the applicant is a Ruritanian.

He does not attempt to attain objectivity by taking a course in sensitivity to the foreign-born, or in learning to value diversity; he simply acts so as to defeat any unfair prejudice he may be guilty of, and gets on with his job. The exemplar of objectivity is the double-blind protocol employed by those testing a new drug or therapy; they do not protest that, as medical scientists, they could not possibly, consciously or otherwise, distort the results of the trial — they simply make it impossible for any prejudice to have an effect on the outcome of the trial, and move forward.

For the scholar in the humanities, being objective means being as explicit as possible about the assumptions and purposes with which he begins a study; citing and quoting his sources accurately; and exposing his reasoning completely. Having done this, the scholar has attained objectivity — he may not have attained *truth*, but that's not what objectivity promises; all it does mean is behaving in such a way as to help expose your own errors if you have committed any, and defeat your own bias if you're guilty of any. In short, just as 'random number' denotes not a special kind of number, but simply a number produced by a randomizing process, so 'objective position' is not one known to be certain, but one arrived at by an objective process — one that makes a systematic effort to preclude or defeat error and bias.

Note that objective behavior does not presuppose honesty; on the contrary, it is a means of attaining, so far as possible, reliable results even in the face of weakness and bad character — its glory is to force a scoundrel to refrain from malfeasance by putting his actions in the public eye. We are particularly concerned here not with cases of good faith — cases in which the subjects are truly determined that no unfair prejudice be permitted to affect their judgment — but rather with those who would be glad to cheat, but are forestalled by a general agreement as to methods. Objective procedures are the tools of those who believe that we can devise systems so good that no one needs to be perfect.[156]

The belief that objectivity can be attained, and in fact is often attained in civilized societies, is not an 'idealistic' one; it is not the position of those too innocent to know, or too high-minded to admit, that there are scoundrels and weaklings in the world. Champions of objectivity are only too aware that there are great numbers of people who are not in the least embarrassed by their prejudices, or interested in defeating them; we even know that almost all of us, on occasion, fall into that category. We are in fact just those with an unshocked awareness of human weakness in general, and in particular the tendency to fudge evidence when we believe that our cause is so noble as to justify fudging — as virtually all causes seem to be, at some time and to most people.

When the confused or the cunning charge that a decision rendered by some authority is invalid because it is not 'objective,' they mean either that those authorities have committed a specific act of injustice in arriving at it, or that the justice of their decision is not *demonstrable* — that is, it cannot be shown to be founded on apodictic knowledge. If they mean the former, the burden is on them to specify and document that act of injustice (we will waive, of our charity, the question of how they can demonstrate the injustice of any act, given their claim that it is impossible to be 'objective'); if they mean the latter, they are simply rehearsing the general truth that we have no apodictic knowledge, a truth that has no bearing on any particular dispute, any more than the existence of gravity has any bearing on an investigation into a plane crash.

On second thought, let's *not* waive the question of how the critic can know that someone else is not being objective, let's ask it. When we are charged with a failure to be objective, our accuser is implicitly claiming to know what an objective position or view would be; how does he know this? If he has achieved objectivity, then objectivity is not only possible in principle, but has actually been achieved by at least one person. How did he achieve it? Why can't we achieve it too? If he has *not* achieved objectivity, how does he know that *our* position is not objective? The kindest way to think of those who have succumbed to Wittgenstein's Fallacy is that they are a bit confused.

Postmodernism as reaction to the loss of certainty

Abandoning the idea that objectivity is attainable and worth striving for — a dangerous step in itself — seems to lead inexorably to the even more pernicious step of thinking that there is no such thing as objective reality: not only can we know nothing, really, but there is nothing, really, for us to know. Even the findings of the hard sciences and mathematics have been called simply stories that we like to tell ourselves, and stories very different from those that other cultures, or at least alien beings in distant galaxies, might tell themselves with equal justification.[157] And this doctrine, in itself so abstract as to seem to have no bearing whatever on sublunary life, has in fact had some very curious effects on Western politics and cultural life.

Nietzsche was the first philosopher of stature to proclaim the death of God and the loss of belief in objective reality that is its frequent concomitant, and to attempt to base something like a system of thought and morality upon that loss. (The general educated public in the West has been a little slower to follow this path; it took the horrors of the twentieth century to make that public accept in large measure that they were no longer — if they ever had been — looked after by a benevolent personal God.) Thinkers since Nietzsche have reacted to the loss of belief in God in one of three ways: by attempting to replace the lost belief with one founded on science or Marxism or some other secular authority; by inventing or reviving some substitute religion, such as New Age spirituality, Wicca, or millenarian cults; or by accepting the loss without regret, and welcoming the absence of belief as a positive development.

The most extreme and doctrinaire followers of the third way are variously called Postmodernists or Relativists or Antifoundationalists or anti-Platonists or antimetaphysicians or antiessentialists or anti-dualists or pragmatists or any of several other names, but I think Postmodernism is the most common name, and it is the one I will use (usually abbreviated "PM") here. Of the two men who are commonly regarded as leaders of the PM movement here in America, Richard Rorty is the most rewarding to study for our purposes; the other — Stanley Fish — is more a literary critic, much less a philosopher. So the discussion that follows will look into the causes and consequences of PM, and in particular at the work of Rorty as it affects our cultural and political life, especially after The Attack of September 11, 2001 — and only that. This is not the place to assess Rorty's work in general, and in any case that task has been performed more than once by his professional colleagues.[158] All I am concerned to do here is to assess the effect of Rorty's campaign against objectivity on our ability to act or even think with assurance.

The Rorty flavor of postmodernism (which I will call postmodernism *tout court*) seems to be unique among nominally philosophical doctrines in having no roots in philosophy. And far from feeling the lack of such roots as a weakness, it explicitly repudiates any need of them; it regards virtually all of Western philosophy from the pre-Socratics to John Dewey as misguided or worse. Although many of postmodernism's champions are, like Rorty, members of departments of philosophy, and lard their writings liberally with quotations from and references to philosophical works, they themselves do not practice what has traditionally been called philosophy. Nor do they point to a philosophic path to be taken by their followers; they look at philosophy from a position outside that discipline, occasionally even hostile to it.

This makes PM so unusual among nominally philosophic doctrines as to arouse intense curiosity; what made people formulate it, and others then accept it, I wondered? What changes would we need to make in our thinking and our projects if we did accept it? It was with these questions in mind that I read several of Rorty's books, as well as a few by other PM spokesmen,[159] but nowhere in them did I find what I'd hoped for. Most of their message seems to consist of variations on one theme: "you only hold the Realist-Objectivist position because you've been trained to; you simply can't imagine an alternative way of looking at things."

And one keeps wanting to ask Rorty and his allies, "Suppose I *could* see things your way — what good things would result? What problems would be solved, what advantages would I enjoy?" But no answer is offered to these questions; we simply get told, in effect, that we have to have faith. When we are told by an orthodox religious believer that faith must come first, we are offered some powerful inducements: salvation, the beatific vision, eternal life, the ministrations of a bevy of virgins — but Rorty and the others make no such promises, don't even tell us just how our life here on earth will change for the better if we adopt their views. Is it possible that the only reason that the postmoderns can offer to induce us to join them in their war against Absolute Truth is that their doctrine is Absolutely True? How did such a doctrine ever come to be formulated? What makes anyone hold it? The PM champions offer no answers; I offer mine here.

Three roots of Postmodernism

PM has three main roots:

1. The first, already discussed here, is the need to come to terms with the "death of God" — that is, the awakening from the illusion of apodictic knowledge. PM is the result of taking the welcoming approach to this loss, and taking the welcome to an extreme.

2. The war against absolutism and other abuses of religious and

intellectual authority, and the rapid degeneration of that war into one against authority as such.

3. The special problems of intellectuals, and especially academic intellectuals, in maintaining their own position and self-esteem.

The war against absolutism: abolishing the abuse by abolishing the use

The central tenet of PM is that "objective reality" — meaning the way things inescapably are, independent of human thoughts and wishes — is a myth, and along with it, of course, the notion that a statement is true to just the extent that it accurately describes its correlative in objective reality, that part of the world it asserts something about. A principal root of this rejection of objective reality, I believe, is the urgent desire of some modern philosophers to combat religious fundamentalism, bigotry, dogmatism, and intolerance. They have noted with dismay that people who think they have absolute knowledge, especially those who believe they have had a unique revelation from God, often behave despotically and cruelly toward others, feeling that their monopoly of enlightenment justifies such behavior toward the unenlightened. The absolutists often go even further: they come to feel that it is their *duty* to behave so, and that the unenlightened — if they survive the process — should be grateful for being coerced into enlightenment.

It is in response to that triumphalism, I believe, that the PM spokesmen try to convince us not merely that no one has such absolute knowledge, or can have such knowledge, but even that there is no such knowledge to be had. They apparently believe that if we give up our absolute beliefs and our belief in the absolute, what will remain is sweet reason. Rorty usually (he speaks with more than one voice, as we shall see) seems to think that if we give up our belief in objective reality, we will become liberals or progressives or whatever Utopian socialists are called these days. I think he is wrong; what would remain, for a great part of the public, is moral emptiness and confusion. The only effect on most educated Westerners of an exposure to PM is to undermine (or *subvert,* to use one of PM's favorite terms) the assumptions that form the basis of their thinking. For some PM believers this is a welcome consequence, and perhaps their main reason for talking PM up; but for many others, I think, PM is a runaway doctrine, an ideology that has escaped the seminars and academic journals in which it was conceived, and has become a monster its creators can no longer control. And as seems to be the habit of monsters, this one, now loosed, is turning on its creators.

Last infirmity of noble mind: the predicament of the Western intellectual

The infiltration of PM throughout our culture, even among many who do not describe themselves as PM believers, is largely traceable to the difficulties inherent in being a Western intellectual or academic. If a large part of your life is devoted to thinking, reading, and writing, and especially if you've taken years to get a Ph.D while others were forging careers in business or the professions, you can't help feeling you need to show results in the form of advanced ideas and deeper knowledge — what was it all for, if you can't? If your subject is one of the sciences, even one of the social sciences, you'll have no trouble doing that; you know many things that laymen do not, and can do many things they cannot.

But what if your studies were in the humanities, where little or nothing can be demonstrated, and where you cannot get the laity to see you as a master of esoteric knowledge? And what if your studies seem to lead to conclusions very close, even identical, to those reached by ordinary intelligent people outside academia? What if, to look squarely at the worst case, the non-intellectuals have arrived at the right answer without your help? For many intellectuals, the need to distinguish themselves from the crowd is so great that they will take a position that is outrageous if that's the only alternative to simply agreeing with the popular view. Their behavior has been amusingly described by Clive James:

> ... those desperate commentators, omnipresent now in our multiple media outlets, who must always advance an outlandish opinion because they don't write well enough to make a reasonable opinion interesting.[160]

And the academic intellectual, in particular, suffers not only from the need to differentiate himself at almost any cost from the laity, but also from the common human desire to stand out among one's peers. The academic has more than ordinary problems here, too, because he is usually too high-minded (or simply unequipped) to compete with peers in possessions, power, or worldly achievement. But many academics have found another way to gratify the unquenchable human drive for distinction and fame: they compete among themselves to see who can be more radical, more critical of the West, more sympathetic to every person, doctrine, and movement hostile to the United States, more 'understanding' of everyone who has hurt us. Debarred from the usual forms of showing off, academics flaunt what Veblen would have called Conspicuous Compunction. They thereby earn admiration for their courage in defying Authority, which in the United States is well known for hauling dissident professors off to re-education camps or oubliettes. If anyone pays attention to them at all, professors who bravely *speak truth to power* are in danger of receiving a MacArthur "genius" grant (note the terrible fates that have befallen Professors Chomsky and Said for their defiance of the powers that be). What takes real courage in academia as in public life is speaking truth to the powerless.

Rorty: the priority of politics

The PM project of which Rorty is a leading spokesman is at bottom a political campaign, not a philosophical doctrine. Rorty is, so far as

I know, the only PM philosopher who says this, explicitly and proudly:

> Those who share Dewey's pragmatism will say that although it may need philosophical articulation, it does not need philosophical backup. On this view, the philosopher of liberal democracy may wish to develop a theory of the human self that comports with the institutions he or she admires. But such a philosopher is not thereby justifying these institutions by reference to more fundamental premises, but the reverse: He or she is putting politics first and tailoring a philosophy to suit.[161]

And seeing what they usually try to sell us politically, it is no wonder that postmodernists open by trying to discredit the concept of objective truth. Those who ask us to abandon the traditional Realist concept of truth never say, as one might expect, "There's no objective truth, so do your own thing!"; their cry is always, "There's no objective truth, so do what I say!" And all too often the beast that their chase has in view turns out to be a mangey donkey; in Rorty's case, all of Western philosophy from Plato until John Dewey is to be junked so that, in effect, the results of the American presidential election of 1972 can be reversed, and George McGovern be declared the victor after all.

But because he is pleading for a political cause rather than a philosophical thesis, he cannot give any *philosophical* reason why anyone else should join him in his pseudo- or anti-philosophical position. The claim Rorty makes for his position is not that it is true, but simply that it leads to a more salutary state of things in general. Rorty asserts that if we accept PM, we will be better people — better friends, better parents, better citizens, living in a better world: one that is kinder, more tolerant, more inclusive, more joyous. He makes this quite clear in many of his writings, perhaps most fully in his essay "Solidarity or Objectivity?" From Rorty's point of view, then, the only relevant objection that might be made of PM would be that it does *not* make us happier and healthier — if adopting the PM position does not improve our well-being as individuals and citizens, then PM fails. (It may well be the only philosophical doctrine that is in need of testing and approval by the Food and Drug Administration.)

Rorty wants us to stop talking about objective reality, and turn instead to talking about ideas that help us become happier, better people. But the idea of objective reality is one that has long made Western man happier, perhaps even on balance better, so by Rorty's own criterion, we ought to retain that notion. Rorty himself might be happier if we abandoned the idea of Objective Reality (OR), but he has not offered us any evidence that *we* would be happier. For another thing — or maybe it is just another aspect of the same thing — many people find little comfort in a doctrine that that has obviously been formulated just to give them comfort; we metaphysical prigs (a Rorty term for those curmudgeons who *will* keep insisting on OR) are so purblind that frankly feel-good doctrines are no more likely to succeed with us than a medication that openly advertised itself as a placebo. In short, if Rorty really wants to see philosophy help us cope with our total situation, he ought to support OR, however much pleasure it would give him to see it abandoned; if we are metaphysical prigs, the PM bunch are epistemological sluts.

213

Rorty thinks that we should stop debating all the traditional questions of Western philosophy, and simply ask of any proposition, does this help us realize our objective of becoming nicer people? He writes as if the proposition "human progress consists essentially of becoming ever more friendly, trusting, unprejudiced, non-judgmental, and accepting of others' needs" has been established, and that further debate is pointless — in fact, was always pointless, but just wasn't fully recognized as such until PM came along. This suggests that it must be a pleasure to be a campus neighbor of Rorty's, but likewise that he may have nothing very cogent to tell us about life off-campus. At his most typical, he seems to be saying — gracefully, at length, and very learnedly — "everything important that I know, I learned in kindergarten," and his essays seem simply well-written and documented position papers sponsored jointly by the ACLU, NOW, and the local PTA.

He seems also to believe that his own principles are not controversial propositions, but such obvious common sense that they need only be mentioned to win assent. He writes:

...we [pragmatists] see both intellectual and moral progress not as a matter of getting closer to the True or the Good or the Right, but as an increase in imaginative power.[162]

This is argument by typography; one might with equal justification write "not as An Increase in Imaginative Power, but as a matter of getting closer to the true or the good or the right." Why is the pragmatist's goal a simple good, while the Realist's are rigid ideologies, to be mocked with copybook capitals?

Rorty's postmodernism and the world after the Attack

But Rorty is by far the most interesting writer of the PM party, and unlike most of his allies, has more than one dimension — so much so that sometimes there seem to be two of him, Rorty Major and Rorty Minor. In the next few paragraphs I am (still) dealing with R. Major, the senior and far better known of the two, but his döppelganger or kid brother will be looked at shortly, too. R. Major's principal claim for PM is that it makes us more receptive to new and foreign ideas, more open to the pleas and arguments of outsiders, more ready to sympathize with the claims of aliens. And in urging this course on us, he recognizes no limit — he ignores the case of irresolvable conflict; the case in which we encounter those who will not sit down and reason with us, who believe they already know the truth, and will not stay for an argument.

Rorty Major is concerned exclusively with preventing *us* from becoming such absolutists and bullies, and ignores the possibility that we are at least equally in danger of meeting those from other cultures who are just such threats themselves, and who have killed, imprisoned, or exiled all their own Rortys, who might have pointed out the error of their ways. He worries that even Dewey's pragmatism (Rorty's special term for the PM faith) was not sufficiently thorough-going, even while millions of those whose marginalization he deplores are plotting to kill yet more of us. But for R. Major, human progress consists solely in ever-increasing inclusiveness, ever-increasing readiness to allow the claims of others, ever-increasing sympathy with whatever was once regarded as alien; he has no advice for those faced with an adversary unwilling not only to talk, but perhaps even to accept surrender.

Whether the cheery consequences that Rorty envisions following on the adoption of PM, if they actually came about, would justify the adoption of PM is debatable; what is clear is that, so far as one can see today, PM does not tend to bring them about, but rather the reverse. The effect on most people of exposure to PM is — again — to sap their confidence in their own values, weaken their will to resist aggression by others, and confuse them on moral issues — and some at least of the postmodernists are quite aware of this, and seem not at all unhappy about it. (As I noted in an analysis[163] of one of Stanley Fish's post-Attack writings, the fact that Edward Said was one of those who have called for the rejection of "false universals" suggests that not every postmodernist is simply trying, as Fish suggested, to arm the West better for its battle.)

But Rorty has more than one persona, as I said, and can spring surprises on us. His most common message, by far, is that we need to extend imaginative sympathy in ever-widening circles so as to embrace the marginal and even the hostile, and that the great merit of PM is that it prevents us from thinking that we are The People, and everyone else the Barbarians. But then there is Rorty Minor, who occasionally peeps out from behind the Professor of Niceness; in one of the essays that has already been quoted from, R. Minor speaks:

> …we heirs of the Enlightenment think of enemies of liberal democracy like Nietzsche or Loyola as, to use Rawl's word, "mad." We do so because there is no way to see them as fellow citizens of our constitutional democracy, people whose life plans might, given ingenuity and good will, be fitted in with those of other citizens. … They are crazy because the limits of sanity are set by what *we* can take seriously.[164]

And later in the same essay,

We have to insist that not every argument need to [*sic*] be met in the terms in which it is presented. Accommodation and tolerance must stop short of a willingness to work within any vocabulary that one's interlocutor wishes to use, to take seriously any topic that he wishes to put forward for discussion.

And in a closely related essay (italicized words in square brackets, are mine, not Rorty's),

> Yet their connoisseurship forces them to realize that most of the globe's inhabitants simply do not believe in human equality, that such a belief is a Western eccentricity. Since they [*it doesn't matter for present purposes who "they" are*] think it would be shockingly ethnocentric to say "So what? We Western liberals *do* believe in it, and so much the better for us," they are stuck.
>
> Anti-anti-ethnocentrists [*a category in which Rorty includes himself*] suggest that liberals should say exactly that...[165]

I find R. Minor a very refreshing and hope-inspiring fellow; it is a shame that he's so little known, even — apparently — to R. Major. It is my fond hope that the two Rortys might meet, and that the senior recognize that his kid brother is no longer a mere kid.

Incommensurability

This point of R. Minor's, that there are some political and social positions that we must simply reject, and cannot hope to 'understand' or empathize with or accommodate, seems to be the practical counterpart of the more abstract notion, often found in PM, that there are cultures or schools of thought or Weltanschauungen that are simply 'incommensurable' — that are radically different all the way down, that admit no common ground on which one might stand while trying to bridge the gap, that cannot even communicate with each other. PM finds this notion fits in well with its rejection of absolutism in the usual sense — if there are such irreconcilable differences between human groups on such fundamental matters, how can there be any one Objective Reality? — but the cost of making this argument is very high; in its insistence on so unprovable a position, it arouses the suspicion that PM is itself an example — perhaps the best current example — of what it seems to be deploring. PM philosophers, here as elsewhere, get hold of the wrong end of the stick; on the conceptual level, where they might be expected to be determined to understand everything, they find some strains of human thought hopelessly incomprehensible, while on the practical level, they cannot bring themselves to wholly condemn even those who try to kill us. Rorty, again distinguishing himself from the ruck of PM believers, explicitly repudiates the 'incommensurability' thesis,[166] but PM in general is stuck with it — and Rorty, in rejecting it, is to some extent at odds with many of those he elsewhere refers to under such labels as "we pragmatists" and "we liberals" and similar implied claims to unanimity.

There have been a number of theories offered within living memory that prided themselves on being incommensurable, that is, inexpressible in any language but their own: Freudianism and Marxism were the most notable among them. Each was a closed system: one that protects itself from attack by explaining away all possible criticisms as so many vestiges of a now discredited mode of thought, so that to seek to criticize it is simply to reveal ignorance or prejudice. PM is yet another of this genus, and thus an example of just what it claims to find throughout the world, a system or paradigm so radically different from others as to be incommensurable with them; no neutral vocabulary exists in terms of which anyone outside the system can talk about it so as to make sense within it. Postmodernism, then, is a mousetrap so cunningly made that no mouse, once inside, can escape — but one that will catch few mice, because it contains no bait that many will find attractive.

The postmodernist suggestion that there are incommensurable outlooks or weltanschauungen that preclude agreement or even mutual comprehension between parties who subscribe to different flavors of them is very like the notion behind the gadfly's questions, "How do you know that anyone except yourself exists?" or "How do you know that everything didn't double in size overnight?" or "How do you know that the world, including your memories of the past, didn't come into being just fifteen minutes ago?" And the answer to the incommensurability-monger, like the answer to the gadfly, is "I haven't the faintest idea; now go away, I'm busy." There may be no such thing as a stupid question, but there certainly are impudent and time-wasting questions. And those pushing the 'incommensurability' thesis may find they have generated yet more unintended consequences: if we are persuaded to accept that thesis, we may well wonder why we need to be concerned about members of cultures so different from ours that communication is impossible. We may see such beings as less than human, and treat them accordingly — an especially unwelcome outcome for a movement one of whose chief motivations was a fervent desire to end bigotry and oppression.

To get back to Rorty: he would not agree, I think, that there are two of him. He would say, I think, that what I see as Rorty Minor, the tough Rorty, has always been implicit in his writings, and that I simply failed to see it. Let it be so; if it is my failure as a reader not to have realized when reading Rorty that these other sentiments, the ones I think of as coming from Rorty Minor, were right there all the time, then I accept the blame. But my fault or not, it is a fact that such tough words as I have just quoted from him are not *explicit* in any but a very few passages in his many books and papers. And it would be of the greatest interest — *practical* interest — to know if he sees the Islamic fundamentalists by whom we are now threatened as being on a par with Loyola and Nietzsche in unacceptability as fellow-citizens, and as equal candidates for the epithet *mad.*

It would be of practical use, I think, to be able to say to the droves of academics to whom Rorty's is a name to conjure with that he, the arch-pragmatist and co-doyen, with Fish, of PM, has had it up to here with those who attacked us on September 11, and gives permission to his allies, even the most serious readers of the German sociologists and the French literary theorists, to simply hate the attackers' guts. Rorty might do both his country and his philosophy a large service if he could bring himself to say so, loudly and clearly.

I say this because I believe that the United States, and most of the Western world, is living in what psychologists call a fugue state; the true meaning of The Attack of September 11, 2001, is so terrifying that very few can face it fully, and events have not yet broken through our shell of complacency and self-imposed blindness to force us to. We are, I think, fighting for our lives, and our peril is all the greater because for the great majority of us nothing has yet happened to drive that message home. In our situation, the harm done by a false philosophy, which would ordinarily be contained within academic circles, is visited on all of us. PM, problematic and potentially dangerous even in normal times, is for a civilization under deadly attack a corrosive acid that weakens us where we are most vulnerable: not in our airports or office buildings or shopping malls, but in our will and our spirit. It is bitter beyond irony to observe that what began as an attempt to prevent us from being tyrannical and intolerant to others has become a weapon in the hands of those who would be so to us.

CHAPTER 9

Plagiarism and Misquotation: the Use of Others' Thoughts and Words

What is plagiarism? The old rules recapitulated

The misconception of the relation between thought and words that is the underlying cause of virtually all the phenomena studied here has led to some remarkable changes in our attitude toward plagiarism, quotations, and generally the use of words that in some sense belong to others. To the extent that words and thought are decoupled, our respect for accuracy in reproducing the words in which a thought was originally embodied diminishes, and so does our scrupulosity in assigning particular utterances to their authors. These degenerative changes can be seen in many recent events and writings.

During the first quarter of 2002, the press was full of stories about plagiarism. Several well-known popular historians and science writers were charged with passing off as their own substantial passages from other writers' books.[167] Most of the writers so charged admitted to some degree of culpability, but usually claimed that they had been simply careless and hasty, not intentional plagiarists. (One or two of them tried, rather disgracefully, to put some at least of the blame on their "research assistants," whom they were just too busy to supervise. And many also asked for leniency on the grounds that their research methods, which apparently consisted of jotting attractive words down on scraps of paper and dumping them in a shoebox, were too primitive to allow noting that the words happened to be someone else's — there was just no room, or time, for the opening and closing quotation marks that would have reminded them of that.) But even when their pleas of carelessness and haste were accepted, their reputations suffered serious injury, and even their publishers and editors suffered some injury. It is not only historians and writers who have been so exposed; a United States Senator (still in office in 2006, and frequently quoted in the press when lecturing his political opponents about their misbehavior) was caught a few years ago delivering a speech of which much was taken, without attribution, from one originally delivered by Neil Kinnock when leader of the British Labour Party.

Plagiarism has, of course, always existed, but seems to be getting more serious and more frequent, partly because of the increased pressure on students to get good grades, job seekers to get hired, and everyone to get ahead generally, but also because of that dissociation of words and thoughts that is the theme running through, and uniting, all the many phenomena we have been considering. With words seen as merely the dress of thoughts, what harm in assuming the garments of others? There are perennial stories in the press about cheating in the schools and colleges of the United States, in which students turn in as their own work entire essays written by others — sometimes finding them through the Web, and paying cash for them. The practice of presenting others' material as one's own is becoming so common, in fact, that some of the perpetrators have moved from the defensive to the attack, claiming that since "everybody does it," it is unfair to punish those who happen to be unlucky enough to be caught. So far, at least, only a few seem to have been corrupted into thinking that theft becomes excusable when it becomes common, but even professional writers and editors are sometimes a little confused on the question of using the work of others. I will begin by stating what I believe is the standard, traditional way of using the ideas and words of others.

Using other people's ideas

When a writer uses an idea (other than a commonplace) that he has found in someone else's writings, he is required by professional ethics to acknowledge that fact. If his own book is a scholarly one, with foot-notes or endnotes, the standard way of acknowledging indebtedness for some specific idea is in such a note: "I owe the idea of totalitar-ian tolerance to ..."; if his debt is broader, going beyond the use of a single idea, an appropriate way to acknowledge that would be to say, in a preface or introduction, "My thesis in this book is heavily indebted to the work of Professor X, especially his *The Erotics of Double-Entry Bookkeeping*, which first broached the idea that ...." There are two distinct reasons for making such acknowledgements, of which the first is simply courtesy. Someone else has done some work, and produced something of value; you are now benefiting from that work and that product, and owe him a tip of the hat for the service he has done you. The second reason is that such acknowledgements are a vitally impor-tant way of maintaining clarity and coherence in intellectual life; they explicitly link together the many different voices in the on-going pub-lic conversation that is created by all those contributions, and make their inter-relationships clear.

If Mr X has written an article that attacks Professor Y's arguments, I want to know if he has read Y's latest book, which came out very recently, and I want to know if he's made use of Ms Z's doctoral dissertation, which brought to light some facts that have an important bearing on Y's work. If Mr X is doing a proper job of acknowledging his sources, in footnotes or otherwise, those questions will be answered; I will learn, for example, whether he fails to mention Y's recent book because it came out too late for him to use in his discussion of Y's work, or because he simply thinks it unimportant for that purpose.

In recent years, publishers have become increasingly reluctant to accept footnotes; their claim is that potential readers are put off by pages that are "disfigured" by notes, and that no one pays any atten-tion to footnotes anyway (publishers are not troubled by the contra-diction between these two reasons.) Whether sales really are lost because readers are esthetically repelled by pages that have notes at the bottom, or intellectually intimidated by all the learned references and *ibids*, isn't clear; what is very clear is that setting a page with notes is more expensive than setting one with nothing but plain text, and that publishers are doing everything possible to cut costs.

Authors and in-house editors may not have much voice in the matter of allowing or disallowing footnotes, but they must be aware of the issues, and prepared to do what is necessary to ensure that the decencies are observed. If you are writing or editing a scholarly work, one dealing with a topic on which much has already been said by many others, then you must see to it that the relationships — especially the indebtedness — of the present work to those of other scholars are made clear, even if the publisher won't let you use footnotes. There are other mechanisms, as noted earlier, to do this: endnotes, prefaces, "bibliographical essays" at the end of the book, and so on; use whichever of them is most convenient, but get the job done somehow.

Using other people's written words

The rules about using other people's *ideas* aren't perfectly clear, if only because the facts in specific cases can be difficult to establish: when does an idea enter the public domain, and cease to be someone's private property? For that matter, what counts as an idea — how original and important and clearly expressed must a notion be before its author deserves a tip of the hat every time it is used by someone else? There is room for some amount of honest disagreement on these points, and hence for some difference in the way acknowledgements are treated by different authors. But in the matter of using someone else's *words* there is much less room for such differences; although debaters can dream up ambiguous or otherwise problematic cases, there is in practice seldom any honest doubt about whether we're using someone else's words or not. And the mechanisms for dealing with quotations are clear, and not yet forbidden by the economics of publishing.

If you find a passage — even if it is just a brief phrase — in someone else's book so well worded, or so supportive of your own thesis, that you want to use it in your own text, then it is a quotation, and to be treated as such in your document. The way to do that is, in a nutshell, to surround it with quotation marks if it is brief, or to present it as a *block quotation* (also known as *display quotation*) if it is lengthy. The question of when a quotation is lengthy is settled by whatever style guide is being used; if no such guide is involved, here is a rule of thumb: use block quotations whenever the passage you're quoting is more than a couple of lines long, or whenever the passage, whatever its length, contains some potentially confusing internal punctuation.

Putting it in block-quotation format has the double advantage of making it instantly clear that the passage in question *is* a quotation, and of making opening and closing quotation marks unnecessary. Even when no confusion about punctuation is possible, the substitution of formatting for punctuation is a relief to the eye. Where confusion *is* possible, as when the quoted passage itself begins with a quotation, or where quotation marks are being used within it for other purposes — ironic or "distancing" quotation marks, for example — the absence of beginning and ending quotation marks minimizes the chance of confusion, eliminates clutter, and makes unnecessary such expedients as changing internal double quotation marks to single ones.

There are times when you want to incorporate in your own text the substance, but not the exact words, of another writer — a *paraphrase.* If you do, you are especially responsible for accuracy and faithfulness, since you are claiming that although the words are yours, the thoughts and tone are exactly those of someone else. You must make it absolutely clear that what you are presenting *is* a paraphrase, and — as should go without saying (but nowadays nothing goes without saying, and some things don't go even *with* saying) — you must not use quotation marks when the words are yours, not the other writer's, no matter how certain you are that you've expressed his meaning perfectly.

Sometimes you will want to insert something into a quoted passage — typically, to replace a pronoun with an antecedent without which the passage may not be clear — and sometimes you will want to eliminate part of a quoted passage, typically because that part is irrelevant to your purposes in quoting it. The rules here are quite clear: if you add anything to the quoted passage, even if it is just replacing a pronoun with the original author's own antecedent, you must place all added material in brackets: [ ] And if you omit anything, no matter how trivial or irrelevant for your purposes, you must indicate that omission by inserting an ellipsis: ... And finally, if you need to add emphasis to some part of a quoted passage to direct attention to a particularly important point, something typically done by italicizing that part, you must state explicitly, either just before or just after the quotation, that the italics or other emphasizing device are yours, and not in the original.

If there is something questionable within a quoted passage — a misspelling, for example — that may cause your reader to wonder if it was really in the original, or is something you introduced in the process of quotation, you may need to add [*sic*] immediately after that item. *Sic* is Latin for "thus"; it tells the reader that the usage in question really appeared just that way in the original. It is unfortunate that in some writers' hands, *sic* has become a standard way to sneer at a quoted remark, a shorthand way of saying "Yes, believe it or not, this fool really did say this foolish thing!" What makes this especially unfortunate is that some writers, in reaction to the sneering use of *sic*, have refused to use it ever, even in its original, unobjectionable sense — and thereby deprive themselves of a simple way of reassuring their readers that a quotation is accurate. They are like the cat who, having once jumped onto a hot stove, has learned never to jump onto a hot stove again — but cannot bring himself to jump onto a cold one, either, to his disadvantage.

Finally, beware of quotations taken "out of context" — that is, significantly changed in meaning simply by being extracted from their original settings. Such extraction can substantially modify the meaning of a quoted passage, even to the point of making it directly contradict the meaning it had originally. The charge that one has been quoted "out of context" has to be supported by particulars, however; the mere fact that a critic has quoted less than an entire work does not justify the charge, or virtually all quotations would be "taken out of context."

Using other people's spoken words

The possible pitfalls in using other people's words are greatly multiplied when those words were not written but spoken. In that case, doubt may honestly exist not only on how to handle those words, but even as to what those words were — a problem that is dealt with in courts of law by employing a court stenographer who takes down every word, every intelligible sound, uttered by a participant in a trial, and can ask any speaker to slow down if he's speaking too fast to be recorded accurately; unfortunately, such services aren't generally available outside a courtroom. The problem is exhibited in the letters-to-the-editor page of almost every issue of almost every serious journal of opinion: someone has been quoted in an article the journal printed a week or a month ago, and now writes an angry letter to say that he has been misquoted. The reporter says that the letter-writer is wrong; her interview notes show that the interviewee did say just what her story quotes him as saying, and she closes with "I stand by my story." Everyone loses in this very common situation; the interviewer feels her professional integrity has been impugned; the interviewee feels betrayed and vows never to speak to that reporter, perhaps any reporter, again; and readers don't know which to believe.

And is plagiarism so bad, anyway? A judge's injudicious view of the matter

The subject of plagiarism has recently been treated by Richard A. Posner, a judge on the United States Court of Appeals for the Seventh Circuit, in two essays, one titled "The Truth About Plagiarism,"[168] and the other simply "On Plagiarism"[169] (apparently he was not as much concerned with the truth in this piece), and I find in them further evidence that even for so highly regarded and widely read a public intellectual, the issue of plagiarism — the use of others' words and thoughts — seems to cloud the mind. (But perhaps it is just the fact that Posner is not merely a judge, but a frequently published author on a wide variety of public issues, that explains his confusion; plagiarism may well be one of those issues that Orwell told us could be misunderstood only by an intellectual.) The first of these was published in *The Atlantic Monthly* for April 2002, the second in *Newsday* for May 30, 2003. The two pieces are the same in substance, and I will treat them as if they were one, except that direct quotations will be marked *A* (for *Atlantic*) or *N* (for *Newsday*) to help anyone who wants to check their accuracy.

"The Truth About Plagiarism" is subtitled, undoubtedly by a *Newsday* editor, "It is usually a minor offense and can have social value." I assumed before reading the piece that this subtitle was the usual dollop of hype that editors apply to every piece that passes across their desk in an effort to get readers hooked, but in this case the subtitle is a fair one. Posner *is* engaged in trivializing the offense of plagiarism, which he does by ignoring its accepted meaning, and he *does* suggest that plagiarism — at least what he calls plagiarism — is socially beneficial. But what he is mostly engaged in is muddying the waters of discourse.

Here are his arguments, in each case followed by my comments.

Posner (A): We must distinguish in the first place between a plagiarist and a copyright infringer. They are both copycats, but the latter is trying to appropriate revenues generated by property that belongs to someone else ...

Comment: I know of no one who needs to have the difference between plagiarism and copyright infringement expounded, but if there is any such person, he will be really confused by this misinformation. Copyright infringement is the use of copyrighted material without the permission of the owner; it need not (and usually does not) involve the pretence that the material so misused is the work of the infringer, nor need it involve the misappropriation of revenue.

Posner (A): "Plagiarism," in the broadest sense of this ambiguous term, is simply unacknowledged copying ....

Comment: There is nothing in the least ambiguous about *plagiarism,* nor does it have broader and narrower senses; it means illegitimate appropriation of another's words; that is, falsely claiming, usually implicitly, someone else's work as your own.

Posner (A): [paraphrase by me, since the original passage is too long] Shakespeare, in the famous description of Cleopatra that he puts into the mouth of Enobarbus, is simply copying, almost verbatim, a passage from North's translation of Plutarch's life of Mark Antony. In *The Waste Land,* T. S. Eliot in turn "stole" that passage from Shakespeare, and in *West Side Story* Leonard Bernstein copied the plot of Romeo and Juliet. ... [verbatim quotation of Posner resumes at this point.] If these are examples of plagiarism, then we want more plagiarism. They show that not all unacknowledged copying is "plagiarism" in the pejorative sense. Although there is no formal acknowledgement of copying in my examples, neither is there any likelihood of deception. And the copier has added value to the original — this is not slavish copying.

Comment: Yes, if these were examples of plagiarism, we would want more of it. And if my grandmother had wheels, she would be a trolley car. As Posner acknowledges in both papers, none of his examples consists of simple copying, and all of them except the Shakespearian adaptation of North's passage do not merely permit, but require, their audiences to understand the derivation of the material it adapts. (The Shakespearian example differs merely in that it freely permits, but does not *require,* the audience to recognize it as an adaptation of earlier material.) So even in Posner's own "broadest sense," none are examples of plagiarism.

Posner's thinking here is close to incoherent, and hard to disentangle. Within a single sentence of the last-quoted passage he agrees that the examples of plagiarism he has just offered, although they do not "formally" acknowledge being copies, are such that no acknowledgements are necessary, because everyone understands, indeed is expected to understand, the relation of these examples to their several originals. But plagiarism is not copying that is so obvious as to need no explicit acknowledgement, it is copying that conceals the fact that it is a copy; the essence of plagiarism is deception. He then implies that if a copier adds something of value to the material he copies, he is not guilty of "slavish" copying, and presumably not a plagiarist at all, or at least not guilty of plagiarism in "the pejorative sense." Posner here implies a couple of interesting ideas one wishes he had enlarged on: first, if a thief takes the diamond he has stolen from you, and mounts it in a fine gold setting, is he no longer guilty of theft, or at least less guilty? And what exactly is the *non*-pejorative sense of plagiarism?

Posner (N): Plagiarism ... unlike real theft ... is not a crime. If a thief steals your car, you are out the market value of the car; but if a writer copies material from a book you wrote, you don't have to replace the book. ... The real victim of [the plagiarist's] fraud is not the person whose work he copies, but those of his competitors who scruple to enhance their own reputations by such means.

Comment: If a plagiarist publishes something of mine as his own, he may be stealing from me something far more valuable, even in a crass monetary sense, than a car. If I was the first to write "$E=mc^2$", and you publish it as yours, you may have stolen the Nobel Prize from me. If I was the first to say "Hypocrisy is the tribute vice pays to virtue," and you publish it as yours, you may have stolen from me a reputation as a wit or philosopher. But even if the words you steal from me are far less valuable than these examples, still you are both depriving me of the credit earned by those words (they do earn credit, otherwise you would hardly trouble to steal them), and enhancing your own reputation at my expense. You are also misleading your readers, some of whom may go on to utter statements or perform acts of their own on the basis of the misunderstanding you have caused, and get into trouble because they've done so. But Posner thinks that if writer A plagiarizes from writer B, it is not B who is damaged (if anyone is), but writers C, D, and E, who have refrained from plagiarism.

"You don't have to replace the book," says Posner, confounding *book* in the sense of intellectual property with *book* in the sense of a physical object. Indeed, not only need the victim not replace what has been taken from her, she will usually be unable to replace it. For one thing, it is usually only by chance, and in exceptional cases, that the victim of plagiarism learns of her victimization; and in those few cases where she does learn of it, there will usually be little she can do about it. The law — especially in Judge Posner's court — offers little remedy to a plaintiff in a plagiarism case, but generates lawyer's fees, and consumes time and energy, without end. One of Posner's reasons for trivializing the act of plagiarism seems to be that the law takes no great interest in it — and to a lawyer, where there's no legal remedy, there's no crime; if there's no cure for a disease, the disease must be unimportant or imaginary.

233

The doctrine implied by Posner's argument that since the victim of plagiarism has suffered no material loss — she doesn't have to replace the book from which material was taken without her knowledge, let alone permission — she has not really been harmed, is a curious one. I wonder if it applies to a woman who is raped while unconscious, and learns about it only by chance, long afterward? She too has suffered no material loss, and assuming that she was not impregnated by the rape, nor infected with a disease, nor physically injured in any way, what kind of case has she in Posner's court? (I'm aware that Posner's is an appellate court, and that he would hardly be presiding over a rape case; maybe his remoteness from substantive criminal trials is part of his problem in dealing with such matters.) If material loss is the criterion, what grounds has she for seeking a legal remedy?

This analogy, sound up to this point, fails in one important respect: rape is a recognized crime on which there is a large body of legislation and case law, so its victims are not likely to be fobbed off with "You don't have to replace your virginity," or remarks along those lines — but it can still provide some illumination. Posner differentiates between the crime of theft and more nebulous offenses, like plagiarism, by pointing out that the former deprives the victim of something of value — a car, for example — while the latter deprive their victim of nothing — nothing material, at least. It is hard to see, on this basis, why rape, another offense which leaves its victim apparently deprived of nothing, should be taken very seriously. We have long since learned, however, to see the rape victim as someone who has suffered a serious wrong; we think that her dignity and autonomy are important, and that the rapist, even if he has done her no other harm than to diminish *them*, has committed a felony.

Just so the plagiarist damages his victim; deprives her of credit for her work and of the gains in reputation that she would have made if she were recognized as the rightful author — in general, deprives her of the fruits of her labor. I do not mean to suggest that the injury she suffers is as great as that suffered by the rape victim, or that plagiarism should be made a felony; I suggest simply that the two are of the same pattern, as a tiger and a house cat are of the same pattern, though substantially different in magnitude. And if our pet cat claws the furniture, brings in dead birds, and thinks outside the box, we take measures to correct him — nothing like the measures we would take if a tiger were loose in the neighborhood, but measures nevertheless.

Posner (N): *Paradise Lost* plagiarizes the book of Genesis in the Old Testament. ... "My Fair Lady" plagiarized Shaw's play *Pygmalion* ... Woody Allen's movie *Play It Again, Sam* "quotes" a famous scene from *Casablanca*. ... Many of these 'plagiarisms' were authorized, and perhaps none was deceptive ... But what they show is that copying with variations is an important form of creativity, and this should make us prudent and measured in our condemnations of plagiarism.

Comment: I foresee having a problem here in getting the reader to believe that Posner really said the things in the passage quoted above, and meant them seriously. I can only urge the skeptical reader to turn to Posner's essay to see if I've quoted him out of context or otherwise misrepresented him. And neither in this essay nor in any of his other published writings, most of them polemical and sharp-tongued, is there the slightest sign of humor or teasing. If Posner is pulling legs, he has certainly succeeded in pulling mine.

In this passage Posner simply re-defines plagiarism to mean such things as:

- the construction of a work of art (*Paradise Lost*) based on material in the public domain (the Jewish Bible, also known somewhat tendentiously as the Old Testament) by a writer (John Milton) who, so far from wanting his readers to remain ignorant of the dependence of his work on the earlier text, totally depends on the reader's recognition of that relationship, and would be horrified and despondent if he thought his readers failed to see it.

- the construction of a work of art (*My Fair Lady*) on the basis of another one (Shaw's *Pygmalion*), with payment of a fee to the earlier author or his estate, and with the fullest public acknowledgement — indeed, with flaunting — of the relationship between the two.

235

- the construction of a scene or passage in some literary or theatrical work (the *Casablanca* allusion in *Play It Again, Sam*) that depends for its effect on the audience's awareness of its relationship to an earlier one, and has no point without it.

If these examples given by Posner of the use by one artist of material originated by another were indeed cases of plagiarism, then plagiarism would not be even the most venial of offenses, it would be one of the crowning glories of human imagination and creativity. But a material element of what we commonly call *plagiarism* is missing from these examples: the claim, explicit or implicit, by the later artist to be the originator of the material he is adapting or alluding to. If we are to overlook that weakness in Posner's case, we should in fairness overlook the comparable weaknesses in the cases for the propositions that 2+2=5, up is down, and night is day. But let us be fair: Posner does allow, rather handsomely, that "perhaps" no deception was intended. And he does put quote marks around *plagiarism* in the passage in question, showing that he is at least dimly aware that the examples he has given are simply irrelevant. Why, despite his uneasy suspicion that they were irrelevant, he nonetheless built his whole case on them, is something that I hope Posner will explain to us one day. Until he does, I conjecture that the reason is that lawyers are trained to play whatever cards they hold, however poor, as if they were trumps.

Posner suspects that complaints about plagiarism are not always wholly altruistic and disinterested, saying (N) "But I think the zeal to punish plagiarism reflects less a concern with the real injuries that it occasionally inflicts than with a desire on the part of leaders of professional communities, such as journalists and historians, to enhance their profession's reputation." If Posner is right, think of the shame of it! Imagine people so degraded and benighted as to want to protect their profession's reputation for integrity! And while we are facing brutal truths, we may want to consider that perhaps some oppose murder on no better grounds than that they don't want to be murdered — a thought that calls the whole criminal justice system into question; how can we be sure that any of our laws are not tainted by the ignoble motive of self-protection?

Posner's defense of plagiarism, then, consists of assembling a list of artistic adaptations, homages, and allusions; calling them examples of plagiarism; and then claiming that these examples show that plagiarism can be pretty wonderful sometimes. Allowed this form of argumentation, I will gladly undertake to prove any proposition you name; even more exciting, I can see myself making a fortune representing clients in appellate proceedings, at least in one appellate court I know of.

What is a quotation? The Masson-Malcolm case

A useful case study is the lawsuit, or series of suits, brought between 1984 and 1996 by Jeffrey Masson against Janet Malcolm and the *New Yorker* for a profile of him she wrote for that magazine, and later expanded into a book.[170] I single out this rather than any of the innumerable other cases in which misquotation and libel are charged simply because so much material about it is available (do a Web search on either party's name to get some idea of how much literature it generated). Because Masson and Malcolm had their day — indeed, several days — in court, their views, and the evidence in the case, are far better documented than in most such conflicts, where the only record left behind is that in letters to the editor. And it is not only the principals and their attorneys, but many uninvolved critics and journalists, who have recorded their views on the issues raised in this case, giving us further material to chew on.

There were a number of issues in the Masson-Malcolm case, all concerned in some way with the validity of what Malcolm presented as quotations from Masson in her *New Yorker* profile of him. The key issue, and the one of interest for present purposes, is whether it is permissible to present as a simple direct quotation a passage synthesized from separate remarks made by an interviewee over the course of several interviews. Malcolm, the journalist who had done just that in her *New Yorker* piece, said it was, arguing that journalism could hardly exist without it. Masson, the interviewee and subject of her piece, said it was not, arguing that a proper quotation must be not just a passage of which every word was indeed uttered by the subject at one time or another, but one whose constitutive words had been uttered in the order the quotation presents them in, and uttered as one continuous stream rather than piecemeal over the course of a number of distinct occasions and different contexts.

There was little or no dispute about the facts as they bore on this narrow issue: Malcolm did not deny composing such synthesized quotations when reporting on her several interviews with Masson; her contention was that she was entirely justified in doing so, since her business as investigative reporter was not to record and reproduce his words verbatim, as if she were a court stenographer, but to organize and interpret what he told her so as to produce a coherent account for her readers. Masson, for his part (after initially claiming that the most damaging of the remarks attributed to him in Malcolm's piece were simply made up by her), conceded that the words of which they were composed had come from him, but claimed that synthesizing longer passages out of the fragmentary remarks he had made over the course of several lengthy interviews, and made in a variety of contexts, had falsified his views and misrepresented him, greatly damaging his career and reputation in the process.

After years of legal proceedings, including an opinion rendered by the U.S. Supreme Court, Masson lost his case. His loss did not come as a surprise to those with some knowledge of U. S. libel law; the burden on the plaintiff in such cases is practically impossible to sustain, since it involves proving that the accused told deliberate or reckless falsehoods. But although the legal case is settled, the central issue of what constitutes a valid quotation, and in particular whether composite quotations may fairly be presented as simple quotations, is not — and for those concerned with the trustworthiness of documents, and the relationship of words to thought, it is one that is far from closed.

Masson vs. Malcolm in the light of the proposed principles

I think that Masson, whatever his faults on other points, was in the right on the narrow issue that is the crux of his case. Malcolm is correct in saying that it is her job to put together a coherent account of whatever she learned in the course of interviewing Masson, but she had the further responsibility of making it clear to her readers in each case whether she was simply presenting unadorned fact, or arranging the facts to be seen as she thought they should be seen. What Malcolm did in silently composing apparent sustained quotations from Masson's scattered remarks may be common practice among reporters, but it is not clear that that fact is common knowledge among readers, even readers of the *New Yorker*. And since she knew that her profile would be damaging to Masson, she should have been particularly careful to state what she was doing, if only to protect herself from just the sort of trouble she got into. Yes, we want Malcolm's interpretation; we welcome her views — but we also want to know when that's what we're getting, and when we're getting the raw material she's collected.

Of course there are often gray areas where it is all but impossible to completely disentangle fact from interpretation — the very items a reporter will regard and present as facts will depend to some extent on what she makes of the story as a whole — but in this case Malcolm could easily have told us that what she was presenting as a quotation from Masson was not the exact stream of words that had come from him, in the order he uttered them, and all on the same occasion and in the same context, but rather a composite of several remarks he had made on several distinct occasions, and possibly in significantly different circumstances.

One way to avoid the problem might have been pre-publication review, in which the subject of a journalist's story is given the opportunity of reviewing it before publication — not to censor it or veto its publication, but just to have a chance to offer evidence of inaccuracy if he thinks he sees any, with the story's author remaining the final judge. But this precaution, which to many readers might seem only common sense, is anathema to most journalists (for discussion of it by a professional journalist, see Steve Weinberg, "Thou shalt not concoct thy quote," at www.journalism.indiana.edu/Ethics/shaltnot.html). And even if pre-publication review was unthinkable for Malcolm, she might have been able to indicate, with a little ingenuity, which passages came from which interview, and what the atmosphere and mood for each had been.

We might have been told, for example, whether she and Masson were being totally business-like when he made each of his remarks. Had they been joking? Flirting? Conscientiously observing the recommendations of such authorities as St Paul and Thomas Jefferson about good wine? If any of these conditions did prevail, I would find it hard to be very stern with them; two interesting people of opposite sex enjoying a long, lazy lunch at Chez Panisse, paid for by the *New Yorker*, makes almost irresistibly for an occasion on which total seriousness and even ordinary discretion might be relaxed. Certainly several of Masson's remarks about himself suggest someone who is completely off guard, speaking with a candor, even a recklessness, that most would allow themselves only when speaking to an intimate friend, a psychiatrist, or a priest — in short, to someone whose discretion

239

one could rely on, someone who could be counted on not to let those remarks go any further. Masson may well have been foolish in opening up to a journalist as he would to such a confidant, but even foolish people have rights.

A full account of such details about her meetings with Masson is perhaps too much to expect from Malcolm or any reporter, but there is one thing that she should have included in her story, and did not. Had she told us how she was handling Masson's remarks, I would have no quarrel with her; as it is, I think she was at fault in presenting as simple fact what was actually her own reconstruction of some fragments of fact she had gathered. She was an archaeologist who had reassembled some newly unearthed shards of pottery into a plausible pot. One admires the skill and diligence that the reconstruction exhibits, and is grateful to be shown a complete pot rather than a basketful of shards, but one requires one more thing of the archaeologist: that she tell us that the pot was not dug up as we now see it, but was reconstructed by her. Malcolm did not do this in her Masson story, and in failing to do so injured Masson and misled her readers.

CHAPTER 10

What is To Be Done?

*Language ought to be
the joint creation of
poets and
manual workers.*
– George Orwell[171]

Where will linquists and their projects go?

What the future holds, I believe, for linguists on the one hand, and the usage arbiters that William Safire calls "usagists" on the other, is divorce — with the latter getting custody of the language. And not only will linguists lose their bid for recognition as usage experts, they will lose their status as practitioners of an autonomous discipline; linguistics itself will be broken up, and its fragments annexed by its neighboring departments. Some linguistic projects and investigations will be absorbed by anthropology, some by archaeology, and some by ethnology; probably the most fruitful projects will be taken over by departments of cognitive development and neuroscience. The good work being done by many linguists at present will go on, but under different auspices, and within different scholarly contexts. Those linguists who continue to pursue the traditional sort of linguistic studies will no longer call themselves, or aspire to be, scientists; but they will try to be, and at their best succeed in being, scholars. And they will regard themselves, and be regarded by others, as the great pioneers of their discipline did and were: as philologists.[172]

Who inherits, or reclaims, stewardship of the language?

It should be unnecessary to say that I do not call for an 'English Academy' on the model of the French Academy, but experience has taught me that that is exactly what some critics will charge if I do not explicitly repudiate the idea — and perhaps even if I do. Nor has any serious writer made such a proposal, so far as I'm aware, since the 18th century. The last thing I would propose is the establishment of any kind of central authority over language, and for the same reason that I reject the idea of a central authority over the economy. A cautionary example of an attempt by officialdom to regulate language is that by military authorities to get the troops to call their weapons and other equipment by the official, dignified names coined by some Pentagon committee. Those who fly and service the United States Air Force A-10 attack aircraft, for example, refuse to call it the "Thunderbolt II," and instead have affectionately dubbed it the Warthog because of its ugliness and the fearsomeness of its up-front weaponry. Similarly the members of U.S. Navy Fighter Squadron VF-143, whose squadron emblem is a predatory heraldic beast that appears to be stalking its prey with head lowered almost to the ground, decided with fighter-pilot cockiness to call themselves the Pukin' Dogs. And tell a New York City cab driver that you want to be taken to an address on the Avenue of the Americas, as the city fathers dubbed it some years ago, and he will take you to what he and all New Yorkers know as Sixth Avenue, and put you down for a hick.

No, I do not propose an official organization to attempt to impose on the public what even generals and admirals cannot impose on their subordinates; what I do propose is a recovery of nerve by teachers, editors, writers, and other such *users* of language, particularly the written language. No Committee of Public Grammatical Safety is needed, no body of elderly worthies toiling away and forever losing ground to the wave of new usages is wanted.[173] What is both necessary and sufficient is that the expert users of language, those whose fortunes, and sometimes whose very lives, depend on their ability to write clearly and forcefully, should cease to look fearfully over one shoulder at the linguists in their role as "scientists," and over the other at the same figures in their role as champions of The People, before daring to perform their duties of discrimination and guidance. They will regard the kind of dictionaries that have prevailed since the mid-20th century as mere unfiltered recordings of random samples of speech, and as having no authority either to bless or curse. (They will regard the lexicographers who are responsible for such dictionaries as they would fishmongers who, in hopes of being taken for ichthyologists, have neglected their proper jobs: offering their customers fresh fish.) It is the main purpose of this book to help liberate them from the pseudo-authorities who have cast such a chill over all use of language for so long, and realize that they themselves are the authorities, insofar as anyone is — when half-gods go, the gods arrive.[174]

Questions of usage — judgments as to how we should write today — will be recognized as lying within the purview of those who read and write, with philosophers, literary critics, editors, and poets taking the lead. They, the new usage arbiters, may occasionally turn for information on particular points to what is now called linguistics, if they judge such information to be relevant to their own objectives, but if they do, they will be looking not for judicial rulings, but for expert testimony on technical points, whose value they will assess by their own lights. They will of course have access to the *OED* and to the works of Saussure and Humboldt and Sapir and Bloomfield and Jakobson and Chomsky and all the rest, but will regard these great figures as expert witnesses only, and witnesses whose testimony is only occasionally to the point. And in the hands of its most skillful users rather than in those of its academic observers, the language will take on the dignity and efficiency of a tool that is being shaped and wielded by its proper masters.

To begin with, we should see an end to the use of the "living, growing language" fallacy as an excuse for misuse of the language — meaning not just the solecisms that can create trouble by causing ambiguity and obscurity but that truly abusive practice, the building of prejudices into the language so as to shut down criticism before it can even raise its voice. A good example of this stratagem, as I noted at the outset of this book, is the term *progressive*, which is now generally accepted, even by conservatives, as the proper name of a loosely-defined cluster of controversial views, and tacitly awards those views the twin crowns of virtue and inevitability. For such a linguistic manipulation, designed to bypass critical thinking by building a desired conclusion into the language itself, I propose the term *mindshunt,* meaning "a term so tendentious that one cannot use it without at least seeming to share the attitude of the term's coiner." (The mindshunt was a well-known stratagem at least as long ago as the middle of the 19th century — James Fitzjames Stephen noted in 1862 that "Men have an all but incurable propensity to try to prejudge all the great questions which interest them by stamping their prejudices upon their language."[175])

Editors and teachers in this new world, freed of their nervous subservience to the linguists, will be able to take the reader's point of view, forever testing the texts before them with the question, does this serve the reader well? Will he be able to read it without wondering what the writer's position is, and what the writer is trying to do in this book or paper? Will he be able to read it straight through without discovering, halfway through a sentence, that he should have turned left, not right, at the last comma?

They will not be antiquarians or inflexible reactionaries; they will often accept, as Fowler did in creating the category 'Sturdy Indefensibles', well-established usages that are on their face illogical or were, when they first appeared, simply errors. For example, when Auden said Freud had become "no more a person now but a whole climate of opinion," he was thinking of a phrase coined by Joseph Glanvill in his *Vanity of Dogmatizing* (1661) — but misinterpreting it, as we all do unless we have actually read Glanvill. The obvious meaning of "climate of opinion" to any modern reader is "the prevailing, relatively constant and pervasive set of assumptions we all share; the consensus"; but Glanvill wrote "Climates" — the plural — and meant almost the exact opposite: "the variability, the non-uniformity of opinions."[176] But to insist that we censure Auden, and return to Glanvill's 17th century usage, would be madness; for all ordinary purposes the phrase now means what Auden and the rest of us assume it does.

What principles will the new language stewards adopt?

The rules that the new guides in language usage will employ are, of course, meant to apply in full rigor only to *expository writing*, not to speech on the one hand nor to *belles lettres* on the other. This is not to say that either of these latter uses of language is simply exempt from the jurisdiction of the rules for expository writing, but merely that those rules may, and frequently will, have to defer to other considerations that take higher priority for those uses. I said earlier that in the case of speech, especially highly informal and elliptical speech among family and friends, the ordinary rules are almost completely replaced by the requirements for the right tone of voice, and the verbal and syntactic economies possible within a circle of those who know each other very well. At the other end of the spectrum, where language is used as art medium, the ordinary rules will frequently be superseded by the need to do what is esthetically required (but note that, as we have been told by one of its most eminent modern practitioners, poetry must be at least as well written as prose). For written non-fiction, though, and for the other two sorts of language use insofar as their course is not dictated by more urgent considerations, the general principles behind all useful rules are these:

Clarity. Until a sentence, a paragraph, an essay, is absolutely clear in meaning, there is nothing else to be said about it. Any lapse into obscurity makes it impossible to know what the author was aiming at, and without that knowledge we have no basis for any further comment. Of course you may, at least in principle, achieve perfect Clarity, and yet have written something not worth reading; but Clarity is the *sine qua non*, the always necessary even if not sufficient quality. The ideal is to write so that the reader is never even for a moment misled, never has to back up to pick up a dropped thread or take a different turning, and cannot misunderstand, no matter how contrary your words are to his expectations or his wishes. His experience in reading your text should be like a walk along a path that is bordered by unobtrusive but insurmountable barriers that never let him stray from the path you intend him to travel. (Of course the path should be so attractive that he isn't tempted to depart from it — the next principle deals with that — but readers are infinitely perverse, and will wander if allowed to.)

Grace. Clarity achieved, Grace is next. It is achieved by looking at the text with the reader's eyes, and dealing in advance with everything that could impede his stroll along the path. It includes constructing sentences whose rhythm supports their message, with emphasis falling naturally on the word or phrase that deserves it, and picking up the thought of the preceding sentence with neither unneeded overlap nor a puzzling gap. It includes a refreshing variety in sentence length and complexity. This list could be greatly extended, but this is not a guidebook on good writing, nor would such a list, in the absence of many examples, accomplish much; the key to Grace is, again, to be able to read your own text with fresh, innocent reader's eyes. Some part of this task may be done for you if you are blessed with that very rare thing, a good editor, but even given such luck, the writer must do most of it for himself — the best of editors can only point to problems and perhaps offer suggestions for their remedy; only the author can fix what's wrong without risk of causing damage elsewhere.

Pietas. Your text, although clear and graceful, and thus good in itself, is not alone in the world — it is a member of a select company of such texts, starting with those produced in antiquity. It will benefit if it honors and preserves, wherever possible, its inheritance, just as it hopes that future texts will in turn honor and preserve it. One manifestation of this respect for the past is the preservation, where possible without sacrifice of Clarity and Grace, of words as they were used in the past, so that the works of the past remain readable. Another manifestation of that respect is the principle that a word that has been used by numbers of good writers in a distinctive and useful sense that is not conveyed by any other word should be reserved for use in that sense; this is the principle a prescriptivist is acting on when he urges that *disinterested* be used exclusively in the sense "having no personal stake in the matter." This is not mere temperamental resistance to change, but a positive determination to see that your text takes its place in the order of literature, and joins gracefully in the ongoing conversation among all the good writers who have preceded you. If you are a great genius, like Shakespeare, you may need to introduce something utterly new, abrupt, even shocking, as Shakespeare did in breaking all the classical dramatic rules — and if you must, you must. But do so only if you must, only if the Muse will have it no other way, not because you don't even know what the rules are, or think you are a hell of a fellow for breaking the rules.

Sample applications of the principles, with derivation of secondary rules

The list that follows applies the principles just discussed to identify and discuss a number of solecisms or other misuses of language. In each case, I try to give a reasoned account of the way the usage offends, and where possible formulate a rule that extracts from one of the general principles just discussed a more focused guide to the handling of some particular case. Some of the examples have already been introduced and briefly discussed, but I have thought it so useful to have all examples in one place that I have not hesitated to repeat them here — and even in cases of repetition, the discussion here will usually be much fuller than that offered earlier.

Although I regard some of the examples offered as offenders, and hope their treatment here will be instrumental in abolishing them, the more important purpose of this listing is to demonstrate the bases on which I think that usage judgments should be made, and what facts are relevant to such judgments.

Usage Example	Discussion
arguable [and *arguably*]	This is a legitimate word — for lawyers. Used by them, it distinguishes between arguments that are presentable to a judge or jury, and those that are not. In the hands of journalists, interviewers, and columnists, it is usually an abuse: it enables them to advance a thesis or accusation while hiding behind some hypothetical third party, just as "Some would say" or "What is your reply to critics who charge ...?" do. And as their victims must be longing to reply, "I don't respond to 'some' or nameless 'critics'; name someone, and quote him exactly," I want to say to the abusers of *arguable*, "Don't tell me what's *arguable*, argue something."
brave new world; sea change	The abuse of these two phrases almost makes one wish Shakespeare had drowned his books, and never written *The Tempest*. Journalists seem to know no change that is not a sea change, nor any change that does not introduce a brave new world. We have taught them language, and our profit on't is, they weary us endlessly with mindless allusions.
connive [at]	Another word with a unique and useful meaning — "to turn a blind eye to [someone else's misdeed]" — that through sheer ignorance is being lost; to many it has come to be just another way to say "complicit in." Whether it can be saved is not clear; it is in any case a cautionary example of Sheer Ignorance at work, weakening the language.
contact (as verb)	Despite the strong revulsion the use of *contact* as a verb aroused in Nero Wolfe (see Rex Stout, *Gambit*), I see nothing objectionable in it. There is a need, especially as our technical means of communication with each other proliferate, for a verb that means "to get in touch with someone, manner unspecified." I see objections to using *contact* in that role as springing merely from automatic rejection of the new and unfamiliar, a reaction that only brings thoughtful prescriptivism into disrepute.
demean	I have used *demean* in a section subtitle in the sense "to degrade, to diminish, to reduce to mean condition," although a strict prescriptivist would insist that it means "to behave," as its relationship to *demeanor* implies. My reason is simple: I think that it is too late to save *demean* in the sense *behave;* its apparent derivation from *mean* has overwhelmed etymological fact, and our choice now is to accept the popular usage or simply refrain from using the word at all. I want linguistic activists to fight hard when there is a chance of winning a battle, but only then; you have to know when to fold as much as when to fight.

Usage Example	Discussion
disinterested	Amply discussed in the text; included here just for convenience.
encourage	You cannot properly say "I encourage you to ..." any more than you can decently say "I charm you ..." or "I convince you ..."; it is for the object of our efforts to say whether we have encouraged, charmed, or convinced him. What is almost always meant by "I encourage you to..." is "I urge you to ....."; say that.
enormity	Like *demean,* this word is the victim of folk etymology: its resemblance to *enormous* has doomed it to be taken as referring to the size of something huge rather than, as it should, the abnormality of something monstrous. And like *demean, enormity* is now ruined; seeing it in print (practically the only place one does encounter it), one can never be certain whether the writer means it in the old, 'correct' sense, or the new popular sense. Usually the context, or the quality of the writer, enables the reader to make a good guess — but readers should not be asked to guess.
he/she [& derived forms], and *man* for *human.*	*He/she* is one of the makeshifts that have been proposed, although seldom used consistently even by those proposing them, to avoid the supposedly sexist use of *he* to mean "anyone, regardless of sex." As the discussion in the text shows, this usage was accepted by all until recently; it is only within the last few decades that it has been declared offensive for excluding women. It seems to me that the very example offered in the text by a feminist writer to illustrate the absurdity of the older usage (in this case, of *man*) in fact implies just the opposite: that no one felt the term as referring to men only. If this usage is now deemed "sexist" and hence offensive, it can only be because someone decided that it was good tactics to make it so. For this reason, and because no decent alternative forms have been offered, I recommend sticking with the traditional usages. That usage may offend some women for a while. If so, that is something that they must bear, precisely because women are just what feminists want us to see them as, full-fledged human beings, and no members of the human race can have everything their way.
ilk [in *of that...*]	The career of *of that ilk* is a good example of the degeneration of a specialized and unique term into a weak member of a large family of general terms — a pure loss to the expressive capability of the language. Its original, specialized meaning is "[of that] place or race," said of one whose family and estate or clan names are the same. For example, the Wedderburn who is proprietor of Wedderburn, an estate granted by royal charter, would be referred to as "Wedderburn of that ilk"; the Cameron who is chief of clan Cameron is "Cameron of that ilk."

Usage Example	Discussion
literally used for *figuratively*	This usage would make *literally* join the class of words with the curious property of meaning both A and not-A, such as *sanction* and *fast;* we don't need more of them. The potential ambiguity of most members of the class is almost always averted by the distinctive contexts in which the two senses are used, but *literally* and *figuratively* are used in the same context, so one sense will be lost if they come to be regarded as synonymous: if *literally* becomes another way of saying *figuratively,* how shall we convey the idea that we mean something *literally*?
oversimplified	A charge that is often brought by controversialists against arguments they can't accept is that of *oversimplification.* The charge is hard to refute, for any argument that can be stated by mortal man in a finite number of words must leave out much, and it is impossible to show that nothing that has been omitted has any relevance. It should not, of course, be necessary to refute this or any charge until some evidence supporting it is offered by the accuser — at least enough to make a *prima facie* case. But curiously, the charge of having oversimplified some state of affairs is one that seems to need no supporting evidence; the burden of proof seems almost always to rest on the accused. So compelling is the bare charge, in fact, that the accused, like a defendant in the Moscow State Trials of the 1930's, is often eager to confess, and sometimes even brings the accusation against himself before any critic can level it at him. An example, a little more defensive than most: "… it is only a slight oversimplification to see the Roquefort cheesemakers as the party of particularity…"[177]

The writers who admit to being guilty of oversimplification do not, however, follow up their admissions with "and therefore I will refrain from saying what I was going to say (or withdraw what I have already said)"; they go right ahead and say it (or stand by it). And in doing so, they show that their confessions were nonsense, just ritual obeisances to some imaginary standard of scholarship, and attempts to disarm criticism by anticipating it. If *oversimplification* means anything, it means simplification beyond what is permissible, simplification to the point of falsification. Since the writers, after their obligatory confessions of sin, go right ahead with their oversimplified theories and analogies and judgments, it is clear that all they mean is that they have not taken into account all things in heaven and earth. It is touching to see them preface their arguments by what might be called the Scholar's General Confession, but two objections remain: first, it is unnecessary, since no one would suppose in its absence that any finite argument dealt with every consideration imaginable, and second, it corrupts the word and the idea of *over*-doing something. |

Usage Example	Discussion
prequel	Meaning "in a multi-part work of fiction, an installment dealing with events that chronologically precede those of an already-published installment"; formed on supposed analogy with *sequel.* A word that some find offensive because of its cavalier treatment of classical-language roots. I find myself on the one hand uncomfortable with the word, perhaps for the reason just imputed to "some," yet unable to object to it on more impersonal grounds. Since the thing the term denotes exists, it is clear we need a word for it, and as nothing better is on offer, I suppose we must accept *prequel.*
progressive	As noted in the text, this term is a classic example of the *mindshunt* — the attempt to silence opposition to a controversial position or doctrine by commandeering some honorific for its standard name, so that dissent would seem to be outlawed by definition — who wants to be against progress? What is remarkable in the case of *progressive* is that even conservatives have accepted the usage. Perhaps that acceptance will have the effect of neutralizing the term — but if so, it will be a loss to the language; there are times when we need *progressive* to describe something that all parties would agree constitutes *progress.*
quantum jump (or *leap*)	A *quantum jump* is seen, as its name implies, only on the quantum level, and it is a "jump" that involves the disappearance of a particle from one point in space simultaneous with its reappearance — or at least the appearance of a particle indistinguishable from it — at another point, with no trace of its passage from the first point to the other. The question of whether the particle that appears at the new location is the very particle that disappeared at the old one is, literally, metaphysical. The journalistic use of *quantum jump* to mean a very significant jump, one that causes a change in kind, is luckily so far removed from the physicists' sense that it is unlikely to cause any dangerous confusion, and can be disregarded by prescriptivists, although they will refrain from using the term themselves except when publishing in *Physical Review.*
read (noun)	Would you willingly eat in a restaurant that offered *great eats*? If not, do not be surprised that when you recommend a book as a *great read*, people who care about words will not only decline to read the book, but will regard you as having a tin ear. I had supposed this usage restricted to the "book review" supplements to minor newspapers, but have discovered in a recent advertisement[178] for Yale University Press books blurbs by three critics that exhibit it. One says "a not-to-be-forgotten read," the second "A first-rate read," and the third "A luscious read."

253

Usage Example	Discussion
reticent (for *reluctant*)	Discussed sufficiently in the text; remarkable for being a completely gratuitous error, based on pure ignorance, and without the slightest redeeming feature.
share (verb)	*Share* should be reserved for occasions of generosity, those in which a person willingly deprives himself of something desirable for the sake of another, as when Sir Philip Sidney, badly wounded, gave the last of his drinking water to a dying fellow soldier. When one person tells another how he spent his summer vacation, he should not be thanked for *sharing* his memories; he retains them completely.
stereotype	Discussed sufficiently in the text; remarkable in suggesting that anything that has been believed and asserted by many people for a long time must be false, or at least dubious. The danger of the new use of *stereotype* is that it easily shades into an attack on *generalization,* that indispensable tool of intelligence. The prevalence of the new, pejorative sense of *stereotype* is shown in a left-handed manner by the publication of a book (Schauer 2003) that was regarded by reviewers as daring for suggesting that stereotypes may sometimes, in special circumstances, have a valid purpose.
verbal (for *oral*)	The distinction between *verbal* — "having to do with, or by means of, words" — and *oral* — "by word of mouth, by speech as opposed to writing" — is a valuable and necessary one. If *verbal* is allowed to take over the role of *oral,* while retaining its own, the result is either confusion, or an attempt to overcome confusion by means of a wordy, awkward makeshift like "funny ha-ha or funny peculiar?" There is no argument for this misuse; it is pure loss, caused by pure ignorance. It is to be corrected gently when encountered — but corrected.

What will the world be like when all this is done?

In an earlier chapter the linguist Dwight Bolinger was quoted as saying "the same number of muggers would leap out of the dark if everyone conformed overnight to every prescriptive rule ever written." I am sorry not to be able to assure Professor Bolinger that the new world I hope to help bring about will see a decline in violent crime; it might, but I make no such promise. I do think there will be visible improvement in many aspects of our cultural life. When linguistics is absorbed into its neighboring disciplines, as geography has been, and when language change is understood to be not something that hidden laws impose upon us, but something that we bring about ourselves, the full results can only dimly be seen from where we are. But one thing is clear even now: it will bring greater clarity, coherence, and honesty to our cultural life, as is always the result when a process swathed in mystery is brought into the light, and we begin to understand and take responsibility for our own actions.

Linguistics as a Science

How
did linguistics
come to be
regarded
as a science?

The confusions and errors that we have noted so far delude not only ordinary citizens, but — even more — professional students of language, because they are in the grip of a more fundamental delusion that laymen may be spared: the notion that linguistics is a science. In explaining why that claim is not to be granted, I must make it clear that I am not using the label "science" as a prize to be awarded or withheld depending on how one feels about the discipline in question. I think the term science is one with a sufficiently clear and well-established meaning that one can determine, with the degree of precision attainable in such matters, whether it fits a candidate discipline or not.

A *science* is, first of all, the study of a subject that can for most purposes be isolated from other phenomena in the universe; it has boundaries, and it is almost always possible to say whether a given phenomenon lies within them or not. Then, it is a study whose practitioners regularly form hypotheses, and then conduct experiments that test those hypotheses. The result of a well-designed experiment is either to refute a hypothesis decisively, or grant it the right to survive to face further tests; a scientific experiment yields one of two possible answers, No and Maybe. And finally, a science is cumulative and imperial: it subsumes ever more phenomena under its explanatory theory, without resort to special pleading and ad hoc constructs, That theory may itself get more complex, and further from "common sense," but its additional complexity is small compared with its increase in explanatory power. When a science finds it necessary to postulate more and more special cases and auxiliary suppositions to reconcile theory and observation, it starts looking for a better theory. Linguistics satisfies none of these criteria. But the term *science* has since Victorian times been for many an honorific and a prize; scientists are held in high repute, get their projects funded, and get away with referring to the rest of us as *laymen.*

The first major exploiters of the term *science* as an honorific were Karl Marx and — especially — Friedrich Engels, who insisted that their socialism was no mere sentimental yearning for a happier human estate, nor variety of Utopianism, but the discovery and analysis of an inexorable historical process, and hence deserving of the name *scientific.*[179] But the blame for miscalling linguistics a science is more

directly traceable to the use by some 19th century philologists and humanistic scholars of the term "scientific" to distinguish their own rigorous methods from those of their more dilettantish colleagues, past and present. A few editors of classical texts, for example, claimed to be working 'scientifically' as a way of distinguishing their own practices and products from the looser belletristic writings and speculations of others.[180] Thus A. E. Housman:

> Textual criticism is a science .... It is the science of discovering error in texts and the art of removing it.[181]

Of course he did not mean to say it was like physics or chemistry:

> The study of Latin is a science conversant with literature: there are therefore two ways in which it ought not to be pursued. It ought not to be pursued as if it were a science conversant with the operations of nature or with the properties of number and space, nor yet as if it were itself a branch of literature, and no science at all.[182]

It was the triumphant public progress of the physical sciences, particularly after Newton, that made "science" an honorific that more and more scholars tried to capture for their own disciplines. And some of these aspirants to the title "scientist" were not as scrupulous as Housman in disclaiming for their own disciplines the rigor of the physical sciences. But despite all the care he took to disclaim for textual editing, even as practiced by him, a literally scientific character, he unwittingly helped to create an atmosphere in which *science* ceased to be simply the neutral name of some studies dealing with the natural world, and became one that could not be denied to any study without implying that it was in some sense weak and fuzzy. (A sympathetic reader of Housman knows that he would be horrified to learn that he had been in the slightest degree instrumental in creating such a scene of confused terminology and injured vanity, and indeed he was far from being the chief miscreant, if miscreant at all.) I repeat, however, that *science* is being used here simply as a technical term, and a matter of accurate classification; to deny the title science to any field of study is no more a demotion or slap in the face than it is to deny the title "fish" to a whale.

Why linguistics isn't a science, and won't become one

Linguists continue to be very busy, but their busyness seems to be about an ever-increasing number of unrelated topics: some are in effect anthropologists, gathering linguistic data from remote peoples, and compiling dictionaries and grammars of languages spoken by small isolated tribes; some study the minutiae of the grammars of their own or other contemporary languages; some try to find 'language universals' among seemingly unrelated tongues; some, following Chomsky, try to find the Universal Grammar that is the foundation of all particular grammars; some create maps depicting the boundaries of various dialectal usages and pronunciations; some try to decipher the remaining fragments of languages that were dead before Troy fell; some study the way in which children acquire language competence, or explore the cerebral structures and processes that seem to be associated with language acquisition and use; some even study the possible linguistic significance of sounds made by whales and apes, or try to teach these animals the rudiments of human language.

Such a pattern of development suggests that linguistics is not the kind of study that can ever become a science. This is not to say that those investigations and projects have no value or interest, just that they are not what is meant by 'scientific research,' and their results not what is meant by 'scientific findings.' Virtually all the investigations and projects carried on under the name of linguistics have their interest and value, but they give little promise of converging toward a comprehensive and unified theory of language. Linguistics, instead of subsuming more and more phenomena under the umbrella of some general theory or set of rules, is forever proliferating and splitting off into specialties that have little to do with each other.[183] The only thing that these studies have in common is that they all deal with language in one way or another — and this is not enough to unify them and make them all part of a recognizable discipline, an *episteme*. There is no human activity that language is not part of; to take everything language-related for one's domain is to take on too much, to cast one's net too wide. In declaring no aspect of language alien to itself, linguistics has shown itself admirably catholic and open-minded, but undermined its hopes of being a science. In attempting to embrace everything to do with language, linguistics has in fact embraced all of life, and thereby deprived itself of a subject that might be amenable to scientific study.[184]

In another way, though, linguistics is too narrow and selective; while language, whether as speech or writing, is an important part of almost every human activity, it is the whole of very few. Human life is shot through with language as good beef is marbled with fat, and as no edible cut can be without fat, nor composed wholly of it (despite the reported tastes of Jack Sprat and his wife), so no humanistic study can either ignore language or concentrate on it alone. Linguists have tried to carve from reality a cut consisting of all and only the fat, without regard to where the animal's joints are, or the edibility of the resulting cut. It is as if a group of scholars decided to study all and only the things humans do with their left hands, and then claimed for Sinistrics the status of a science. Noam Chomsky has claimed otherwise:

> Linguistics is one part of cognitive psychology: a part that is relatively easy to isolate. Language is a system (very rich, to be sure), but easy to isolate, among the various mental faculties.[185]

But he is mistaken; discrete utterances, spoken or written — Saussure's *parole* — may be isolable; language as a whole — *langue* — is not.

A lesser but still serious problem linguists face is one that besets all studies of human behavior: they are dealing with creatures who are increasingly aware of being studied, and whose behavior increasingly reflects that knowledge, and subverts those studies. We, the tens of millions who have been to college, all own dictionaries, and sometimes consult them; we buy books on usage and style, add interesting new words to our vocabularies, and read (or at least buy) books on usage, like those by William Safire. And while we manipulate and toy with language (with no apology for our ignorance of the goals and methods of linguistic science), linguists try desperately to discern behind all this noise the intrinsic laws of language that they hope and believe are there. One can't help sympathizing with them, however misguided one thinks them, but sympathy cannot alter the fact that too many people persist in "interfering" with language to permit the development of a science, which depends on regularity and reproducibility in its data.

These I believe to be the reasons why linguistics in the twentieth century experienced no triumphs comparable to those of the nineteenth, and seems even less likely to in the twenty-first. And if my reasons are valid, the prospects for a science of linguistics are dim. The language-standardizing forces and the six types of language modification by its users that were examined earlier in this study, although usually pulling in opposite directions, are equally inimical to the concept of linguistic laws that work at some super- or subhuman level — any such laws, if they existed, would continue to be as much overwhelmed by human efforts to control language as would Kepler's laws if every back-yard amateur astronomer could manipulate planetary orbits to suit his notions of elegance. The conditions under which linguistic laws — again, assuming they existed — could be observed are vanishing, if not already gone; it may seem to the linguists that the inmates have taken over the asylum, but it is merely that the guinea pigs are taking over the laboratory. Even in the remotest parts of the earth, it is getting very hard to find naive subjects to observe; more and more we encounter pranksters who are so perverse as to turn the tables on the investigator, and feed him 'observations' fabricated just in order to mislead or embarrass them. One example: the nonsense some Samoan girls fed to Margaret Mead out of mischievousness — and perhaps a little resentment at being used.

Active Eskimo-Language Terms for Snow and Ice

Active Eskimo-Language Terms for Snow and Ice

This list of terms is undoubtedly both incomplete and imperfect; it was gathered from multiple sources (noted for each entry) of uneven authority, and has not received formal detailed scrutiny, as if submitted to a peer-reviewed journal. But as noted at the end of Chapter 5, it has been informally checked by several leading Eskimo-language experts, and they have given it general approval. I hope it will spur some expert on Eskimo languages to replace it with a fully professional version, but I think that as it stands it is adequate to demonstrate the rough size of the active Eskimo snow-and-ice vocabulary, which is clearly at least an order of magnitude greater than that of the corresponding active English vocabulary.

Term	Language: Y=Yup'ik, I=Iñupiaq	Variant forms	Meaning	Source
aayugaq	I		Ice ridging, or long crack across a shallow bay or lagoon	8
agiuppak	I		A smooth wall of ice along the edge of fast ice, formed by moving ice	8
aisitaq	I		Cracked ice made by force of moving ice; part of ayukaq	8
akelrorak	I		Snow newly drifted	2, 4
akillukkak	I		Soft snow	2
alliviniq	I		Ice that was under other ice but resurfaces smooth and dirty	8
aluktinniq	I		Nature-caused hollow area	8

Term	Language: Y=Yup'ik, I=Iñupiaq	Variant forms	Meaning	Source
aluqsraq	I		Young ice punched by seals forming a seal blowhole	8
anaglu	I		Black ice	8
anautak	I		Snow-beater	4
anijo	I (note 7)	aniu?	Snow on ground	1
aniu	I		Snow on ground, packed snow	2, 8
aniuk	I	anio	Snow for melting into water	2, 4
aniuvak	I		Snowbank	2
apingaut	I		First snowfall	2, 4
apiqqaagun	I	apiqqammiaq, apputiqqaaq	First snow	8
apitchiq	I	apitchiqsuq	When female polar bear which bears young allows herself to get snowed under	8
apun	I		Snow on ground	2, 8
aput	I		Snow (spread out)	4
apuuak	I		Snow patch	2
aqilluq	I		Light snow, deep [enough?] for walking	8
aqilluqqaq	I	mauya	Soft snow	8
arguqtagniq	I		Newly-formed thin ice collecting on the downwind side of a polynya (a large area of open water surrounded by sea ice)	8
ataitchuaq	I		Shore ice cut close to the coast	8
atigniq	I		New ice forming a smooth apron around pre-existing ice (which may be thin, or thick enough to walk on)	8
auganaruaq	I		Ice thrust up at an angle (ca. 45°)	8
auiu	I		Packed snow	2
auksalak	I		Melting snow	2, 3
auniq	I		Spring ice with melt holes	8

Term	Language: Y=Yup'ik, I=Iñupiaq	Variant forms	Meaning	Source
auquparaq	I		Shingle ice (dinner-plate size)	8
auverk	I		Snow block (for building)	4
avaaqtinniq	I		Ice caught in a narrow part of river or lead [sic]	8
ayak	I		Snow on clothes	2
ayiupaq	I		Ice chipped off by waves	8
cellallir	Y	cellarrlir	To snow heavily	9
cikuk	Y		Regular ice	6
gengaruk	Y		Snow bank	9
hiko	I (note 7)		ice	1
hikuliaq	I (note 7)		Thin ice	1
ignigluq	I		Crushed refrozen ice, as found in cracks	8
ignignaq	I		Strip of smooth ice between shore and sea ridges	8
iiguaq	I		Ice that is added or pressed onto shore ice	8
illuk	I		Snowblind	8
imaiq	I		Ice broken up but pressed together so that there are no leads	8
imuniq	I		Young ice crushing	8
iqugaaq	I		Westwind opening ice at leeward ice of point	8
isaamaniq	I		Ice formed as a long peninsula	8
ivuniq	I		Pressure ridge (rough ice, blocking passage)	8
kaatchi	I		To slice [snow?] into layers	8
kaattiq	I	kaatchiruaq	To cut blocks of hard-packed snow for house	8
kaiyuglak	I		Rippled surface of snow	2
kaneglluk	Y		Thick frost that forms on bushes from extreme cold	6
kanevvluk	Y		Fine snow/rain particles	9

Term	Language: Y=Yup'ik, I=Iñupiaq	Variant forms	Meaning	Source
kanik	I	kannik? kaniq?	Frost	2
kaniktshaq	I (note 7)		Snow	1
kaniq	I		To be covered with light frost in early autumn when frost collects indoors	8
kaniqluk	I		Frost on sea water	8
kannik	I		Snowflake	2
kanut	I (note 7)		New ice with snow	1
kaŋiqluk	I		A bay or cove in the ice	8
katiksugnik	I		Light snow deep enough for walking	2
katiksunik	I		Light snow	2
kiksrukak	I		Glazed snow in a thaw	2
kimaugruk	I		Snowdrift that blocks something	2
kisitchat	I		Anchor ice, fast ice touching the ocean floor	8
kuftuk	Y		Hail	6
kusulukkat	I		Icicles on ice, ice caked on structures	8
Iliikaun	Y		Young ice, freshly frozen over, connected to regular shore-fast ice	6
manelaq	I (note 7)		Pack ice	1
mapsa	I		Cornice (overhanging formation of ice, snow, or rock; usually along a ridge), overhanging snow	8
masak	I	misak, missak?	Slush snow/waterlogged/swamp	8
masallak	I	masayyak	To be damp enough for making snowballs of snow/watery snow (inland)	8
massak	I		Snow mixed with water	2, 4
mauragaq	I		Ice used to step across wide crack	8
mauya	I		Snow that can be broken through	2

Term	Language: Y=Yup'ik, I=Iñupiaq	Variant forms	Meaning	Source
mavsa	I		Snowdrift overhead, and about to fall	2, 8
mayuqtitaq	I		Shingle ice, but larger than kaspik	8
milik	I		Very soft snow	2, 8
minik	I		Mist	8
misulik	I		Sleet	8
mitailak	I		Soft snow covering an opening in an ice floe	2
miulik	I		Sleet	2
mugaliq	I		Slush ice on sea	8
mugalluk	I		Slush	8
muruaneq	Y		Soft, deep snow	9
napaayuq	I		Upright ice cake	8
natatqugnat	I		Hailstone	8
natigvik	I	9: =Y natquik	Snowdrift	2, 9
natquiteq	Y		Ground snowstorm at least 15–20 feet, ground to top	6
navcaq	Y		Snow cornice, snow (formation) about to collapse	9
nulagun	I		Refrozen cracks (<10 feet wide)	8
nunagvaq	I		Ice once used by walrus	8
nutagak	I	nutagaq?	Powder snow	2
nutagaq	I	9: = Y nutaryuk	Fresh snow, powder snow	8
nutagun	I		Snow covering a water hole (with no ice), snow on water with no ice	8
nutaqiiq (?)	I		Smooth ice covered by snow with wetness between snow and ice	8
nuvugaq	I		A pointed area of ice, peninsula or corner surrounded by water	8
paagiiq	I		Ice pushed by the wind and current one way and the other, making it appear to move	8

Term	Language: Y=Yup'ik, I=Iñupiaq	Variant forms	Meaning	Source
patuqliq	Y		Ice that forms over bushes & houses from moisture in air	6
peqalujaq	I (note 7)		Old ice	1
perksertok	I		Snow drifting (it is drifting)	2, 4
piagnaq	I		Snow condition good for sled travel	8
piqaluyak	I		Salt-free ice or old ice gone through several seasons, perhaps glacial ice	8
piqsiq	I	agniq	Snowstorm	8
piquniq	I		Ice mounting that has bottom air, also used by sea mammals	8
pirtuk	Y		Blizzard	6
pokaktok	I		Snow like salt	2, 4
pugtaq	I (note 7)		Drift ice	1
puiniq	I		Hole in ice made by seal or other sea mammal	8
pukak	I	milak	Sugar (crystallized) snow under soft snow, thawed for drinking water	2, 3, 8
puktaaq	I		Ice cakes	8
puktaaqat	I		A small cake of ice	8
puktaat	I		Scattered floes (navigable)	8
puktaat	I		Small ice chunks away from others	8
qaapaaq	I		Slush ice piled up on beach, ice ridging	8
qaigiitchuq	I		Rough ice	8
qaigilu	I		Ice not rough nor smooth, but with some irregularity	8
qaimnugniq	I		Kulusiq-type ice over a large area, a type of ice seen at Gambell early in the fall	8

Term	Language: Y=Yup'ik, I=Iñupiaq	Variant forms	Meaning	Source
qaimnuq	I		Cake of ice smoothed by sea spray	8
qaisqinaq	Y		Thick, fresh mushy snow in sea or water	6
qaisuatat	I		Smooth ice between areas of rough	8
qaivagniq	I		Round cakes [of ice] frozen together (flat ice)	8
qakuunaq	Y		First frost during beginning of winter on sidewalks, rocks	6
qanainaqtuaq	I		Main pack moving in directly toward sea ice	8
qanattaaq	I		Snow or ice with one end partly off the ground	8
qanigniq	I		Uulsugnaq after it has spread out	8
qanik	I (note 7), Y	qaniq	Falling snow	1, 6
qanikula	I		To snow intermittently	8
qanipalaat	I; W. Green-landic		Feathery clumps of falling snow	5
qaniqtaq	I		Slightly refrozen but fragile ice; will quickly spread out if stepped on	8
qanisqineq	Y		Snow floating on water	9
qannik	I		Snow on ground, snowflake, fresh falling snow without wind	3, 8
qayuqlak	I		Snow formation caused by prevailing wind	8
qetraq	Y		Wet snow frozen, making a hard outside crust on top	6
qimaktinniq	I		Ice between anchor and shore (usually with open water on either side)	8
qimuagruk	I		High snowdrift	8
qinu	I		Slush ice	8

Term	Language: Y=Yup'ik, I=Iñupiaq	Variant forms	Meaning	Source
Iñupiaqruqqaq	I; W. Green-landic		Glaze on snow in thaw time, (upingaksragman)	5, 8
quahak	I (note 7)		New ice without snow	1
qugraq	I		ice pinching off a lead or crack against either other ice or the shore	8
quvlunaruaq	I		Ice with small ripples (bouncy)	8
sagrat	I		A few cakes of ice in mostly open water or lead	8
sarri	I		Good, thick ice from the north (pack ice), floating pack ice (across from land-locked ice)	8
siku	I		Ice	8
sikuaq	I		Freezing hole/confined area, thin ice, dangerous to walk on	8
sikuliagruaq	I		Thick ice (> 3 feet)	8
sikuliaq	I		Ice that is not thick (ca. 1 foot deep), the first ice to arrive near Barrow in the fall, may be smooth or broken, not formed locally, able to hold a walrus/already thick ice, safe to walk on, one of the first types of ice to arrive at Gambell in the fall	8
sillik	I	silliq	Hard, crusty snow	2, 8
sisuuk	I; W. Greenlandic		Wet snow that can slide and cause an avalanche	2, 5, 8
stenkiteq	Y		Ice crystals in frozen fish	6
tiluktok	I		Snow-beater	4
tiluktortok	I		Snow-beating (is beating snow)	4
tsikut	I (note 7)		Large, broken up masses of snow	1
tuaq	Y		Sea ice	6
turagruaq	I		Old ice	8

Term	Language: Y=Yup'ik, I=Iñupiaq	Variant forms	Meaning	Source
tuuniq	I		Cracked ice made by force of main pack ice	8
tuvaiq	I		Once shorefast ice, now floating due to gradual breakup	8
tuvaiyagaaq	I		Once shorefast ice, now floating due to high winds (mostly in water)	8
tuvaq	I		Shore ice	8
tuvaqtaq	I		Shore ice over only part of beach	8
uiniq	I		The edge of the ice	8
umiaglu	I		Ice used for raft/bottom ice	8
utvak	Y		Snow carved in block	9
uullukkuu	I		Snow [that] melts instantly	8
vuneq	Y		Huge piled-up sea ice in water	6

NUMBER OF ENTRIES: 123

SOURCES

1. Cecil Adams, *The Straight Dope*, page 297; quoted by Mary L. Herrick, Stumpers e-mail, 10 March 1994.
2. Webster & Zibell, *Iñupiaq Eskimo Dictionary*, and Thibert, *English-Eskimo Eskimo-English Dictionary*; quoted (indirectly) in http://einstein.et.tudelft.nl/~arlet/puzzles/sol.cgi/trivia/eskimo.snow
3. *The Kobuk Iñupiaq Dictionary*, cited by John Rife, Stumpers e-mail, 27 April 2001.
4. Arthur Thibert, *English-Eskimo Eskimo-English Dictionary*, University of Ottawa: Research Center for Amerindian Anthropology, 1958.
5. *West Greenlandic, an Inuit Dictionary*; cited by John Riffe, Stumpers e-mail, 27 April 2001.
6. Harley Sundown (school principal, Scammon Bay, AK), private communication, 14 February 2002

7. Dialect of the Umingmaktormiut group, considered part of the Inuit-Iñupiaq division.
8. Elise Sereni Patkotak (Public Information Officer, North Slope Borough, Barrow, AK), private communication, 26 March 1996.
9. Steven A. Jacobson, *Yup'ik Eskimo Dictionary.* Fairbanks, AK: University of Alaska, Alaska Native Language Center, 1984. Cited by A.C. Woodbury, "Counting Eskimo Words for Snow," Stumpers e-mail, 3 March 1997 (Edwards > Halpern, but confused nesting of messages)

CAVEATS

A. Note that some spellings may be unreliable; there seems to be no universally accepted system for representing Eskimo-language words in the Latin alphabet.
B. There has been no attempt in compiling this list to reproduce diacritics or other special symbols except in one case, where two distinct words could not be differentiated in print without the use of the special character ŋ.
C. Note that a few definitions contain Eskimo words — presumably snow/ice terms — that are not themselves defined.
D. No attempt has been made here to observe the finer geographical or ethnic distinctions, such as 'Norton Sound, Unaliq subdialect'; only the simple distinction between Iñupiaq and Yu'pik has been observed with some regularity.
E. There are, as Professor Jacobson has noted in a private message, several dictionaries of various Eskimo languages and dialects that I did not draw upon in compiling this list: the *Siglit Inuvialuit Eskimo Dictionary,* 2nd edition, revised & expanded by Ronald Lowe, 2001; Amos & Amos, *Cup'ig Eskimo Dictionary;* and the *Naukan Yupik Eskimo Dictionary* that was in press at the time I compiled this list. While I wish I had been able to avail myself of these additional resources, I don't think my failure to do so in any sense invalidates my conclusions; indeed, the only effect such consultation could have had is to lengthen the list.

AI and the Golem project – the reverse-engineering twins

The
Golem and the
Hidden Entity
of the
Turing Test:
brother monsters

Within a very short period during
1956–7, two important projects concerned with the nature of human
intelligence sprang up at the Massachusetts Institute of Technology:
the work of Noam Chomsky in linguistics, already discussed at length
here, and the project called Artificial Intelligence (AI), which was
named and set in motion by Professors Marvin Minsky and John
McCarthy, who had been inspired by the writings of Alan Turing. AI
became an organized effort with official academic and industrial support at the Dartmouth conference that Minsky and McCarthy led during the summer of 1956; the Chomskyan revolution in linguistics
effectively began with his first important publication (Chomsky 1957)
the following year.

That either project should have had its inception at MIT is remarkable — that institution was hardly known as a center of humanistic
or psychological studies; for both of them to spring up there, and at
virtually the same moment in history, is astonishing. But the mystery
is readily cleared up; as Chomsky has explained,[186] it was the very
absence of a significant department of linguistics at MIT that made
it possible for him to carry on his research there. His views were so
contrary to those of the linguistic establishment of the time that, as
he observes, he could not have gotten a position in any well-
established linguistics department. In fact, he was employed by
MIT's Research Laboratory of Electronics, and supported largely by
Department of Defense funds.

As for AI, that research program was founded not by psychologists and other investigators primarily concerned with human intelligence, but by computer scientists inspired by the paper[187] in which Turing described a computer-based experiment that he called The Imitation Game, and by the availability of computers sufficiently powerful to allow rudimentary attempts at realizing that thought-experiment. Turing's Imitation Game — now universally called the Turing Test — conjectured that a computer might be programmed to answer any question put to it in a natural language exactly as a human being would — so well, in fact, that humans questioning it would not be able, in general, to tell that they were conversing with a machine. And Turing proposed that if human judges conversing with such a machine could not guess from its answers to their questions whether they were conversing with a human or a machine, there would be no reasonable grounds on which to deny that the machine was thinking.

There is no need to go into detail about the Turing Test (those who want to know more might begin by reading the treatment of the subject in [Halpern 1990], which includes an extensive reference list) in order to see the close connection between these two superficially very different research programs. The computer program that Turing postulated would have to deal with any question or remark that its human interlocutor might address to it, just as the Golem (that is, the complete "grammar" that Chomsky and his followers are working toward) would. The Golem's task would be much simpler: it would not need to fabricate a response to the sentences addressed to it so as to convince its questioner that he was dealing with another human, or indeed respond at all, except with a "pass" or "no pass" — but it would need to discriminate with the same skill as a human between well-formed and ill-formed questions and remarks, and in doing so would have to "understand" them in the same sense as Turing's computer program; it would not be allowed to get away with giving the notorious "colorless green ideas sleep furiously" a pass, even if by the then-prevailing linguistic criteria it is judged *syntactically* correct.

But the strikingly significant point is that both the Artificial Intelligence embodied in the Turing Test computer's software, and the

Golem that the modern linguist is trying to achieve, are brother monsters: mechanized processes that infallibly distinguish between the meaningful and the meaningless, though perhaps not in the way that a human would. The AI enthusiasts claimed, with Turing, that if the computer could deal with any question in a manner that caused humans to think they were dealing with another human, it must be allowed to be thinking; the linguists claimed that if the Golem could discriminate correctly between the grammatical and the non-grammatical word strings submitted to it, it must be allowed that it had explained how humans process language. And many of the lessons learned in the course of attempts to realize AI might benefit linguists, just as many of the criticisms leveled against AI projects might also apply to them.

What both projects were doing is what has since come to be called *reverse engineering*. Ordinarily a technical product begins with an idea or discovery, then goes through a stage of detailed design that generates such things as blueprints, specifications, and flowcharts, and finally yields the product as a tangible object or working computer program. But sometimes that process is reversed: if a product has already been built by company A, the engineers working for company B may be asked to study their rival's product so that their own company can build a competitive one. Company B's engineers will then start not with a notion but with a finished product, and seek to produce blueprints or their equivalent so that their own company can build a similar product — hence *reverse engineering*. And since the original product they are studying may well incorporate patented components or processes, it is often important for company B's engineers *not* to realize the function of company A's product in the same way that company A realized them, lest they lay themselves open to a suit for patent infringement. So company B will often go to much trouble and expense to protect itself from that charge, even to the extent of setting up an isolated engineering group who are forbidden to analyze or disassemble or otherwise "look inside" the product whose functions they are seeking to replicate; they are not allowed, that is, to truly "understand" that product, but rather forced to think of it as a "black box" about which they know only what output it yields for any possible inputs.[188]

The Turing Test and the Golem are both examples, with minor variations, of such reverse-engineering projects. Both aim at achieving a competence otherwise seen only in human beings; both do so by emulating certain aspects of human linguistic behavior as seen by an external observer, and neither can show that it is operating in just the way that the human mind does in realizing that behavior. Turing doesn't seem to care whether the successful AI program actually gets it effects the same way the human mind does, but the Golem-builders are in this respect more ambitious and aggressive than their more modest AI brethren. Chomsky in particular claims that the realization of the Golem would yield deep insights into the actual functioning of the human brain; indeed, that claim is the basis of his interest in linguistics. A complete and perfect Golem, if such a thing could be realized, would be of little interest to Chomsky if it yielded no insight into the human speech faculty, and through that into the human mind in general.

But how would one know that a complete and successful Golem had been achieved? Since humans disagree among themselves on many points of grammar and usage, there will frequently be some disagreement between the Golem's judgements and those of at least some humans. Here Chomsky invokes a practice that is common in the more traditional sciences: there is, he notes, a very large body of sentences about whose grammatical correctness there is virtually universal agreement. If the Golem agrees with the human consensus about all of *them,* then the Golem's view should prevail when some people disagree with it on the relatively few controversial or ambiguous cases. The theory or grammar embodied in the Golem, in other words, will have earned the right to declare certain data points "outliers" that we needn't worry about or trouble to account for — they are just "noise."

This is a defensible method when the theory in question is a very well established one — we don't expect something as thoroughly tested and solidly verified as the General Theory of Relativity, for example, to be abandoned as soon as some solitary and little-known investigator reports an apparent anomaly in applying it. But that method cannot be used to defend Chomskyan linguistics, where the "theory" is little more than a working hypothesis that not even every linguist finds plausible. If the Golem's judgment about the correctness of certain examples is allowed to prevail over that of some humans, we will be creating just that sort of irrefutable, closed system of thought that Karl Popper taught us is the sure sign of unscientific thinking, and losing sight of the Chomskyan goal of learning about the human mind.

If even a few human speakers of English judge as "acceptable" expressions that the Golem considers "unacceptable," or insist that the rules the Golem uses are not those that they use, why is the Golem's judgment to be preferred? On what basis could the judgment of a theoretical construct be preferred to that of the speakers whose behavior it is merely an attempt to emulate? And if it cannot be so preferred, what becomes of the project to create an artificial discriminator between acceptable and non-acceptable expressions? And finally, if *per impossibile* such a discriminator could be built, what would we have learned about *language*? Under what theory would it constitute a great achievement?

The resemblance that I have noted between the Golem project and Turing's Artificially Intelligent computer appears again at this point, but with a slight difference: Turing claimed that there would be no good reason to deny the attribute *intelligent* to the computer that passed the Turing Test, but he did not claim that that computer would be doing exactly what human minds do. Chomsky, on the other hand, does claim that the Golem would be the image of the human mind in its linguistic aspect, even perhaps a map of the very brain paths involved in human understanding of language. The question central to both projects is that of the Black Box: if I can build a device that responds to any input or stimulus with exactly the output or behavior it would evoke from a human being, have I therefore built something that must be internally just what a human mind is, when active in the same realm of experience? Chomsky seems to believe the answer is yes — a strange position for one who first came to the notice of most of his colleagues with a devastating attack on behaviorism.[189]

Another parallel between Chomskyan linguistics and computer

science is to be seen in the essential identity between the formalisms used by linguists of his school to express transformation rules and the analogous expressions used by computer scientists to describe programming languages. When employed by computer scientists, these formalisms were known as metalanguages;[190] when employed by linguists, they described or represented "grammars." In both cases they enabled users to construct hierarchies of linguistic entities, starting by defining the terminal symbols (the alphabet or other primitive elements of the system); then proceeding to generate first-order constructs defined in terms of the terminal symbols, then second-order constructs defined in terms of the first-order constructs (and if necessary further terminal symbols), and so on until the highest-order construct, a complete grammar or language, had been defined.

Both of these very similar formalisms emerged in the 1950s; it is not clear whether one derived from the other, or if they were invented largely independently. Since some early computer programmers came to the craft from linguistics, and some linguists — Chomsky himself is an example, having started out at MIT in the Research Laboratory of Electronics — were familiar with computers, it is likely that the idea was "in the air" where both groups found and exploited it, and that much cross-pollination must have occurred.

Computer programming languages and — in the hands of Chomskyan linguists — natural languages are similarly treated as sets of permissible strings of primitives, with the meanings of the various permitted strings taken for granted when needed, ignored otherwise. When Chomskyans describe a transformation, for example, the units of interest within the sample sentences that they use to illustrate it are already marked as "noun phrase" or "copula" or "verb phrase" and the like. These units are recognized largely by their meanings — case endings and other formal identifiers are seldom sufficient — but after that, transformations work by moving such units around according to formal rules that forbid some movements and allow or require others, and so on. This concentration on the formal aspect of language, the aspect in which a sentence in primarily a string of words whose admissibility is judged with little or no regard for its meaning as a whole or the meaning of its constituent words, may be necessary if language is to be treated scientifically, but scientific treatment does not guarantee interesting results.

Some programming language analogues to natural language features

The parallel I noted in the text between the attempt to realize a Golem and the attempts, very early in the computer era, to realize Mechanical Translation (in full, Fully Automatic High Quality Mechanical Translation) is in fact more than an analogue, almost an identity; the two are very similar in their aims, and have failed for the same reason: they are dependent on information that is simply not available within the data at their disposal. In both cases, an utterance is handed over for translation to a system which attempts to deal with it on the basis of (a) its graphical or audible representation, and (b) such general rules as the system designer has thought of and been able to incorporate in it. MT so conceived has failed; no system demonstrated to date has succeeded in producing fully automatic high-quality machine translation of arbitrary, or even of somewhat constrained, running text from one natural language to another. Good translations, as Yehoshua Bar-Hillel told us at the time (Bar-Hillel, 1964), and as that failure should have taught us permanently, depend on an enormous amount of background knowledge on the part of the translator, including familiarity with the idioms of both source and target languages, of the subject matter the text deals with, of the style and idiosyncrasies of the author, and of the way the world works in general. The most sophisticated systems can often produce rough and serviceable translations of plain expository prose, but even these generally need so much editing by humans that they offer little if any saving of time.

The failure of linguists generally to understand the importance of what the recipient brings to the communication process, and the lessons that computer programming has to contribute to linguistics, is illustrated by a problem that Chomsky discussed in 1963, and was still a subject of controversy between Chomsky and James McCawley in 1971 and perhaps later: the role of *respectively* in such a pair of contrasted statements as:

(a) John and Mary went to dinner and a movie.

(b) John and Mary went to dinner and a movie, respectively.

The difficulty existing linguistic models have in accounting for the way in which *respectively,* when appended to (a) to create (b), changes the meaning of that statement, is due to their failure to appreciate that the recipient of a verbal statement is a fully active partner in the communication process, and the fact that some elements of such statements are there to give the recipient information not about the subject of the statement, but about the statement itself, and how the recipient is to interpret it. They are not, in other words, part of the text of the message, but elements of a different language — a metalanguage — and are addressed to a different process within the recipient's mind. They convey exactly the same sort of information that a transformational analysis would, in fact, if sent along with the message proper.

This distinction can be seen with perfect clarity in the processing of "higher-level" computer programming languages, those that enable programmers to write programs that are more or less readable by humans. The price paid for this human readability is that those programs are not immediately executable by the computer, and have to be translated into "machine language" before they are. The translation is carried out on the computer itself by a program (a "compiler" or "interpreter") built for just that purpose. The main input to such a translation program is of course the human-readable program, but embedded within that program are statements of quite another kind (compiler directives) that are not themselves to be translated, but rather understood by the compiler as instructions directing its own operations while it is compiling. *Respectively* plays in English the role of such a processor-directive; it tells the recipient nothing, directly, about John and Mary — it is not part of the message — but rather instructs him on how he is to analyse the message. Programmers cannot help being quite conscious of the distinction between matter to be translated and directives to the translator, because they are the builders of the translators themselves, and of the application programs that contain both input to be translated and directives aimed at the translators. Linguists and others dealing with human processors frequently take those processors for granted, and fail to see that English, too, contains such special orders directed to *its* processors.

Notes on Chomsky and the Chomskyan literature

To learn more about Chomskyan linguistics

This appendix offers guidance to those who want to know more about the revolution in linguistics caused by the work of Noam Chomsky. I begin with a warning: it is far from easy to understand Chomsky, not because he hasn't explained himself, or been explained by others, but for the opposite reason. His own publications are voluminous: he is continually writing, lecturing, and being interviewed, and every word he utters is soon in print. The number of papers and books by others about him and his ideas is probably even greater than that of his own writings, and many of them have been reviewed before publication by Chomsky and endorsed by him, making them quasi-official statements of his position on a good many issues. Then there is the Chomskyan vocabulary: some of the key terms in modern linguistics — *universal grammar, deep structure, transformation, generative grammar,* and a few others — are either his coinage, or so reworked by him as to be considered in his custody. And he takes advantage of his ownership of those terms to extend and modify them as his ideas evolve; probably none of them means now exactly what it meant when he first coined or adopted it.

Further complicating the task of understanding his work is Chomsky's habit of developing his ideas in the course of debating with and criticizing the work of other linguistic philosophers. He is clearly stimulated by verbal battle with his peers, but when he expounds some new idea in the course of rebutting assertions or theories of others, he frequently makes it necessary for the reader who would thoroughly understand what's going on to have read the work of Searle or Putnam or Quine or Dummett[191] that he is engaging. Finally, there is the turning of some ordinary words into terms of art whose meanings have only the most glancing relationship to the familiar ones; in particular, it must not be supposed that such central terms as *language*[192] and *grammar* have, in Chomsky's writings, anything like their ordinary meanings. So complex is the history of Chomskyan thought, and the twists and turns of his technical vocabulary, that an entire book (Botha 1989) has been written just to elucidate — and have some fun with — that history.

In preparing my account of modern, Chomsky-era linguistics, I of course read many of Chomsky's own writings, but on some topics, particularly highly technical ones, I found more enlightenment in secondary works — that is, studies of various aspects of his work by other critics and commentators. I have also profited from general overviews by others of his work, among which I restricted myself to those that Chomsky himself has approved of. Here are five that substantially fit that description:

First, that by Justin Leiber (Leiber 1975), a book that bears on its back cover the following statement by Chomsky:

> It is the book that I would recommend to people who ask me what I'm up to. In fact, I think it is a good general introduction to recent work in linguistics, particularly valuable because of the way this work is placed in the setting of questions and issues in psychology and philosophy.

Second, there is (Lyons 1978), of which the preface to the first edition opens:

> I should like to record here my gratitude to Noam Chomsky for reading and commenting upon the manuscript of this book. The fact that it has been read in advance by Chomsky (and corrected in a number of places) encourages me in the belief that it gives a

reasonably fair and reliable account of his views on linguistics and the philosophy of language.

Third, there is a valuable little book (Chomsky 1979) which bears Chomsky's name on its title page, but whose history is so unusual that one might ordinarily approach it with caution: it began as a report, in French, of taped conversations on linguistics between Chomsky and the French linguist Mitsou Ronat (*Dialogues avec Mitsou Ronat*, Paris: Flammarion, 1977), with Chomsky's side of the conversation translated into French by Ms Ronat. Later it was decided that an English-language version of the book should be published, and since the tapes had by then been lost, Ms Ronat had to translate Chomsky's remarks, originally in English, back into English from her French versions. With all this decanting of the wine from one bottle into another, it would not have been surprising if the resulting text turned out to be turbid, but in fact it reads smoothly and coherently, and since Chomsky has allowed it to be published under his name, it is fair to assume that it truly represents his thinking.

Fourth, there is an overview (Searle 1972) of Chomsky's linguistics by John Searle, himself a distinguished philosopher and writer on the mind and language. In recommending it, I rely for assurance of Chomsky's approval of it on the Holmesian principle that the most significant fact may be that the dog did nothing in the nighttime: Searle's essay did not provoke an immediate and forceful reply from Chomsky, which constitutes a sort of left-handed endorsement by him. Chomsky is well known for writing sharply worded corrections of any descriptions of his views that he regards as erroneous, so his silence in this case may be taken as significant. (Chomsky was, of course, well aware of Searle's piece; he refers to it explicitly in a letter printed in the July 19, 1973, issue of *The New York Review of Books*.) Chomsky did later dispute (in Chomsky 1976) some parts of Searle's presentation, but the mildness, brevity, and delayed appearance of his response suggests that the disagreement is not very serious. For someone with absolutely no background in linguistics, Searle's overview would be a good place to begin.

Fifth, there is a long piece (Mehta 1971) on Chomsky and modern linguistics by Ved Mehta, which comprises a profile of the man based on extensive interviews, an account of transformational grammar, and subsidiary interviews with Charles Hockett, one of the most outspoken of Chomsky's critics, and of Roman Jakobson, then widely considered the doyen of linguistics. Mehta fully engages Chomsky's arguments, even correcting them once or twice, and offers diagrams to illustrate the way transformations work. (The piece was later reprinted in a book of Mehta's essay-interviews, also called *John is Easy to Please*.) Highly recommended, especially for readers who want to get a feeling for the resistance to Chomskyan linguistics.

For Chomsky's own efforts at explaining himself to a lay audience, see (Chomsky 2004, pages 575–579), probably the simplest explanation he has ever given of his work; it is his reply to this question from an interviewer: "Dr. Chomsky, many of our teachers are unfamiliar with your work, because the study of linguistics is not required in their professional training. It would be helpful and would arouse some interest in this field, if you answered the following questions. Your 1957 publication, entitled, *Syntactic Structures*, presented a completely new way of looking at language. What was it that started you on this exploration?" While his reply is simple and clear so far as it goes, it will not fully satisfy anyone who really wants to understand what he hoped to accomplish and what he actually accomplished. (Chomsky 1968) and (Chomsky 1980) are fuller expositions of his views on language and on the role of linguistics in investigating the human mind; I recommend reading them before any of his more technical writings. On the special topic of reconciling Chomsky's views on the origin and development of language with Darwinian evolution by natural selection, see (Pinker 1994).

Some thoughts after pondering the Chomskyan revolution

- Chomsky did not enter linguistics, as so many linguists do, because he was "fascinated by words"; his main interest is the way the human mind works. His work in linguistics is motivated by his belief that a complete grammar of a natural language would reveal some fundamental facts about the human mind and the structure of the brain. As a result, Chomsky isn't much interested in actual language — what people say and write — he's interested in psychology and philosophy, and if he thought that the royal road to understanding how the mind works was through philately or oneiromancy, he'd be working in one of those domains.

- Chomsky is determined that his study of language be scientific. He is willing to accept the possibility that transformational generative grammar is too abstract, too far removed from actual language usage to yield interesting results about the mind, because he knows that as a scientific hypothesis, even its failure will reward us with useful results, however negative: we will *know* that one hypothesis about language is false. To take such a risk is courageous and deserving of respect; even more courageous and respect-worthy would be an admission that just such a failure has occurred.

- Chomsky's great service to linguistics was to get it moving again, rescuing it from the doldrums, giving it something to do. As younger linguists take over, more and more of the specifics that Chomsky introduced will of course be replaced or modified beyond recognition, just as more and more of Freud's notions have been, but Chomsky is becoming what Auden said Freud had become, "no more a person now but a whole climate of opinion."

- Chomsky, in the course of criticizing some contentions of John Searle's, has rejected the idea that language is 'primarily' or 'essentially' a tool for communication, contrasting that view of language with

    a very respectable tradition … that regards as a vulgar distortion the "instrumental view" of language as "essentially" a means of communication, or a means to achieve given ends. Language, it is urged, is "essentially" a system for expression of thought. I basically agree with this view. But I suspect that little is at stake here, given Searle's concept of "communication" as including communication with oneself, that is, thinking in words. We do, I am sure, think without words too — at least so introspection seems to show. But insofar as we are using language for "self-communication," we are simply expressing our thoughts, and the distinction between Searle's two pictures collapes.[193]

Continuing in a later work his critique of the idea that language is primarily for communication, Chomsky goes on to give examples of non-communicative uses of language, such as phatic communion (although he does not use that term), private musing, and talking to someone who, one knows, will not understand what he hears. These uses, Chomsky contends, show that language is used also for non-communicative purposes, and hence that there is no basis for the proposition that language is primarily for communication. He sums up his position in the words

It is difficult to say what "the purpose" of language is, except, perhaps, the expression of thought, a rather empty formulation. The functions of language are various. It is unclear what might be meant by the statement that some of them are "central" or "essential."[194]

I think that Chomsky goes badly astray here. First, he appears to have forgotten in 1980 (the publication date of the passage just quoted) that in 1976 (the date of the preceding one) he had no difficulty in agreeing that language does have an essential function, and even named it:

Language, it is urged, is "essentially" a system for expression of thought. I basically agree with this view.

Whether this formal contradiction simply represents a change of mind that Chomsky did not bother to acknowledge, or is a sign of momentary confusion on his part, there are more important problems to be considered in his position. One such problem is presented by his contention that there is no sound basis for singling out as "essential" any one of the many uses to which language is put; another by his rather reductive notion of why we use words, or "talk to ourselves," even in the absence of a receptive audience.

Certainly language is used for various purposes, but this does not preclude the possibility that one of them is primary or essential. A book, too, can be used in many ways: as a paperweight, a doorstop, a murder weapon, a flowerpress, a cache for love letters or money, a splash of color relieving an otherwise drab corner of the room, a trophy for impressing or intimidating others — even, to be sure, as a medium of verbal communication. Despite this multiplicity of roles, though, we have no hesitation in declaring the last of these its primary or essential role. We do so because all its other roles it shares with other things — indeed, these others are roles for which it is less than ideally suited, and into which it is pressed only when we lack an artefact better designed for the purpose. But as reading matter, the book comes into its own, and stands unrivaled; that is a role that it alone can play, and is hence its primary, essential role. In the same way, there are many incidental uses to which language can be put, but only one — the one I earlier called the *linguistic* use of language — to which language alone can be put; and this we rightly regard as its primary use.

That use includes the function that Chomsky once honored as part of "a very respectable tradition," but which he later rejected as "a rather empty formulation": the expression of thought. But language does far more than just *express* thought; it enables its user to capture and preserve and stimulate thought, even when we are not trying to convey the thought to anyone else. Chomsky misses a promising line of investigation in failing to consider why, even in the absence of an audience, we talk — put our thoughts into words. If the term *communication* necessarily meant the conveyance of ideas or feelings or information to another, then it would indeed burst if stretched to include the antithetical notion of talking to oneself, but this is simply a red herring; we are not concerned with the proper meaning of the word *communication,* but with the nature of language. In fact the most common use of language is talking to ourselves, whether we are in company or alone, and the purpose of that talking is something for which *communication* would not be a misnomer. As I have argued in the section of Chapter 7 called *Thinking without words,* we need words to capture and preserve our own thoughts for later use by ourselves, and when we talk to ourselves we are addressing "another" — we are addressing ourselves as we will be in the future.

If Chomsky brushes aside the idea that language is essentially for communication (or for the expression of thought, if that function is seen as a different one), it is because he sees no way to deal with it scientifically; it suggests no research program to him. As he puts it:

> While it is quite commonly argued that the purpose of language is communication and that it is pointless to study language apart from its communicative function, there is no formulation of this belief, to my knowledge, from which any substantive proposals follow.[195]

The educated world will have to judge whether his refusal to deal with what most non-linguists — and even some linguists — see as the essential role of language is compensated for by the insights and discoveries that result from his decision to follow a different path.

• Chomsky has been much concerned with the question of how an infant acquires language. Broadly speaking, he sees two possible ways of accounting for the ease with which the very young child learns his native tongue: one is that he is a genius at drawing wide-ranging inferences from the random bits of language that he hears during his first few years, the other that he has an innate faculty specifically fitting him for the acquisition of a natural language, a faculty that Chomsky calls a "universal grammar" — a built-in understanding of what underlies all human languages, and perhaps of human capacity for learning anything — which is then tailored (or "parameterized," to use Chomsky's usual term) during the infant's early language experience to become the grammar of the particular natural language he is exposed to.

Since the first is extremely implausible, he concludes that the second must be the case — and of the two, he is surely right in regarding the second as the more plausible. But there is, at least at this level of conjecture, a third explanation: it may be that the infant mind possesses neither general powers of inference so magisterial as to enable it to extrapolate virtually the whole grammar of a natural language from the fragments it is exposed to, nor a highly specialized faculty for language acquisition that enables its owner to learn a natural language even while his general intellectual abilities are still infantile. The third possibility is that the mind of the infant — or perhaps better, his brain — is so plastic, so malleable, so much more impressionable than even the traditional philosophic *tabula rasa,* that it is formed by the language it hears. What would account for a child's ability to pick up his natural language so quickly and effortlessly, under this hypothesis, is not that his brain is already structured in a certain way, but just the opposite: that his brain at birth is completely unstructured, and does not learn a language, but is shaped by it, literally organized by the language it hears. If this is the case, it might be more accurate to say not that the child acquires the language, but that the language acquires the child. It may be language that turns the brain into a mind.[196]

I'm sure that some, at least, of these observations and objections have been made before, sometimes by linguists themselves. But if they have, that does not mean that they are somehow thereby neutralized, on the principle that if one has acknowledged one's faults, they cannot be counted against one. To admit that you have blundered is not to wipe out the blunder; at best, it is a first step toward correcting the blunder, or at least not blundering in the same way again. Not only do I reject the notion that to acknowledge one's error is to wipe it out, I go further: if linguists noted some of my points before I ever made them, they are all the more at fault; mere ignorance is much more forgivable than a refusal to fully confront and resolve a difficulty that one has observed. As a Chinese sage observed, *He who knows and does not do, does not know.*

A **L**anguage
of
Mathematics?
A Proof
of Programs?

$\mathbf{A}$ Language of Mathematics? A Proof of Programs?

This appendix deals with another harmful consequence of that mistaken view of language that is at least in part due to linguistics, but one so specialized that even many readers who have found the text so far easy going may wish to skip it. I hope that some, however, will be ready to work their way through it in order to see another, and quite different, aspect of the cost of misunderstanding language. I have done everything I could think of to ease the path for these stalwarts, hoping that any difficulties they find will be in the substance, not in the exposition.

Yes, it looks like a duck ...

The visible work product of the mathematician presents itself to the observer as a written text: part of it in natural language, and another part consisting of statements constructed from a finite repertoire of symbols, the mathematical symbols — that is, the numerals; the operators over them ($+$, $\times$, etc.); some purely syntactic marks such as parentheses, brackets, and ellipses; the Greek letters that have conventional mathematical meanings (Ω, Δ, π), and so forth. The symbolic parts of mathematical texts seem perfectly analogous to natural-language texts, which are likewise sequences of statements constructed from a finite repertoire of symbols, in this case the alphabetic characters. And this, in turn, supports the notion that mathematical notation constitutes a language, just as Galileo seemed to claim when he told the world that the book of nature is written in mathematical characters.

So the resemblance between a mathematical text and a natural-language text, taken together with that divorce between symbol and meaning that we have seen involved in so many misconceptions about language, has convinced many that mathematics is a language itself, analogous to, and on an equal footing with, a natural language like English. And like so many of the misconceptions examined here, the mistaking of mathematical terminology and symbology for a distinct language has led or at least contributed to some practical blunders. That mistake is, for example, at least partly the foundation of the view held by so many computer scientists that programming languages — the body of commands that evoke action from computers — can and should be modeled on the language of mathematics. It is also at the root of the notion that a computer program is analogous to a mathematical proof, and is subject to being proved correct, as a mathematical theorem is proved correct. Each of these mistakes will be examined in turn.

The erroneous views to be examined get support also from the circumstances of the computer's origin. The historic link between mathematics (especially numerical analysis) and the computer is so strong that many still think of the computer as an arithmetic engine. The very name "computer" seems to imply that, and the notion was further supported by the prevalence of mathematically trained people in the early days of computing, and by the fact that early computers were indeed used mostly as fast calculators. Although the computer is now far more involved in business and personal data retrieval and other such clerical work than it is in calculation, and although programmers today are more likely to have a degree in computer science or business than in mathematics, there still lingers some feeling that the mathematician has a kind of childhood-friend intimacy with the computer that no later comer can hope to attain.

Among the effects of these circumstances of the computer's early history is the feeling on the part of an influential school of computer scientists that mathematics needs to be brought to bear on programming, and in two ways. One is the feeling that programming languages should be recast along the lines of mathematical notation, so as to capture that notation's rigor, precision, and economy — and perhaps even its supposed creative power — for the practice of programming. The other is that programs can and should be validated, or proved correct, by means very similar to that used in the proof of a mathematical theorem. The computer scientists holding these opinions will be called *calculists* here, since they have as their objective the transformation of the conventional procedural programming language into something like a calculus — or see it as being one already. What the calculists' campaign demonstrates though, as I hope to show, is that mathematicians are no better than the rest of us at analyzing what lies closest to hand; they have misunderstood the relation between the two disciplines of mathematics and programming, largely because they think that mathematics is a language. In particular, they err in supposing that the contribution that mathematics can make to programming lies in its notation.

Mathematical Notation and Natural Languages

The rigor, precision, and economy that the calculists see in mathematical notation, and hope to capture for programming languages are regularly contrasted with the ambiguity, sloppiness, and redundancy of natural language, the opposite end of the spectrum of conceivable programming languages. But the belief of the calculists that mathematical notation constitutes a distinct language, that it is the vehicle of mathematical thought, and that mathematics and programming are analogous disciplines, is simply unfounded. The calculists have overlooked or forgotten the ancestry of their notation.

Both historically and logically, mathematical notation is an encoding of a subset of natural language, and not itself a language. A *language* reflects (and perhaps to some extent shapes) its users' views about what fragments of experience are interesting enough to merit names; because no two cultures take exactly the same view of this matter, no two languages will map element-for-element into each other. Eskimo languages, as one might expect, have judged worthy of distinct names many more states of frozen water than has English. Even within what is nominally one culture — that of the United States, for example — it is found that dialectal variations exist that have no direct counterparts in other dialects (e.g., southern "you all" has no simple northern equivalent[197]); to some degree, each individual speaks a private language — an idiolect — completely shared by no one else. A *code*, by contrast, reflects no cultural peculiarities, still less personal ones, but is simply a special representation of a language, derived by some mechanical procedure from its ordinary representation.

A language, in short, is a representation of experience; a code is a representation of a language. A language is, from its speakers' point of view, given, natural, and fundamental; a code is artificial, arbitrary, and derivative. Codes add no information to the messages they are applied to (nor subtract any, unless they are faulty); the purpose of encoding a message is to improve the representation of that message with respect to economy, security, or memorability. They do so not by virtue of any inherent intimacy with the subject matter of the messages they encode, but of such extrinsic properties as brevity, secrecy, and mnemonic power.

The primitive operations and operands of mathematics (and logic) are definable only in natural language[198]; composite and higher-level terms are then defined in terms of those primitives (with, often, further natural-language support). If natural language is incorrigibly imprecise, then all mathematical notation is congenitally infected with imprecision, since natural language is the ground from which it sprang, and to which it returns from time to time for refreshment. The historical process by which the notation was formed, with words and phrases first abbreviated, then transformed into stylized and abstract symbols, has been traced in minute and sometimes fascinating detail in (Cajori 1928), the study that is the foundation of all serious discussions of the subject.

Mathematical notation, then, is a shorthand representation of a subset of natural-language terms, designed to facilitate the compact written expression of propositions belonging to a sharply circumscribed universe of discourse. In principle, all mathematical discourse could be carried on in the natural-language vocabulary of which the notation is just a condensed representation. What justifies the notation is that it permits the expression in compact, standardized form of the manipulations undergone by the axioms stated at the outset of a proof. By using the notation to sum up at convenient intervals the transformations that have so far been applied to the object under discussion, the mathematician in effect establishes new base camps for his argument as it ascends toward the summit, letting his readers forget everything that preceded so as to clear their minds for the next step. Given the limited capacity of even the most highly trained minds for following and remembering long chains of close reasoning, the periodic purging and freeing of the short-term memory for fresh input is an invaluable step, and by itself justifies the mathematician's feeling that his notation is an indispensable tool.

But the indispensability of that notation must not blind us to its merely ancillary role in the actual development and presentation of mathematical results. The propositions expressed in the notation — equations, for the most part — do not form the fabric of mathematical argument, much less the means by which mathematical results are obtained. The notation is used in mathematical papers for the purpose of summing up at critical junctures the results obtained so far; the burden of the argument itself is carried by a prose narrative typically starting "Let $F(x)$ be a Hausdorff space such that ..." and ending "...which completes the proof." The equations and other symbolic expressions embedded in the prose serve to record and isolate for inspection the important milestones along the way; their study is seldom necessary for comprehension of the argument, and unless the reader suspects an error in formal manipulation, he will not dwell on them. Supporting this observation is the fact that a non-Russian-speaking mathematician will generally be unable to read a paper in a Russian mathematical journal.[199] The need of mathematicians to learn foreign languages, or employ the services of translators, shows that little of the meaning of even the most formal mathematical discourse is carried by the internationally accepted notation of the discipline. Mathematical notation is not the language even of the most formal and rigorous mathematical papers; they are written primarily in their authors' national languages or — if the author has the misfortune to be the speaker of a national language other than one of the most common three or four — English.

Insofar as the call for a programming calculus is a demand that any programming insights we manage to achieve should, as far as possible, be reflected in our programming tools, it is unexceptionable. Calculism, however, is based not on achieved insight, but on a mere hope that if we mimic the outward forms of mathematical practice, insight will follow. It errs again in taking mathematical notation as analogous to a programming language when it is only homologous to it. If we are to compare things of like function rather than merely of like form, the parallel between the two disappears, since they play quite different roles in their respective worlds. (To the extent that mathematical notation does have an analogue in programming, it would be the "comment" facility offered by most programming languages, particularly when used to create procedure headers.) Consider these fundamental differences:

1. Mathematical objects are imaginary and malleable; programming objects are almost always real and unalterable. A mathematical object is created by fiat, and has exactly and only those properties given it explicitly, and those inferable from them. The objects of interest in programming (except when we use the computer just as a tool in a proof or other purely mathematical procedure) exist in the external world, and can be neither altered nor exhaustively defined.

2. Mathematical goals are flexible and opportunistic; programming goals are fixed and predetermined. If a mathematician trying to prove an intuitively obvious theorem finds it not only impossible to prove, but demonstrably false, he has a much more important result than he was trying for. A programmer unable to reach his original goal is simply a programmer defeated.

These differences are so radical and far-reaching that any argument founded on the superficial resemblance between a proof and a program should be held suspect. The argument is particularly liable to be specious if it assumes that that resemblance implies an identity of goals, methods, or problems in the procedures employed by the two disciplines.

Achieving a calculus: active versus passive notation

What differentiates mathematical notation from a natural language is that it is an encoding of such a language, not a language itself; what differentiates it from a programming language is that it is a *calculus* — something that may be described as an *active notation*. Many mathematicians have claimed for the notation of their discipline that it is more than a static representation of mathematical propositions, but is to some extent an engine for generating such propositions. In this they are clearly right; what they are saying is that their notation is a *calculus*, as described in (Braithwaite 1953):

> A representation of a deductive system in such a way that to each principle of deduction there corresponds a rule of symbolic manipulation will be called a *calculus*. The use of a calculus to represent a deductive system has the enormous practical advantage that it enables deductions to be effected merely by symbolic manipulation, and the correctness of these deductions can be checked automatically merely by inspecting the relationships between the symbols ....

Or, as a writer whose name I have regrettably forgotten put it aphoristically and almost palindromically, "The sum of the representations is the representation of the sum." The enormous practical advantage of which Braithwaite speaks is worth elaborating on. The beauty of working with a calculus is twofold: it immediately makes available to the user all the tools developed by its earlier users, and it gives us a means of carrying on, if only for a short way, after insight and inspiration have departed — which gives them a chance to return before we have bogged down completely. The first of these advantages is obvious: express an idea as an equation or symbolic-logic formula, and at once all the mathematical and logical machinery developed since the Babylonians is at your service, enabling you to perform endless transformations of that idea without sacrifice of its original validity.

What may not be so immediately obvious to those not actively practicing one of these disciplines is that such notational manipulation can be invaluable in getting unstuck when at a hard place in the unfolding of a line of thought. Simply by giving its user a way of transforming, if not necessarily advancing, the representation of his thought, the calculus keeps the argument moving, living, open to good ideas or good luck, even when the worker's original impulse is spent, and when if left to his own devices he would stand becalmed. Using ordinary language here as one's reasoning vehicle is driving a car — run out of gas, and it stops dead; using a calculus is riding a horse — drop the reins, and the horse may find his way back to the barn, taking you home as well.

This double power of the calculus — to endow its user with all the tools developed by the cumulative genius of several millennia, and to let thought progress for a while by coasting when the engine has quit — has won for it volumes of tribute from its users. The tributes are deserved; the development of mathematics, and of the physical sciences that depend on it, would be impossible without the power the calculus gives us of exploiting the vast array of devices in the mathematical armory, and of making progress almost absent-mindedly through symbolic transformations. But unfortunately for programmers, this power of mathematical notation lies in its being a calculus — a representation of a deductive system — and the development of a program is not an exercise in deduction.

Proof ≠ Program

Among other differences between program and proof, note that a theorem, once proved, can immediately be used as a building block in further mathematical work regardless of its length, inelegance, or other shortcomings. Mathematicians may be so dissatisfied with that original proof that they labor for years, even generations, to come up with a better one, but the original — provided that it *is* a proof — is enough to let the theorem take its place as part of the established stock of mathematical results. A program in a correspondingly unsatisfactory state — a program that is functionally correct, but too big or slow to run economically — is a useless program. Unless it can be trimmed to size, it is nothing but a waste of time and effort. A mathematical proof is the establishment of a truth, and as such constitutes an achievement, no matter what its incidental shortcomings; a program is an engineering project operating within economic constraints; it has no redeeming value if it cannot run within the time and space allotted to it.

As was done in the parenthetical part of item 1, above, an exception must be recognized here — an exception that, in the proper sense of "prove," proves the rule just laid down: on those occasions when we use the computer to establish truth rather than to achieve a merely practical result, a program's value is not contingent on its costing less than some specified amount. This is not to say that a program is, even then, proof-like, only that when it executes an algorithm created to supply a proof, as in the case of the four-color problem, it no longer has to justify itself economically. Perhaps this difference can be summed up by pointing out that proofs, to be valid, need only be consistent with established mathematical results; programs in general must pay their way in the outside world. As a corollary, mathematicians need only be very intelligent; programmers must also be sane.

Finally, note that a formal mathematical or logical proof is an exercise in transforming an initial set of statements — the "axioms" — into a desired final statement — the "theorem" or "result" — by means of some sequence of accepted deductive steps. A computer program is likewise a sequence of approved steps toward some desired final state, but the program's objective is not to reason its way to its own concluding statements, but to achieve some external effect: to cause the answer to some computation to appear at the printer, or some picture to appear on the screen. The program is an extrovert, the mathematical proof an introvert.

What all these differentiae point to is the fundamental characteristic that distinguishes mathematics not only from computer programming, but from all the scientific and engineering disciplines: its subject matter. In ordinary human affairs, even flawless reasoning does not guarantee correct conclusions; the imperfection of the data with which we work taints every step like an intellectual original sin. The only objects about which correct reasoning guarantees perfect conclusions are those whose nature is known absolutely because they have been invented, not discovered, and only those disciplines prepared to limit their universe of discourse to objects likewise created by stipulation — imaginary objects — can enjoy the same certainty of

results. To attempt to secure that certainty by aping mathematical symbology, jargon, or other superficial features is to practice homeopathic magic, with its promise that eating our enemy's heart will endow us with his courage.

What has just been said implies a definition of mathematics; let us make that definition explicit: *mathematics is logic, applied to objects that can in principle be exhaustively described.* By "exhaustively described" I mean that all possible truths about such an object are either stated or implied by its definition. A mind able to see all the implications of its definition would immediately know everything knowable about such an object. No need to leave the matter open pending the discovery of new facts; we will never have any new information about the circle or the triangle, any more than we will about Falstaff or Sam Spade — and for the same reason. The qualifying phrase "in principle" is not a hedge, it is of the essence. If an object can be described exhaustively in practice, it is indeed a mathematical object, but a trivial one. The intellectual interest of mathematics, like that of chess, requires that the game be much too rich to be won by brute-force exhaustion of the possibilities; that is why the Appel-Haken solution of the four-color problem left so many mathematicians cold.

Proving the correctness of a program: "Formal Methods" raises its head again

The misleading surface resemblance between the work products of mathematics and those of programming has led to the idea that the same methods by which we test a purported mathematical result to see if it is valid can be applied to computer programs to ensure that they have no bugs. The idea, called "Formal Proof Methods" or just "Formal Methods (FM)," has never yielded important results, but is so seductive, especially to the mathematically trained, that it keeps getting revived as each new generation of "computer scientists" emerges from graduate school. This perennial error is presented once again in an article[200] in an issue of *IEEE Spectrum* devoted largely to the problem of faulty computer software. That problem posed by software bugs is indeed one with very serious consequences in the real world, and therefore erroneous thinking about it must be exposed as such as often as it occurs.

313

To start with basics: what FM means is treating a program or some representation of a program as if it were a mathematical proof — a chain of deductive steps — and testing it just as such formal arguments are tested, checking each step for validity by scrutinizing its derivability from already established steps. This idea has been under consideration since the computer itself came into existence; it has never quite proved itself in practise, nor has it ever quite been refuted. There are two reasons for its survival: first, to some extent it works — it requires that very close attention be paid to the subject program, and such attention will often disclose some bugs, no matter how faulty the theory on which the programmer is working as he examines the program. Second, it has an irresistable appeal to the mathematically-trained "computer scientists" who dominate programming research projects in both academia and industry. These quasi-mathematicians — the "calculists," as I have called them — feel intuitively that the solution to the bug problem must lie, if not within currently available formal methods, then in some development of them; the key, they feel sure, must be mathematical. Their feelings are groundless; there are such fundamental differences between programs and mathematical procedures that FM can never be really successful.

The essential difference is that a mathematical proof is an exercise in deduction: its objective is known at the outset, and is expressible in the notation of the procedure — the theorem to be proved or logical proposition to be demonstrated is, in fact, just another step in that procedure, singled out as a "result" only because it is a step that is especially interesting to mathematicians or logicians. The proof is an attempt to show that, starting from given premises, there is a finite sequence of steps, each of unquestioned legitimacy, that leads to the wanted expression. It is easy, at least in principle, to check the legitimacy of each step — so easy that the process of checking can, again in principle, often be relegated to the computer. In summary: in a mathematical proof, the desired output is specified in advance; the task is to show that it can be arrived at it by a series of of legitimate steps.

The objective of a computer program is radically different: the desired outcome, whether the result of a calculation or the retrieval of a piece of information or the establishment of a connection to the Internet, is not a symbolic expression, nor does it make any sense to ask whether any particular step in the program is deducible from any or all of the preceding steps. There is no such thing as an invalid step in a program — all that matters is that the program's objective be achieved, and within some time constraint. In short, programming is not a science, let alone a branch of mathematics; it is an engineering discipline.

The fact that programming is an engineering discipline is sometimes recognized by calculists, but to little or no avail, since they persist in misunderstanding engineering. In the article cited, the difficulty of getting software engineers to use formal methods is noted, and the following explanation offered:

> But still, the perceived difficulty of formal tools repels the rank-and-file programmer. After all, coders don't want to solve logical problems with the help of set theory and predicate logic. They want to, well, code. "Few people, even among those who complete

computer science degrees, are skilled in those branches of pure mathematics," says Bernard Cohen, a professor in the department of computing at City University, in London.

In every other branch of engineering, he insists, practitioners master difficult mathematical notations. "Ask any professional engineer if he could do the job without math, and you'll get a very rude reply," Cohen says. But in programming, he adds, the emphasis has often been to ship it and let the customer find the bugs.[201]

Professor Cohen's explanation of the unpopularity of FM exhibits some of the confusions that mar many discussions of its usefulness. FM, as embodied in the programming systems described earlier in the Ross article, does not require its users to be expert in set theory or predicate logic or any other branch of what he calls "pure mathematics"; the mathematics is implicit in the tools, and all the user has to do to eliminate ambiguity, supposedly, is use the FM tools to specify his program. The resistence on the part of rank-and-file programmers to the use of FM is due not to their insufficient acquaintance with pure mathematics, but to their belief, right or wrong, that such tools are more trouble than they're worth. And in telling us that other sorts of engineers would not be willing to do without mathematics, Cohen knocks down a straw man; of course no engineer would want to work without those mathematical tools relevant to his branch of engineering, but this does not imply an endorsment of the use in software engineering of the specific mathematical approach called FM. Cohen's final observation about software being shipped prematurely is likewise quite true, but equally irrelevant to the question of whether FM would enable us to do better.

To understand the limitations FM labors under, note that it calls for abstracting from an actual program[202] that part that can be treated as if it were a formal proof, and proving that part correct. There are two difficulties that this approach encounters immediately: first, it is only a part of the typical subject program that can be so treated, and second, the approach gets more and more difficult to apply as programs get bigger and more complex — that is, just as help is more and more needed. And that part of the software-creation process that FM lends itself to is just that part that the programmer understands best and will have least trouble with. All serious computer programs have two sides: one faces the real-world problem that the program was built to deal with, such as computing the orbit of a satellite or processing a transaction initiated at an ATM. The other side faces the computing hardware and the operating system, dealing with such things as memory management, semaphore testing and setting, buffer overflow, garbage collection, data structures, and other such matters that are of no interest to the customer, but have to be dealt with if he wants his program to work.

The program designer and implementor usually understands the real-world problem whose solution is the raison d'être of his project far better than he does the details of the computing system he is using, which is something he did not design, and whose internal mechanism he may have little interest in. This side of his program — the program's infrastructure or overhead — is therefore far more likely to be the seat of troublesome bugs than the more familiar and more logical problem-solving side of the program, and of course this infrastructure is the side of the program that FM is least useful in dealing with — again, it offers no help just where help is most needed. In short, the locus of serious bugs, the ones that are causing so much trouble for so many of our technical projects, lies not in the design phase, where we make high-level decisions about the logical structure of our program, but in the implementation phase, where we write the actual instructions that are to execute our decisions — the devil here, as usual, is in the details.

These limitations do not mean that FM is useless; as noted earlier, it does catch some bugs, just by virtue of forcing programmers to pay more attention to what they're doing. And the cost of bugs in released software is such that almost any method that catches some of them may be justified, especially in those critical applications just mentioned. But those limitations are inherent in FM, and on these grounds alone it is clear that that approach is not the general answer to the problem of buggy software. The reason why FM is not the answer can be put in the form of a reductio ad absurdam. Its usefulness depends on the degree to which the abstract model, while remaining so logically rigorous that it can be treated as a proof, truly mirrors the program being modeled. In the limit, that model would represent the program perfectly, mirroring every step the program takes, while at the same time preserving its own logical rigor. But if the model were that successful, why would we need the program being modeled? We would already have it, to perfection, in the form of the model — the map would have become the territory.

Consider, again, the way in which program requirements or specifications are stated: it is only rarely that they are stated clearly, rigorously, and completely at the outset of a programming project. Even in trivial classroom examples, where specifications *are* stated with some rigor, they are not stated in programming terms. A theorem to be proved is stated in terms of the very calculus that is to be used to prove it; but program objectives are given, not in terms of a final machine state toward which the program is to drive, but in terms altogether external to the program.

This fact alone means that the quest to validate programs by formal, proof-like means is futile, and for reasons that cannot be altered. The task of any program-validation procedure (PVP) would be to show that a given program does, or will, achieve its programmer's intentions. To do so, it would require some independent representation of the programmer's intentions for the program, so as to have something against which to measure the program's actual performance. Ideally, the PVP would report the degree to which the program met those intentions; at the very least, it would have to return a simple Succeed/Fail verdict. Where is this independent "representation of the programmer's intentions" (RPI) to be found? Currently it exists, if at all, as a specification document written in natural language, block diagrams, flow charts, and other such informal notations. None of these is immediately intelligible to the PVP. A RPI, to be usable by the PVP, would have to be expressed in one consistent notation, and so expressed as to be:

- absolutely *complete,*
- absolutely *correct,*
- absolutely *formal.*

About such an RPI two observations may be made: (1) no one knows how to formulate it, and (2) if it existed, the PVP would be unnecessary — the RPI would itself be what we were trying to achieve, a perfect program.

The Principal Players Identified

The Principal Players Identified

As promised in the Preface, I offer here a brief identifying note on every person mentioned in the text, with three kinds of exceptions: first, those whom it is highly unlikely

321

that any reader of this book will need to be introduced to, such as Shakespeare or Marx; second, those who are sufficiently identified in the text; and third, those whose names are mentioned only as examples of a type, and could easily be replaced by other examples with no loss. The few lines devoted to each figure below are meant to provide only a quick means of identification; they are not attempts at thumbnail biographies, nor intended to do anything like full justice to the life and work of the person concerned.

Auden, W[ystan] H[ugh] (1907–1973) English poet who moved to the United States at the outset of World War II; partner with Jacques Barzun and Lionel Trilling in two mid-20th century book clubs. Deeply concerned about the stability and integrity of the English language.

Barzun, Jacques (b.1907) American cultural historian, scholar, teacher, and critic. His many books and essays (most of which appeared in *The American Scholar* over several decades) cover virtually every aspect of intellectual and artistic life, including the music of Berlioz, detective fiction, the craft of historical research, modern editorial practices, and much else. His most recent work, *From Dawn to Decadence* (2000), is a survey of 500 years of Western culture that could have been produced by no other modern writer, and by very few in the past. If Barzun were Japanese, he would long ago have been declared a Living National Treasure.

Follett, Wilson (1887–1963) American editor and writer on English-language usage. His best known book, *Modern American Usage* (1st edition 1966, 2nd editon, revised by Erik Wensberg, 1998), was completed on his death by Jacques Barzun with some help from six other eminent writers and scholars. The book, which also contains a classic essay by Barzun called "On Usage, Purism, and Pedantry," is worthy of the comparison with Fowler that its name invites.

Fowler, H[enry] W[atson] (1858–1933) English teacher, essayist, and writer of guides on language usage. With his brother Francis he wrote *The King's English* (1906), which is still a useful book, but his great work is *Modern English Usage* (1926), which remains a classic for its good judgment, wit, and clarity.

Garner, Bryan A. (b. 1958) Texas lawyer, editor, founder of the H. W. Fowler Society, lecturer and consultant on legal prose, author of *Garner's Modern American Usage*. A moderate prescriptivist. He has reviewed a part of this book before publication, but is in no way responsible for any faults in it.

Housman, A[lfred] E[dward] (1859–1936) English classical scholar, textual editor, and poet. Widely considered the greatest Latinist of his time, and an editor who set new standards for the study and recovery of the texts of Silver Age Latin poetry. He was also the last English poet to be both a critical and a popular success; many British soldiers in World War I carried his *A Shropshire Lad* in their kit bags.

Jakobson, Roman (1896–1982) One of the founders of modern linguistics. He taught at several European universities, ending his career at Harvard, and was widely regarded as the doyen of linguistics. He was unlike most linguists of today, though, in several ways: he was a also a linguist in the non-technical sense — that is, a master of several languages — and much more a littérateur and philologist than most academic "linguistic scientists" of our day.

Jespersen, Otto (1860–1943) Danish linguist and philologist, leading expert on the development of the English language. His fundamental views on language, as presented in (Jespersen 1922) and (Jespersen 1925), are very close, as I discovered after this book was essentially complete, to my own. In particular, he is adamant in holding that language is not a separate realm with laws of its own, but a part of general human behavior, and incomprehensible apart from its full human setting. He even doubted the propriety of applying the term "law" to the so-called sound-change laws. Further, he saw the nearly exclusive concern of linguistics with the formal aspect of speech, and its neglect of the primary *function* of speech, as a shortcoming excusable only because linguistics was a very young branch of scholarship.

Jones, Sir William (1746–1794) British Orientalist who was the first to call attention to the relationships among Latin, Greek, and Sanskrit, and thereby initiate modern historical linguistics.

Kraus, Karl (1874–1936) Viennese satirist, editor, and writer. He is among the most eloquent of those who have fought against the corruption of language. Author of many celebrated aphorisms on linguistic and social decadence.

Lowth, Robert (1710–1787) Bishop of London who wrote on, among many other things, English usage and style. Supposedly an extreme grammatical purist, frequently cited by descriptivists as an arch-prescriptivist.

Mead, Margaret (1901–1978) American anthropologist, student of Franz Boas, writer on sexual mores of Pacific Islanders and of adolescence in several cultures. In later years, something of a television celebrity and all-purpose 'wise woman.' Doubt has been cast on the reliability of some of her early work; it appears that some of her Samoan native informants mischievously misinformed her about their sexual practices and other aspects of their society.

O'Connor, Flannery (1925–1964) American novelist and short-story writer. Lived in and wrote about the South, and rural Georgia particularly. A devout Catholic whose religious and literary life were closely joined.

Orwell, George (1903–1950) English journalist, novelist, critic, and political observer. Notable for, among other things, his determined efforts to cleanse the English language of euphemisms and evasiveness.

Popper, Sir Karl (1902–1994) Viennese-born philosopher of science. His greatest contribution was to point out, repeatedly and forcefully, that the distinguishing mark of a scientific hypothesis is its openness to being tested and — if false — to being falsified, not its likelihood of being proved true.

Rousseau, Jean-Jacques (1712–1778) Swiss-born intellectual and educational theorist. In his *Contrat social* (1762) he introduced the concept of the 'General Will,' according to which the true will of the citizenry, whether they know it or not, is embodied in a strong central government that is hence entitled to act without restraint or consultation with the citizenry. In decoupling the wishes of actual people from the General Will (what I call in the text *The People*) he provided, however unintentionally, a wonderful rationale for despotisms of all kinds.

Safire, William (b.1929) American political analyst, sometime Presidential adviser, and life-long student of the English language. He has written several books on language usage, and still writes a weekly column on the subject for the *New York Times Magazine*.

He coined the term *linguistic activist* to differentiate himself from the hard-core prescriptivists, a practice I gratefully adopt.

Sapir, Edward (1884–1939) American linguist who, like Jakobson, was a literary and cultural critic as well as linguistic expert. He was particularly concerned, in his technical linguistic work, with American Indian languages.

Saussure, Ferdinand de (1857–1913) Swiss linguist, another of the founders of modern linguistics. One of his many contributions was to make a clear distinction between a specific utterance in a language, which he called *parole,* and the language taken as a whole, the *langue.*

Schiller, Johann Christoff Friedrich von (1759–1805) German dramatist, poet, and critic. In his *Über naïve und sentimentalische Dichtung* he contrasted early, heroic literature, unselfconscious and forthright, with modern literature, aware of itself, sophisticated, and ironic.

Simon, John (b.1925) American drama, movie, music and literary critic; an outspoken prescriptivist whose *Paradigms Lost: Reflections on Literacy and Its Decline* (Clarkson N. Potter, 1980; Penguin, 1981) may be the most uncompromisingly prescriptivist book of our time.

Stephen, James Fitzjames (1829–1894) English lawyer and judge who published incisive rebuttals to some of the writings of John Stuart Mill. His critical essays, still in print (see References), are classics of unalloyed conservatism.

Veblen, Thorstein (1857–1929) American economist and sociologist. In his *Theory of the Leisure Class* (1899) he coined the expression "conspicuous consumption" to describe expenditures by the rich intended more to impress others, and thereby enhance their social status, than to gratify their personal appetites and desires.

Whorf, Benjamin Lee (1887–1941) American student of linguistics who, although without formal academic affiliation, was accepted by many academic linguists as a peer. He is best known as co-author of the 'Sapir-Whorf Hypothesis,' which holds that the mental horizons of a language community are to a substantial degree set by the limits of their language; a community having no future tense, for example, would be one whose sense of time would be defective, or at least very different from that of a community possessing that resource. The hypothesis is not taken very seriously today by linguists, but it continues to have a kind of underground life among people with an active if untrained interest in language.

Yeats, William Butler (1863–1939) Irish poet, dramatist, and essayist. Thought by many to be the last great poet of the English language.

What is A 'Foreign Term'?

What is a 'Foreign Term'?

George Orwell's proscription of the use of foreign words and phrases in English-language texts (the fifth of his six rules is "Never use a foreign phrase, a scientific word or a jargon word if you can think of an everyday equivalent.") was recently echoed and expanded on by John W. Nelson in an essay[203] he published in the *The Vocabula Review* under the title "Sayonara, Mr. Fowler: On the Use and Abuse of Foreign Words and Phrases." In doing so, Nelson inadvertently helped to show why this rule of Orwell's, like the rest of them, was poorly thought out, and potentially harmful to the cause of good prose. Nelson's general message was Orwell's: foreign terms are greatly over-used by writers in English, and should as a rule be replaced by native English synonyms. But Nelson did us the service of presenting several examples of the objectionable terms he had in mind, and offering replacements for them. His essay, typical of many that attack the use of foreign terms as pretentious, confusing, or otherwise undesirable, made it clear that the more fundamental problem is not whether to use foreign terms, but to decide what a "foreign term" is.

The problem presents itself with the very first words of his title ("Sayonara, Mr. Fowler..."): I assumed from those words that Fowler, or at least Fowler on the use of foreign words in English, was being dismissed with scorn. But immediately following that title, as an epigraph, is a quotation ("Those who use foreign words or phrases belonging to languages with which they have little or no acquaintance do so at their own peril.") on the very subject from *Modern English Usage* that is respectfully presented, and other references to Fowler within the text show that far from dismissing him, Nelson regards him with admiration. This is all to the good, but it makes it evident that Nelson does not understand the English word *sayonara*. He may understand the Japanese word from which it derives, but he's not writing in Japanese (and the word would be inappropriate even used in its Japanese sense); when you use the English *sayonara,* as Nelson does, you're saying "you're history, dude; bye-bye!" — and this is the reverse of what he means. So Nelson's attack on the use in English of "foreign terms" is undercut by the revelation that he does not realize that the first word in his title is now an English word (as well as a Japanese word), and that he does not understand its English sense.

Nelson recognizes that many of the foreign terms he objects to have no simple English equivalents or synonyms, but suggessts that if synonyms do not already exist, simple word-for-word English translations should be used, and he offers as examples. For the German *weltanschauung* and *Zeitgeist,* and the French *raison d'être,* he proposes to those writing in English "world view," "spirit of the age," and "reason for being." But these supposed English equivalents are equivalent only in the abstract; if used within the contexts in which their originals properly and usually occur — philosophic and historical studies — they would reek of the schoolboy trot or condescension to the reader. They sound, in fact, unEnglish; the natural English terms for the ideas they embody are *weltanschauung, Zeitgeist,* and *raison d'être.* The reader for whom such books are written, coming across "reason for being," for example, would be tripped up for a moment, then realize what "foreign" term that phrase stood for, mentally substitute *raison d'être* for it, and go on.

The great problem with Nelson's essay, as with many other treatments of the same topic, is a failure to understand just what a "foreign" word or phrase is. Nelson himself, curiously, is aware of the predatory and acquisitive nature of English — he even quotes and identifies the source of James D. Nicoll's vivid description of it as a mugger of other languages — but he somehow fails to connect what

Nicoll says to his own thesis. English routinely assimilates words and phrases like those just discussed to the point where they are the natural English expressions for the ideas they stand for; it is pretentious to "translate them into English." (Their status as legitimate elements of the English language is further evidenced by their often acquiring somewhat different meanings in English from those they have in the languages English took them from; English *sayonara* is hardly the only word that we have taken from another language and then bent to our own purposes. Like America, English is populated largely by immigrants.)

And the words lumped together as "foreign" by Nelson and others do not fall into one or the other of just two classes, the native-born citizens and the complete foreigners, they are scattered along a continuum of words in various stages of acquiring citizenship, from the wholly naturalized ones like *rendezvous* or *coup de grâce* to the those like *schadenfreude* or *gedankenexperiment* which are plainly foreign, and used because they convey ideas that cannot be conveyed in standard English without much wordiness. *Sayonara,* to look more closely at the word that Nelson leads off with, is perhaps midway along that continuum — not yet a citizen, but certainly the holder of a Green Card. Ours is a language that has said to all others, "Give me your tired, your poor, your huddled masses yearning to breathe free ..." — and when they accept our invitation, we naturalize the immigrants so quickly that in no time, as someone has remarked, they're as American as tarte tatin.

Nelson tells us that "the only time it is appropriate to use either *rendezvous* or *liaison* is when you are talking about *meeting* your mistress." So much for the poet who wrote that he had "a rendezvous with Death," or the science-fiction author who wrote *Rendezvous With Rama.* The word *rendezvous* is not a synonym for *meeting,* but neither is it restricted to matters of amour; it is used for any highly charged, portentous meeting — with Death, say, or with a mysterious extraterrestrial vessel. As for *liaison,* it is to be met with more frequently today in cookbooks, military memoirs, and treatises on typography than in an amourous context. A pity, perhaps, but true.

The attack on the use in English of terms taken from French goes further:

> If you have a *rendezvous* with two mistresses at the same time, then using *ménage-a-trois* is not only acceptable, it is laudable.

If *ménage-a-trois* is useful only when meeting two of your mistresses (if you have more than two, the term cannot help you, but that is probably the least of your difficulties), it will be of very limited usefulness; the only case I know of in which a man had a meeting with two of his mistresses is that in which Bertolt Brecht met with Helene Weigel and — I think — Ruth Berlau in a meeting the women had called to force him to choose between them. But apart from the narrow applicability Nelson's edict would impose on it, the term doesn't mean what he seems to think it does — a serious handicap in laying down the law on how it should be used. If one has a *rendezvous* with two of one's mistresses, that may justify the *trois* in *ménage-a-trois* — but where's the *ménage*? If a man and two women really formed a *ménage*, there would be no need to set up a *rendezvous;* everyone would normally be right there.

Occasionally, Nelson concedes, a foreign term is in order — but he shows he doesn't understand the term even while allowing it. He asks:

> How better to puncture the exaggerated importance of an issue than to brand it a *cause célèbre?*

To which the answer is, 'almost any way would be better,' because one does not cut down to size an issue that has been treated with more respect that it deserves by branding it a *cause célèbre;* if anything, one would be endorsing its importance by doing so — a *cause célèbre* is not the same as a tempest in a teapot.

This zeal to replace all "foreign words" with good old — or bad new — English equivalents has been remarked and rebuked by others. In a review of the otherwise estimable book *The Coming of the*

Third Reich, Geoffrey Wheatcroft writes of its author:

> ... Mr. Evans has a few quirks, like translating every turn of phrase, even those in common currency.
>
> There may be something to be said for rendering Führer as "leader," but the baffling "struggle for culture" turns out to refer not to some worthy artistic aspirations but to what is well-known in English as well as German as the Kulturkampf, Bismarck's campaign against the Roman Catholic Church. And to translate the names of newspapers — Frankfurt News for Frankfurter Zeitung, Berlin Daily News-Sheet for Berliner Tageblatt, Racial Observer for Völkischer Beobachter — is just silly.[204]

But Richard Evans either failed to see Wheatcroft's comments, or dismissed them, because when he published the second volume of his history of Nazi Germany, *The Third Reich in Power,* an anonymous reviewer commented on the same fault in that volume:

> One final concern: many German titles have been translated into English. While it might work to cast "Mein Kampf" as "My Struggle", some other terms will seem more exotic in English than in German. For example, Julius Streicher's rabidly anti-Semitic paper "Der Stürmer" is translated as the "Stormer", although this term is never used in the English-language literature on the Third Reich. It would be like insisting that *The Economist* should be *Der Volksvirt* when it is cited in Germany.[205]

The state of English prose in George Orwell's day, particularly that of the bureaucratic and mandarin classes in Great Britain, may have been such as to explain, if not fully justify, his wholesale and indiscriminate repudiation of foreign terms, but whether or not it was so then, it is not so now. Bad writing today is very bad indeed, but hardly because the bad writers are over-indulging in foreign terms; it is much more likely to be bad because they are incompetent at writing simple English.

References

All the papers and books that I have used in the composition of this book are listed here, except for those used merely as sources of brief quotations or general facts rather than for substantive contributions to the text. Such sources are generally cited in the relevant endnotes.

Aitchison, Jean (1997), *The Language Web: The Power and Problem of Words.* Cambridge University Press.

———— (1998), "The Media are Ruining English," in Bauer & Trudgill, pages 15–22.

———— (2001), *Language Change: Progress or Decay?* 3rd ed. Cambridge U. P.

Amis, Kingsley (1997), *The King's English.* New York: St. Martin's Press.

Bar-Hillel, Yehoshua (1964), *Language and Information: Selected Essays on their Theory and Application.* Reading: Addison-Wesley Publishing Company, Inc.

Barzun, Jacques (2000), *From Dawn to Decadence: 500 Years of Western Cultural Life.* NY: HarperCollins.

Bauer, Laurie, and Peter Trudgill, eds. (1998), *Language Myths.* Penguin Books.

Bloomfield, Leonard (1933), *Language.* New York: Holt, Rinehart and Winston.

Bolgar, R. R. (1954), *The Classical Heritage.* Cambridge U.P.

Botha, Rudolf P. (1989), *Challenging Chomsky: The Generative Garden Game.* Basil Blackwell.

Braithwaite, Richard B. (1953), *Scientific Explanation.* Cambridge U. P.

Burchfield, R. W., ed. (1996), *Fowler's Modern English Usage,* 3rd edition. Oxford: Clarendon Press.

Cajori, Florian (1928), *A History of Mathematical Notations.* 2 vols. La Salle, IL: The Open Court Publishing Company.

Carpenter, Humphrey (1981), *W. H. Auden: A Biography.* Boston: Houghton Mifflin.

Chomsky, Noam (1957), *Syntactic Structures.* The Hague: Mouton & Co.

——————— (1965), *Aspects of the Theory of Syntax.* MIT Press.

——————— (1968), *Language and Mind.* NY: Harcourt, Brace & World.

——————— (1976), *Reflections on Language.* NY: Pantheon Books.

——————— (1979), *Language and Responsibility.* NY: Pantheon Books.

——————— (1980), *Rules and Representations.* Columbia U. P.

——————— (1988, 2004), *Language and Politics.* ed. C. P. Otero. Oakland, CA: AK Press.

Corey, Peter (2004), "How Linguistics Killed Grammar," in Fiske, ed., *Vocabula Bound,* pages 138–190.

Fiske, Robert Hartwell, ed. (2004), *Vocabula Bound.* Oak Park, IL: Marion Street Press.

Follett, Wilson (1966) (with Jacques Barzun and others), *Modern American Usage: A Guide.* Hill & Wang. (In the edition of 1998, edited by Erik Wensberg, Barzun's valuable introductory essay is slightly revised and relegated to the back of the book.)

Geach, Peter, and Max Black (1960), *Translations from the Philosophical Writings of Gottlob Frege.* Second edition. Oxford: Basil Blackwell.

Graves, Robert, and Alan Hodge (1943), *The Reader Over Your Shoulder.* The Macmillan Company.

Grose, Francis (1785), *A Classical Dictionary of the Vulgar Tongue*. 3rd edition (1963), ed. Eric Partridge. London: Routledge & Kegan Paul.

Halpern, Mark (1990), *Binding Time: Six Studies in Programming Technology and Milieu*. Ablex Publishing Corp.

——————— (1997), "A War That Never Ends," *The Atlantic Monthly* (March), pages 19–22. (A fragment of Halpern 2000, below; listed here to avoid confusion.)

——————— (2000), "Why Linguists Are Not to Be Trusted on Language Usage," *The Vocabula Review*, September. An extended version, "Why Linguists Are Not to Be Trusted on Language Usage — With Some Afterthoughts," will be found in Fiske 2004, pages 85–114.

——————— (2001a), "The End of Linguistics," *The American Scholar* (Winter), pages 13–26. Available also in *The Vocabula Review*, July.

——————— (2001b), "Two Bad Papers on Language Usage," *The Vocabula Review*, October.

——————— (2002), "The Eskimo Snow Vocabulary Debate: Fallacies and Confusions," *The Vocabula Review*, February.

——————— (2003), "Professor Trudgill is Puzzled," *The Vocabula Review*, July, at http://www.vocabula.com/2003/VRJULY03Halpern.asp

Haussamen, Brock (1993), *Revising the Rules: Traditional Grammar and Modern Linguistics*. Dubuque, Iowa: Kendall/Hunt Publishing Co.

Hayden, Donald E., E. Paul Alworth, and Gary Tate, eds. (1967) *Classics in Linguistics*. New York: Philosophical Library.

Hoffer, Peter Charles (2004), *Past Imperfect*. N.Y.: Public Affairs.

Honey, John (1997), *Language is Power*. London and Boston: Faber & Faber.

Hope, Jonathan (2004), "Grimy times," *Times Literary Supplement* (September 17), page 24 (review of Ian Brooks et al. (eds.), *Chambers Concise Dictionary*).

Housman, A. E. (1911), *The Confines of Criticism*, ed. John Carter. (The Cambridge Inaugural of 1911) Cambridge University Press, 1969.

———— (1988), *Collected Poems and Selected Prose*, ed. Christopher Ricks. Penguin Books.

Houellebecq, Michel (2005), *H. P. Lovecraft: Against the World, Against Life*. Translated by Dorna Khazeni. San Francisco: McSweeney's.

Jakobson, Roman (1990), *On Language*, ed. L. R. Waugh & M. Monville Burston. Harvard U. P.

Jespersen, Otto (1922), *Language: Its Nature, Development and Origin*. London: Allen & Unwin.

———— (1925), *Mankind, Nation and Individual From a Linguistic Point of View*. London: Allen & Unwin.

Johnson, Samuel (1950), *Prose and Poetry*, ed. Mona Wilson. London: Rupert Hart-Davis.

Kac, Mark, & Gian-Carlo Rota & Jacob Schwartz (1992), *Discrete Thoughts*, ed. 2 . Birkhäuser.

Kaster, Robert A. (1988), *Guardians of Language: The Grammarian and Society in Late Antiquity*. University of California Press.

Keller, Rudi (1994), *On Language Change: The invisible hand in language*. Routledge.

Knox, Bernard (1993), *The Oldest Dead White European Males*. NY: Norton.

Lakoff, George (2004), *Don't Think Of An Elephant!: Know Your Values And Frame The Debate*. White River Junction, Vermont: Chelsea Green Publishing Co.

338

Leiber, Justin (1975), *Noam Chomsky: A Philosophic Overview*. NY: St. Martin's Press.

Lepschy, Giulio (1992–1998), *History of Linguistics*. Addison Wesley Longman Ltd. Vols I–IV published; Vol V to come.

Lewis, C. S. (1954), *English Literature in the Sixteenth Century*. Oxford: Clarendon Press.

Lyons, John (1978), *Noam Chomsky*. (revised edition). Penguin Modern Masters

Martin, Laura (1986), " 'Eskimo Words for Snow': A Case Study in the Genesis and Decay of an Anthropological Example," *American Anthropologist* 88, 2 (June), pages 418–423.

Mawson, C. O. Sylvester, ed. (1945), *Roget's International Thesaurus of English Words and Phrases* (N. Y.: Thomas Y. Crowell Company (first published 1911). A modern adaptation of Roget 1852.

McWhorter, John (1998), *Word on the Street*. Cambridge, MA: Perseus Publishing.

———— (2001), *The Power of Babel*. N.Y.: Henry Holt.

———— (2003), *Doing Our Own Thing: The Degradation of Language and Music and Why We Should, Like, Care*. NY: Gotham Books.

Mehta, Ved (1971), "John is Easy to Please," *The New Yorker* (8 May), pages 44–87. Reprinted in Ved Mehta, *John is Easy to Please*. NY: Farrar Straus Giroux, 1971.

Meyers, Miriam Watkins (1990), "Current Generic Pronoun Usage: An Empirical Study," *American Speech*, 65:3, pages 228–236.

Morton, Michael (1993), *The Critical Turn*. Detroit: Wayne State University Press.

Nelson, John W. (2003), "Sayonara, Mr. Fowler: On the Use and Abuse of Foreign Words and Phrases," *The Vocabula Review*, August.

Norfolk, Lawrence (2002), "Shaped Like a Violin," *The Guardian,*
July 13. (available at
http://books.guardian.co.uk/review/story/0,12084,753688,00.html)

Nunberg, Geoffrey (1983), "The Decline of Grammar," *The Atlantic
Monthly* (December), pages 31–46.

——————— (1995), "A Touch of Crass," *Natural Language and
Linguistic Theory 13,* pages 173–179. (also on the Web at
http://www-csli.stanford.edu/~nunberg/crass.pdf)

——————— (1996), "Snowblind," *Natural Language and
Linguistic Theory 14,* pages 205–213. (also on the Web at
http://www-csli.stanford.edu/~nunberg/snow.html)

——————— (1997), " 'Best' dictionaries," e-mail message posted
to COPYEDITING-L@cornell.edu, Digest 5365, 14 October.

O'Connor, Flannery (1969), "The Nature and Aim of Fiction," in
Mystery and Manners: Occasional Prose, ed. Sally and Robert
Fitzgerald. N.Y.: Farrar, Straus & Giroux.

Orwell, George (1946), "Politics and the English Language," in
The Collected Essays, Journalism and Letters of George Orwell,
ed. Sonia Orwell and Ian Angus (Harcourt Brace Jovanovich,
1968), Volume 4, pages 127–140; rules stated at page 139.

Patkotak, Elise Sereni (1994), Letter to the editor, *New York,* June
13, p. 8 (reproduced in Halpern 2000).

——————— (1996), Private communication, March 26.

Pedersen, Holger (1931), *Linguistic Science in the Nineteenth
Century.* Harvard U. P. Reprinted in paperback as *The Discovery
of Language.* Indiana U. P., 1959.

Pinker, Steven (1994), *The Language Instinct.* New York: Morrow.

——————— (2002), *The Blank Slate.* Penguin Books.

Pullum, Geoffrey (1989), "The Great Eskimo Vocabulary Hoax,"
Natural Language and Linguistic Theory 7, pages 275–281.

——————— (1990), "The Great Eskimo Vocabulary Hoax," *Lingua Franca* (June), pp. 28–29. A two-page summary of the essay, in the premier issue of this now defunct periodical.

——————— (1991), *The Great Eskimo Vocabulary Hoax*. U. of Chicago Press. Contains the fullest and most authoritative version of the essay.

Ray, Punya Sloka (1963), *Language Standardization: Studies in Prescriptive Linguistics*. The Hague: Mouton & Co.

Roget, Peter Mark (1852), *Thesaurus of English Words and Phrases Classified and Arranged so as to Facilitate the Expression of Ideas and Assist in Literary Composition*. London.

Ross, Philip E. (2005), "The Exterminators," *IEEE Spectrum* (September), pages 36–41.

Sampson, Geoffrey (1980), *Schools of Linguistics*. Stanford University Press.

Sapir, Edward (1921), *Language: An Introduction to the Study of Speech*. NY: Harcourt, Brace.

——————— (1956), *Edward Sapir: Culture, Language and Personality*. ed. David G. Mandelbaum. University of California Press.

Schauer, Frederick (2003), *Profiles Probabilities and Stereotypes*. Harvard U. P.

Schneir, Bruce (2003), *Beyond Fear: Thinking Sensibly About Security in an Uncertain World*. NY: Copernicus Books.

Searle, John R. (1972), "A Special Supplement: Chomsky's Revolution in Linguistics," *The New York Review of Books* (June 29).

Shieber, Stuart, ed. (2004), *The Turing Test: Verbal Behavior as the Hallmark of Intelligence*. MIT Press.

Shippey, Tom (2004), "We're still at it" [review of David Crystal, *The Stories of English*. Penguin, 2004], *Times Literary Supplement* (August 20), page 11.

Sledd, James and Wilma R. Ebbitt (1962), *Dictionaries and* That *Dictionary*. Scott Foresman & Co.

—————— (1996), *Eloquent Dissent: The Writings of James Sledd*. ed. Richard D. Freed. Boynton/Cook Publishers.

Spitzer, Leo (1943), "Why Does Language Change?", *Modern Language Quarterly*, IV, pages 413–431.

Steinberg, Danny D. and Leon A. Jakobovits, eds (1971), *Semantics: An Interdisciplinary Reader in Philosophy, Linguistics, and Psychology*. Cambridge U. P.

Steiner, George (1969), "The Tongues of Men," *The New Yorker* (November 15), pages 217–236.

Stephen, James Fitzjames (1862), "The Doctrine of Liberty in Its Application to Morals," in Richard Posner, ed., *Liberty, Equality, Fraternity*. U. of Chicago Press, 1991.

Strichartz, Robert S. (1989), "An International Language for Mathematics," *The Mathematical Intelligencer 11*, 1 (Winter), pages 12–13.

Taylor, A.J.P. (1965), *English History 1914–1945*. Oxford: Clarendon Press.

Trudgill, Peter (1998), "The Meanings of Words Should Not be Allowed to Vary or Change," in Bauer & Trudgill 1998, pages 1–8.

—————— (2003), "Converse Terms, Polysemy, and Respect for Nonstandard Dialects," *The Vocabula Review* (June), at http://www.vocabula.com/2003/VRJUNE03Trudgill.asp

Turing, Alan M. (1950), "Computing machinery and Intelligence," *Mind* LIX, 236, pp. 433–460. Reprinted in (among other places) J. Newman (ed.) *The World of Mathematics* (New York: Simon & Schuster, 1956) [retitled "Can a machine think?"], vol. IV, pp. 2099–2123; A. R. Anderson (ed.) *Minds and Machines* (Prentice-Hall, 1964), pp. 4–30; D. R. Hofstader & D. C. Dennett (eds.) *The Mind's I* (New York: Basic Books, 1981), pp. 53–67; E. A. Feigenbaum & J. Feldman (eds.) *Computers & Thought* (New York: McGraw-Hill, 1963).

Ullmann, Stephen (1962), *Semantics: An Introduction to The Science of Meaning.* Basil Blackwell & Moss Ltd.

Vickers, Brian (1988), *In Defence of Rhetoric.* Oxford: Clarendon Press.

Whale, John (2004), "Roget's Storehouse," *Times Literary Supplement* (February 12, 2004); review of Werner Hüllen, *A History of Roget's Thesaurus.* Oxford U. P.

Wilton, David (2004), *Word Myths: Debunking Linguistic Urban Legends.* Oxford U. P.

Winchester, Simon (2001), "Word Imperfect," *The Atlantic Monthly* (May), pages 53–75.

Woodbury, Anthony C. (1984), "Eskimo and Aleut Languages," in David Damas (ed.), *Handbook of North American Indians V: Arctic.* Washington, D.C.: Smithsonian Institution.

Yule, Henry & A. C. Burnell (1886), *Hobson-Jobson: The Anglo-Indian Dictionary.* London; reprinted Wordsworth Editions Ltd, 1996.

Notes

[1] One linguist, George Lakoff of the University of California at Berkeley, has turned his professional skills to the task of helping liberal and progressive candidates get elected, and their supporters to win arguments with conservatives. His help consists of advising them on how to 'frame' — that is, word — their views in more attractive language. This linguistic scientist's project seem to be indistinguishable from that of a political consultant, public relations agent, or advertising copy writer, but is presented in a book (Lakoff 2004) that flaunts his credentials as a professor of linguistics, implying that its contents constitute disinterested scholarship brought to bear on a political problem. Some of the beneficiaries of Professor Lakoff's efforts believe that he brings to their party not merely scholarship, but science: Representative Nancy Pelosi, minority leader in the House, said, "… we [Democrats] were just arriving in an unscientific way at what Lakoff was arriving at in a scientific way." (quoted in Matt Bai, "The Framing Wars," *The New York Times Magazine*, July 17, 2005, page 44.) And Professor Lakoff himself apparently believes this; a flyer announcing a lecture of his on "the current state of political discourse in America" offers the following information about him, presumably supplied by Lakoff or his agent: "Lakoff has been a pioneer in applying cognitive science and linguistics to the study of how politicians use, and how electorates are swayed by, metaphorical language and the linguistic 'framing' of issues."

345

[2] Keller, page 8. Keller is Professor of German and Linguistics at the University of Düsseldorf.

[3] Curiously, it was once the boast of the professional student of language to have recovered from just this superstition. The great Danish linguist Otto Jespersen, in lectures delivered in 1925 but not published in English until 1946, says "The most notable advance that has been made in the theoretical conception of the nature of language since the serious study of language first began

consists in this, that we no longer do what was so frequently done in earlier times, that is, conceive language as a self-existent thing or substance, or — to use an expression frequently employed — as an organism, that lives and dies like a plant or any other organism, but have learnt to see that language in its essence is a human activity, an effort on the part of one individual to be understood by, or at least come into relation with, another individual." (Jespersen 1946, page 4). It is not clear whether today's linguists, in insisting that language is a natural phenomenon obeying laws largely independent of actual speakers, have actually succumbed once more to the superstition that Jespersen was congratulating his profession on having escaped, or feel forced to repeat that falsehood in order to protect their pretensions to practicing a science.

4 An allusion to the remark of Max Beerbohm's, as reported by S. N. Behrman: "A tense and peculiar family, the Oedipuses, were they not?"

5 Amy Gamerman, "Rhyme and Reason: Editing the Poet of the Century," *Wall Street Journal,* January 20, 1994.

6 *Cicerone* does not, of course, start with the same sound as *chaperon[e],* but that is not apparent to the eye, which I think is the organ involved in this confusion.

7 Jared Sandberg, "CSI: The Workplace. Which One Is Guilty Of a Double Assault?", *The Wall Street Journal* (November 15, 2005), page B1. For the source of the phrase, see 2 Timothy 4:1 KJV.

8 For examples of rejected changes, glance at Grose 1963, or any of Eric Partridge's collections of slang, or indeed any old dictionary, to find countless examples of snappy expressions that were once thought the cat's pajamas or bee's knees. They were once on everyone's lips, are now on no one's.

9 See, for example, the list offered by Jacques Barzun in Follett, page 13.

10 In Bauer & Trudgill, page 7.

11 Jon Udell, "Tin Ears and the Social Fabric," *Infoworld* (February 16, 2004), page 36.

12 (Jespersen 1922), page 174.

13 Not only are many educated if untitled Britons hazy on the subject of forms of address appropriate to bearers of titles and honors in general, but even some who themselves bear titles and honors are confused on the subject. In an interview (Deborah Solomon, "Knight Moves," *The New York Times Magazine* [August 1, 2004], page 13), the recently knighted editor and writer Harold Evans told the interviewer "An earl is higher than a lord," and "A dukedom is related to the royal family" — both statements utter nonsense. *Earl* is a rank; *Lord* a form of address. And a duke — presumably what Evans meant, and possibly what he said to his interviewer, who was clearly much more concerned with showing how unimpressed she was than with anything he was saying — is not necessarily related to the royal family. It is tempting to think that Evans was pulling the leg of his self-absorbed interviewer, but such mistakes are so common now that I fear that he was being perfectly serious.

14 An interesting example of the dangers posed by oversimplified headlines: in January 2005 Lawrence Summers, president of Harvard University, attracted much criticism by raising the possibility at a semi-private academic conference that one reason for the scarcity of women among academic mathematicians and scientists may be innate differences between men and women. The reaction of one of his critics, Professor Evalyn Gates of the University of Chicago, is described in the last paragraph of a newspaper story (Sara B. Miller and Amanda Paulson, "Harvard flap prompts query: How free is campus speech?", *The Christian Science Monitor,* January 28, 2005) as follows:

> At the recent conference, ... he only suggested that gender differences be studied as a possible reason for women's absence in the sciences. "But the headlines say, 'Harvard president says men are better at science than women,'" says Gates, the University of Chicago professor. "That kind of phrase repeated over and over, especially when it reinforces an underlying concept people have already, can be extremely damaging."

347

It would seem that Professor Gates' complaint should be directed to the editor who imposed that headline on the story in the interests of brevity, rather than to Summers. Some examples of extravagant newspaper headlines, and some interesting comments on them by Sir Kinglsly Amis, can be found in (Amis 1997, s.v. 'Overstatement').

[15] In a newspaper story (Glen Martin, "Park Service wants to eliminate exotic deer at Point Reyes," *San Francisco Chronicle*, February 4, 2005), the exotic deer in question are referred to as "the hefty ungulates."

[16] For example, an admission ticket for June 30, 2004, to the Chabot Space & Science Center in Oakland, California, bears on its reverse an offer from a local ice-cream parlor: "Ask about taking our Artic Survival Tour and see how ice cream is made the old fashioned way — By Hand!"

[17] Schneir 2003, page 135.

[18] Keller, page 141.

[19] In fact prescriptivists approve of many changes, even propose some: terms like *foreword*, *folklore*, and *handbook* were proposed by 19th-century champions of 'Anglo-Saxon' diction, and have been accepted into the English language.

[20] Nunberg 1983, page 46.

[21] This passage of Trudgill's is from Bauer, page 8; the one from Aitchison is from Bauer, page 19. Perhaps the best reply to the "Funny peculiar ... ?" awkwardness is "Peculiar unique or peculiar strange?"

[22] The allusion is to the reply made by that candidate in Molière's *Le Malade Imaginaire*.

[23] Nunberg 1983.

[24] Nunberg 1997.

[25] Trudgill 1998, page 6.

[26] Trudgill 2003.

[27] Shippey 2004.

[28] The imply/infer issue can be a matter of life and death. When Sally Blount appeals to Nero Wolfe to save her father, his first

question to her is, "Do you use 'infer' and 'imply' interchangeably, Miss Blount?" If she had answered anything but No, as she did, Wolfe would have told Archie to show her to the door, and her father would almost certainly have been wrongly convicted and perhaps put to death. (See opening scene of Rex Stout, *Gambit*, 1962.)

²⁹ For an account of the birth of linguistics as a scientific discipline in the 19th century, see (Jespersen 1922) and (Pedersen 1931); for a full history of linguistics in the broadest sense, starting from the earliest surviving evidence of interest in language, see (Lepschy 1994, 1998). Jones' seminal lecture is reprinted in (Hayden 1967).

³⁰ Chomsky 1976, pages 82–83.

³¹ Ullmann, page 71.

³² Ullmann, page 260.

³³ I have also restricted myself, for convenience, to those linguists working in and on English; I have seen nothing to suggest that looking further afield would add anything of significance to my arguments or conclusions.

³⁴ Chomsky 1980, page 133, and Chapter 3 ("Knowledge of Grammar"), passim.

³⁵ Chomsky made the further claim that the general patterns disclosed by transformational grammar were more than just analogous to what occurs in the minds of language users; they represented, he claimed, processes that actually took place in those minds — that is, they were homologous to those processes — and revealed the innate mental structures that enable very young children to pick up their native languages long before their general reasoning powers are fully developed. But these claims, while highly interesting — see Appendix C for some discussion of them — are quite independent of the issues we are concerned with here.

³⁶ I am aware, of course, that language is used for purposes other than communication, but to take them into consideration here would accomplish nothing but to make the inadequacy of transformational grammar even more evident.

[37] This is a difficulty that Lyons, who is to Chomsky very nearly what Huxley was to Darwin, is acutely aware of, and attempts to deal with — in my view, unsuccessfully — in Lyons 1978, pages 36–37.

[38] Chomsky 1957, page 5.

[39] Nunberg 1983, page 37.

[40] Steinberg 1971.

[41] Mathematicians, too, once went through a "formalist" phase, in which a few advanced thinkers proposed that mathematics be divorced entirely from meaning, and regarded simply as a game played with certain symbols. Frege's dissection (Geach 1960, pages 186ff.) of this movement might profitably be considered by the linguistic formalists as well.

[42] The first of the many difficulties faced by the linguistic program of creating a model, or set of rules, which generates all and only the acceptable sentences of a language is that its fundamental terms, such as *sentence* and *acceptable* are anything but rigorously defined. Is a sentence what one's high school English teacher taught it was, a string of words conveying a thought, containing a subject and a predicate (with perhaps some auxiliary structures called clauses modifying either or both), and ending with a period or equivalent final punctuation? Is an utterance acceptable if its meaning can somehow be made out, despite its violent infraction of normal usage?

[43] It is interesting to see that Jürgen Habermas, a theorist who starts from Marxism and psychoanalysis, premises very different from mine, has nevertheless come up with essentially the same idea on the difference between sentences and natural speech utterances. Michael Morton writes (Morton 1993, pages 74–75):

> "In a paragraph headed "Sentences versus Utterances," Habermas writes: "If we start with concrete speech actions embedded in specific contexts and then disregard all aspects that these utterances owe to their pragmatic functions, we are left with linguistic expressions." And he continues:

"Whereas the elementary unit of speech is the speech act, the elementary unit of language is the sentence. The demarcation is obtained by attending to conditions of validity — a grammatically well-formed sentence satisfies the claim to comprehensibility; a communicatively successful speech action requires, beyond the comprehensibility of the linguistic expression, that the participants in communication be prepared to reach an understanding, that they raise claims to truth, truthfulness, and rightness and reciprocally impute their satisfaction. Sentences are the objects of linguistic analysis .... speech acts of pragmatic analysis."

44 For elaboration on this point, see Appendix B.

45 Of course linguists have noted that many, perhaps most, examples of actual speech are syntactically imperfect, to put it rather gently, and try to resolve the difficulty by calling such fragments "elliptical" and the parts omitted "understood"; but this is stretching matters — how much manipulation of one's data can one get away with in order to save the phenomena? Such stratagems — many of them quite ingenious — begin to resemble the epicycles and equants that Ptolemy had to resort to in order to sustain the geocentric model of the planetary system.

46 The philosopher Sidney Morgenbesser is supposed to have refuted J. L. Austin, who had remarked in a lecture that in no language do two positives make a negative, by waving a dismissive hand and muttering "Yeah, yeah!" This riposte would of course be unintelligible to the Golem, since it depends for its effect wholly on the tone of voice in which it was presumably uttered and the accompanying dismissive wave.

47 Another modern piece of evidence: it has been frequently observed that users of e-mail get into rancorous misunderstandings with each other through failure to realize that the body and voice signals that were supposed to convey that they were joking when they said something have not been transmitted over the net, with the result that their words have been misunderstood and caused offense.

351

[48] "Writing, like talking, is the art of expressing thoughts in words
 … . But there is, necessarily, a vast difference between the oral
and the scriptural use of words. When we talk, we have for our
ministers not words only, but also gesture, play of feature, mod-
ulation of the voice's tone, and regulation of its pace, whereby
we may subtly temper or accentuate the words themselves, and
fit them, be they never so carelessly chosen, exactly to our meaning. When we write, we have nothing but words, words, with those
little summary and meagre things whose hard office is to ape the
variable pauses of the human voice… ." Max Beerbohm, quoted
in David Cecil, *Max: A Biography of Max Beerbohm.*

[49] Leonard Bloomfield, who was one of the great figures of 20th century American linguistics, went so far as to say "Writing is not
language, but merely a way of recording language by means of
visible marks." (Bloomfield 1933, page 21). On the importance
of speech sounds, Chomsky says "A grammar of a language …
can be loosely described as a system of rules that expresses the
correspondence between sound and meaning in this language."
— Chomsky, in Leiber 1975, page 120. And "To study this
co-ordination of certain sounds with certain meanings is to study
language." — Bloomfield, in Steinberg & Jakobovits 1971,
page 162.

[50] According to McWhorter 2003, page 18, the oldest recording of
actual speech dates from 1877, when Thomas Edison recorded
"Mary Had a Little Lamb." There is no direct evidence that any
human spoke a word before that date.

[51] I am not here agreeing with Professor Trudgill's claim that we need
not worry about using such terms as *imply* and *infer* interchangeably; precise technical terms like these are too definite, carry
too much weight to be modified, let alone reversed in meaning,
by context — all a contradictory context can do to such a term
is to suggest that something has gone wrong.

[52] Leiber 1975, page 44.

[53] In case the reader is troubled by my conflation of "an infinite number of sentences" with "sentences of infinite length," I point out

that the two notions are, at bottom, the same: if there are to be an infinite number of sentences, then there must be sentences of infinite length. If we put any limit on sentence length — decreeing, say, that no sentence can exceed 10,000 words in length — we thereby put a cap on the number of sentences that can be produced. The total number of sentences that can be generated from a finite lexicon, and not exceeding 10,000 (or any other finite number) of words is length, is great, but finite.

54 The evolution of the game of chess offers an instructive analogy here. Over the centuries, chess has evolved so as to present a challenging, but not demoralizing, problem to human memory and reasoning powers. If chess were much harder, no one could play it; if it were much easier, no one would care about it. That is why the ability of computers to "beat the world champion at chess" is of so little interest, any more than it is of interest to know that many fish can swim faster than the Olympic 100-meter sprint champion. The idea that human language could have evolved — or even begun — without regard to basic human limitations is much like the idea that chess just happens to be so structured as to be playable by nearly anyone, but dominated by only an extraordinary few.

55 It is not only in matters of language and literature, of course, that the modern feeling that rules, memorization, and formal instruction are suppressing and blighting talent. We have all heard the claim that 'all children are artists, but their creativity is crushed by art teachers'; and even mathematics, strangely, is periodically claimed to be a subject that suffers from conventional teaching practices. During the 1960s a project called the School Mathematics Study Group (referred to as SMSG, which was interpreted by cynics as "Some Math, Some Garbage") convinced some California school districts that children should not start their mathematical education by being drilled in basic arithmetic operations and memorizing the multiplication table up to 12 times 12, but should be introduced instead to the most general mathematical concepts, chief among them set theory. My

daughter started elementary school in Palo Alto on a Monday; that Wednesday, I happened to mention in her hearing that her mother had two toothbrushes, and so did I. My daughter, with three whole days of education behind her, said, "Are those equal sets, Daddy?" I nearly fell out of my chair; at this rate, I thought, by next year she'll be proving the Riemann Hypothesis; I'd better brush up on my functional analysis if I'm to be able to talk to her. I need not have worried; she went on to be as cheerfully ignorant of higher mathematics as most California kids, with some shakiness in ordinary arithmetic as a bonus. Possibly because many parents had similar experiences, SMSG was downplayed for a while, but it has come back to haunt us under another name: "constructivist math." When a parent whose child was being trained to "work out problems for himself" under this program begged his teacher to show him a times table, she replied "But that's drill-and-kill." For details see Samuel G. Freedman, "'Innovative' Math, but Can You Count?", *The New York Times* (November 9, 2005).

56 O'Connor, pages 84–85.

57 Halpern 1997.

58 "The Media are Ruining English," in Bauer & Trudgill, pages 15–22.

59 I'm happy to note that I'm not alone in questioning the infallibility of Orwell as a guide to usage. As I found after writing my critique of his rules, a few of his other strictures on usage were rejected by Kinglsy Amis in (Amis 1997), page 136.

60 A. E. Housman, *D. Ivnii Ivvenalis: Satvrae* (London: E. Grant Richards, 1905), page xxx.

61 Winston Churchill, writing in 1932: "I cannot recall any time when the gap between the kind of words which statesmen used and what was actually happening was so great as it is now" (from his *Arms and the Covenant*, page 43, quoted in A. J. P. Taylor, *English History 1914–1945*, page 317); also, Auden's "low dishonest decade," and from Piers Brendon, *The Dark Valley: A Panorama of the 1930s* (NY: Knopf, 2000), pages xvi–xvii: "...

the Depression years witnessed the dissemination of falsehood on a hitherto unprecedented scale."

[62] A survey of the issues raised by the appearance of this work is given in Sledd 1962.

[63] Fiske's attack on the dictionary appeared in the August 18, 2003 issue of *The Weekly Standard*, and — in a slightly revised version — in *The Vocabula Review* for August 2003. McKean's letter was printed, slightly abbreviated, in *The Weekly Standard* for September 22, 2003, and in full in *The Vocabula Review* for September 2003. It is the full version that is reprinted in the text here.

[64] The *Times Literary Supplement* of February 11, 2005, reviews (page 12) the second volume of Julie Coleman, *A History of Cant and Slang Dictionaries* (Oxford U. P.), which covers works of that description published between 1785 and 1858 (the first volume covered 1567 to 1784). Presumably there will be at least one more volume.

[65] Housman 1969 (1911), page 42.

[66] Hope 2004.

[67] The conflation of spoken and written language in gathering data for a dictionary is another example of lexicographers' confusion. Dictionaries are used almost exclusively in connection with writing, not speaking; we don't go to Webster to learn how to say something, any more than we go to a dancing school to learn how to walk.

[68] Mawson 1945, Roget's "Introduction," page xiv.

[69] I must observe in fairness to Winchester and the others I criticize in this section that many writers have fallen into the careless habit of calling Roget a collection of synonyms (and antonyms), even one of his principal editors, Mawson, who subtitles his edition of Roget "A Complete book of Synonyms and Amtonyms ..." But the term *synonym* does not appear in Roget's own title, which is *Thesaurus of English Words and Phrases Classified and Arranged so as Facilitate the Expression of Ideas and Assist in Literary Composition*.

[70] Mawson 1945, Roget's "Introduction," page ix.

[71] Do all enemies of Roget bear the names of English towns or counties? Am I jousting with members of a landed and armigerous aristocracy? If so, why are they so poor at jousting? (And the third member of the trio I criticize here, Whale, bears a name suspiciously like Wales.)

[72] His praise of Fowler has a slightly unpleasant tinge of patronization, though; he pats him on the head with the phrase "that good man, H. W. Fowler," and describes the admirers of his best-known book as "a coterie ... who prize its diffident irony." The *de haut en bas* tone is especially revealing because Nunberg really admires Fowler, and does not mean to put him in his place — it is just the tone that one who thinks of himself as a professional adopts unthinkingly when speaking of or to an amateur or layman; as a surgeon does when talking to a patient, unless forcefully corrected. Apart from the condescension, Nunberg seems to have been thinking of someone else when he said "diffident irony"; there is very little of either diffidence or irony in *Modern English Usage*.

[73] Nunberg writes, "since nonstandard forms of English possess internal logic just as standard English does, they are not inherently inferior; rather, the doctrines of prescriptive grammar reflect covert class prejudice and racism." Here Nunberg, wielding his favorite weapon, the Unsupported Assertion, attacks his favorite opponent, Straw Man. Those of us who regard the patois of the Black ghetto as inferior do so not because we think it lacks "internal logic" — if it did, it could not serve as a medium of communication at all — but because it demonstrably lacks the means of expressing many ideas and shades of meaning that standard English possesses. And since those without a fair command of standard English are at a severe disadvantage in getting good jobs and other good things, we prescriptivists, in urging that African Americans — like all other Americans — be taught standard English rather than be encouraged to speak "naturally" so that they can be studied as interesting linguistic specimens ("native informants"), are helping them attain important economic and social goals. If

prescriptivists were racists, we would want to perpetuate the disadvantages of Blacks, not remove them; cultural elitists we may be, but elitists who want others to share our lofty status.

74 Sapir 1921, pages 154–155.

75 Sapir 1921, page 150.

76 It is headed "Superiority," and appears in full only in the original edition of 1926.

77 And not only his reasoning; he writes "forgone," meant to write "a foregone conclusion," should have written "inevitable."

78 Pinker improves the story in the act of summarizing it; he says "they do not have four hundred words for snow" — but even Pullum does not record seeing a claim greater than two hundred.

79 The statement of Auden's that either Bolinger or Pinker slightly misquotes — Auden said "and this leads to violence," not "that" — appeared in Bernard Weinraub, "Auden: 'A Difference in Memories'," *The New York Times,* October 19, 1971, page 52. I owe this information to Professor Edward Mendelson of Columbia University.

80 Auden's concern for the survival of honest language, and what he meant by the "corruption" of language, are shown in many of his writings; he dealt with them explicitly and at length in his acceptance speech for the National Medal for Literature in 1967, printed in the *Library Journal* (December 15, 1967), pages 4508–09.

81 Carpenter 1981, page 415.

82 The allusion is to the doctrine presented in James Q. Wilson and George L. Kelling, "Broken Windows: The Police and Neighborhood Safety," *Atlantic Monthly* (March 1982), pages 32–36.

83 Barzun, private communication, January 25, 1995

84 The late R. L. Trask.

85 Shippey 2004.

86 In his *New Introductory Lessons on Psychoanalysis,* Freud said "Where id was, there ego shall be."

87 To some linguists, the answer is yes; I was accused of demagoguery by the late R. L. Trask for publishing my views in *The American Scholar,* that notorious rabble-rouser's platform.

[88] Shippey 2004.

[89] McWhorter 2003, page 33 (the final exclamation point is McWhorter's).

[90] The ineptness of this book (Burchfield 1996) begins on the title page, where it is claimed that it was "first edited by H. W. Fowler." A guide to language usage that doesn't know the difference between writing a book and editing one is a fearful thing, but perhaps it was a kindness on the part of the Clarendon Press to warn us at the outset what we were in for.

[91] "Historians of language have traditionally focused on the aspect of change, perhaps tacitly assuming that 'Where nothing changes, there is nothing to be explained'." Keller 1994, page 141.

[92] Halpern 2002.

[93] Nunberg 1996, page 205.

[94] Pinker 1994, pages 64–65.

[95] McWhorter 2001, page 49n9.

[96] Wilton 2004, "500 Eskimo Words for Snow," pages 50–54.

[97] I owe the term to D. W. Brogan, a specialist in modern French history but also the best foreign observer of America since Tocqueville. (I had supposed that it was already in use in the form *Métis* for those of mixed Eskimo-European descent, but I have been disabused of that error by Mr. P. D. Petersen, who kindly explained that *metic* comes from Greek *meta+oikos*, and *Métis* from Latin *misticius*, a different root and a different idea.) More recently I learned from Richard Pipes' autobiography, *Vixi* (Yale U.P., 2003), page xi, that in the British Virgin Islands the term *non-belonger* means the same thing.

[98] Those who agree with Pullum that Eskimos have no more words for snow and ice than English apply very strict standards when it comes to admitting an Eskimo-language word to the list of accepted snow-and-ice terms, but moderate their scholarly rigor when deciding what words are to count as English-language words for the same things. In a e-mail message dated July 1991, printed first on the Linguist on-line site, and reprinted elsewhere, Professor Anthony C. Woodbury of the University of Texas at

Austin offers a list of supposed English-language terms for snow that includes *avalanche, dusting, snow bank, snow cornice, snow fort, snow house, snow man,* and *snow-mixed-with-rain?* [sic]. Note that *avalanche* and *dusting* have no necessary connection with snow or ice at all, and that the various phrases beginning with *snow* are not terms for types of snow, but for types of banks, cornices, forts, and so on.

⁹⁹ A good discussion of the hypothesis is offered in (Sampson 1980), Chapter 4.

¹⁰⁰ Since writing this, I have found the following statement by Lawrence Kaplan, Professor of Linguistics and Director of the Alaska Native Language Center, University of Alaska <www.uaf.edu/anlc/inuitoreskimo.html>:

> *Inuit or Eskimo: Which names to use?*
>
> Although the name "Eskimo" is commonly used in Alaska to refer to all Inuit and Yupik people of the world, this name is considered derogatory in many other places because it was given by non-Inuit people and was said to mean "eater of raw meat." Linguists now believe that "Eskimo" is derived from an Ojibwa word meaning "to net snowshoes." However, the people of Canada and Greenland prefer other names. "Inuit," meaning "people," is used in most of Canada, and the language is called "Inuktitut" in eastern Canada although other local designations are used also. The Inuit people of Greenland refer to themselves as "Greenlanders" or "Kalaallit" in their language, which they call "Greenlandic" or "Kalaallisut." Most Alaskans continue to accept the name "Eskimo," particularly because "Inuit" refers only to the Inupiat of northern Alaska, the Inuit of Canada, and the Kalaallit of Greenland, and is not a word in the Yupik languages of Alaska and Siberia.

What seems clear from this rather complex situation is that (1) no one is certain about the derivation of *Eskimo;* (2) whatever its derivation, there is no reason to suppose it offensive, nor is it taken as such by the Alaskan natives to whom it is applied;

and (3) the term *Inuit* is inaccurate as applied to many Eskimos, and may indeed be a cause of resentment if applied to them.

101 Lewis, page v. The same point is made even more forcefully in Taylor, page v, note 1.

102 In a private communication of January 13, 2004, Professor Steven Jacobson of the Alaska Native Language Center told me that "in Alaska there are Yupik people who are not Inuit ...." In fact, the objection to *Eskimo* seems to be largely confined to Canada, and largely instigated by politicians, social workers, and "activists," not the native peoples themselves. When I used *Eskimo* in a published essay a few years ago, I got a few corrections, all from Canadians, who seemed to enjoy the opportunity to display their superior sensitivity.

103 The list of snow terms referred to is available here as Appendix B.

104 Posted by Tom Collins, a teacher, on the *Atlantic Monthly*'s "Post & Riposte" Web page, 9 March 1997.

105 Some years ago, a fellow employee of a computer software company made me an offer that I declined with the words, "No, thank you." He looked at me in a kindly manner, then gently corrected me: " 'No way, José!' " he said, offering me the formula I should have used.

106 Steven Pinker writes (Pinker, page 371), "A linguist's question to an informant about some form in his or her speech (say, whether the person uses *sneaked* or *snuck*) is often lobbed back with the ingenuous counter question 'Gee, I better not take a chance; which is correct?'" Professor Pinker should consider the possibility that sometimes the ingenuousness is on the other side; the "informant," not altogether content with his role as "native" or guinea pig, may be teasing or seriously sabotaging the stern linguistic scientist. The story of how simple Samoan "native informants" amused themselves at Margaret Mead's expense — and that of the many linguistic sophisticates who swallowed her report whole — is a case in point.

107 Martin 1986.

108 Pullum 1991, page 162.

[109] For more on the Sapir-Whorf Hypothesis, see
http://cs-tr.cs.berkeley.edu/TR/UCB:COGSCI-83-08

[110] Nunberg 1983, page 37.

[111] Meyers 1990.

[112] In this matter as in several others Chomsky is more modest and realistic than many of his epigones. Asked what language speakers of Black English should be taught in in school, he answers "My own personal judgment, for what it is worth, is that speakers of a language that is not that of groups that dominate some society should probably be taught in their own languages at least at very early stages, until basic skills are acquired, and should be taught in the dominant language at later stages, so that they can enter the society without suffering disadvantages that are rooted in prevailing power, privilege and domination. One might hope to modify these features of the dominant society, but that is another question. Children have to be helped to function in the world that exists, which does not mean, of course, they they — or others — should not try to change it to a better world." (from Chomsky 1988, page 581.)

[113] See (Sledd 1996), particularly "Bi-Dialectalism: The Linguistics of White Supremacy."

[114] The question of how one language or dialect can be said to be better than another is discussed carefully in (Ray 1963), Chapter 10, and in (Jespersen 1925), Chapters V and VI.

[115] "To acquire immunity to eloquence is of the utmost importance to the citizens of a democracy." — Bertrand Russell, *Power*, Chapter 18, Section 4, as quoted in the *Penguin Dictionary of Modern Quotations*, 490 (16). The question of the relation between the quality of a piece of writing and that of the thinking it embodies is a difficult one. I have been told by one linguist that my views on language are not worth considering because my writing — or at least one sentence of mine — is so poor, and by another that my writing is excellent, but that I must not presume to pose as an authority on language on that ground.

The late R. L. Trask found the first sentence of (Halpern

2001a) so bad as to discredit the entire paper. He quotes (in a message posted to a Web site called "EvolPsych", then sent privately to me) the offending part of that sentence:

> [I]t's a living, growing thing — so it seems particularly unfortunate that it should be false.

and comments:

> Halpern has used the harmless little word 'it' three times here. On the first occasion, 'it' denotes language; on the second occasion, 'it' denotes nothing; on the third occasion, 'it' denotes a proposition mentioned earlier. Such slovenliness is diabolical style, and people who write like this have no business lecturing the rest of us on the supposed shortcomings of our English.

I think Trask's comment on that sentence is ridiculous, but the validity of that specific judgement is unimportant compared with the general question of whether a single instance of graceless writing can or should nullify a sustained and otherwise sound argument. I was astonished to learn that Trask was so sensitive to the niceties of prose that a sentence using "it" in three ways should so strongly affect him — "diabolical" is strong language indeed for even the worst of solecisms. He didn't complain that the sentence was difficult to understand, or that he had any trouble in identifying what "it" stands for in each of its three appearances — he merely claimed that it is so offensive on (apparently) purely esthetic grounds as to disqualify me from saying anything about language. So for this linguist, bad writing is the unforgivable sin, vitiating whatever argument it was trying to convey.

But Peter Trudgill (Trudgill 2003) takes very nearly the opposite position on how writing — presumably anyone's writing — relates to the quality of the argument it expresses:

> Obviously, Halpern speaks at least one language fluently. And he certainly writes English well. But the fact that he is an expert user *of* language does not mean that he is an expert *on* language, as is painfully apparent from what he has to say.

The views of Trask and Trudgill, taken together, amount to this: the smallest instance of bad writing utterly damns the message in which it occurs, but no amount of good writing in the least validates it. I agree with Trudgill — no matter how high the quality of a piece of writing may be, it does not guarantee that the argument it conveys is sound — but I do not accept Trask's view that one bad sentence discredits everything a writer says about language usage; if that rule were adopted, very few linguists would be able to utter a word about language.

To make the story even more curious, Trask's posthumously published guide to usage, *Say What You Mean!* (Boston: David R. Godine, 2005), shows him to be a staunch prescriptivist, ruling on questions of usage without hesitation or apology; on a number of points he is more prescriptivist than I am. His recommendations on usage, his attitude toward postmodernist jargon and "political correctness", and his views on language in general are so close to those expressed in the essay he was attacking that it's hard to account for the violence of that attack except by supposing that he saw linguistics in danger, and felt that the assault must be repelled by any means available.

116 Judith Butler, "A 'Bad Writer' Bites Back," *New York Times*, March 20, 1999, Op-ed page.
117 James Clerk Maxwell, *Scientific Papers*, ed W.D. Niven (Cambridge, 1890), II, 328.
118 Bolgar 1954, page 31.
119 Kaster 1988, page 11.
120 Vickers 1988.
121 There are many variants on the meat-and-sauce metaphor: the passenger-and-vehicle, the body-and-clothes, the cake-and-frosting, the spirit-and-flesh — all of them ways of making thought the principal and essential thing, and words superficial and dispensable. They are, of course, classic rhetorical tropes, and frequently used in arguments aiming to discredit rhetoric. I will shift freely from one to another of these variants in what follows; this is not mixing metaphors, just looking at the same thing

through a variety of lenses and from a variety of angles.

122 "The unassuming exposition ... may lull the reader into taking these remarks as obvious. It is easy to get used to a display of intelligence. One silently appropriates whatever is said, and on second reading the author seems to repeat the reader's lifelong conclusions." Gian-Carlo Rota, in Kac 1992, pages 236–237.

123 There is indeed one special field of thought where the popular theory holds, at least to some extent: logic and mathematics. These disciplines do indeed successfully separate much of their content — axioms, theorems, propositions, and so forth — from the formalisms — sentences, formulas, or equations — that express them. Why this is so, and why it cannot be so in general discourse, I have discussed in Halpern 1990; I mention here this slight exception to the generality of my argument only to indicate I am not unaware of it.

124 Quoted in Carpenter 1981, page 415.

125 "Then, as to rhetoric: ... we are apprehensive of this sauce by which our parents were persuaded, as we believe, to swallow many impure substances. ... But rhetoric is not necessarily a garnishing added to an idea to make it persuasive; it may invest the idea so closely as to become a part of it, as in some famous speeches of Shakespeare ...." — Kenneth Clark, *The Nude: A Study in Ideal Form* (Doubleday Anchor Books, 1959), pages 303–304.

126 Rhetoric was from antiquity until the Renaissance the art of *speaking* persuasively — until printed books became common, it could be nothing else — but the ideas it embodies have since been largely refocused on written language. The rhetorical teachers of modern times seldom use *rhetoric* in the titles of rhetorical books like *Modern English Usage,* but rhetoric is their subject.

127 Quoted by Robert Craft in his review of Alan Anson, *The Table Talk of W. H. Auden* (Ontario Review Press, 1990) in *The New York Review of Books,* January 17, 1991, page 4.

128 Knox 1993, pages 69–108. The pages explicitly devoted to rhetoric are 86–99.

[129] There are restaurants that do this; rather than try to describe their dishes on the menu, they show pictures of them, or even bring them (or models of them) to your table — an effort to avoid the pitfalls of language that would win applause from the Laputan academicians.

[130] See Barzun 2000, pages xvi and others cited in that book's index under 'decadence.'

[131] I know, of course, that language is used for many purposes other than conveying information or serving as an art medium; there is phatic communion, unconscious vocalization, game-playing, venting, and awkward-gap filling, to name just a few. But all these purposes could be otherwise satisfied if language were not available; what is being considered here is what may be called the *linguistic* use of language: the use of language for purposes that only language can satisfy. Perhaps the most linguistic use of language is that for which we have the subjunctive mood, the mood in which we discuss situations that have not been realized, and that may even be impossible of realization. To be able to contemplate the non-existent or the not-yet-existent is something possible only to those speaking a well-developed language.

365

[132] At least one literary artist, the Peruvian novelist Mario Vargas Llosa, fully recognizes this. In an interview that is partially reprinted in the *Wall Street Journal* for April 6, 1990, he says "Intellectuals and artists have a strength — that comes perhaps from the artist's condition itself — which is the condition of the dreamer; the man who wants to transcend the limits of reality, to go further. Capitalism has nothing to do with that. It has to do with reality. ... The poet and novelist want no part of this reality. They want to transcend it." The interview is well worth reading in its entirety.

[133] Yeats originally wrote "dance attendence" but for reasons unknown to me changed it to "dance attention" shortly before his death.

[134] Anthony Julius, *T. S. Eliot, anti-Semitism, and Literary Form.* Cambridge U.P., 1995.

[135] For the latest such attempt, see the debate on the subject in *Modernism/Modernity* for January 2003. Its gist is summarized on the Web at www.york.ac.uk/admin/presspr/pressreleases/tseliot .htm, and in Emily Eakin, "Another Round in the Skirmish Over Eliot and Anti-Semitism," *The New York Times* (March 11, 2003), page D1 (?)

[136] Carpenter 1981, page 358.

[137] Lovecraft has now (2005) been canonized by the issue of a volume of his stories in the Library of America series.

[138] H.P. Lovecraft, "The Whisperer in Darkness," in Robert Bloch (ed.), *The Best of H. P. Lovecraft* (NY: Ballantine Books, 1982), page 172.

[139] Quoted in L. Sprague de Camp, *Lovecraft: A Biography* (Garden City, N.Y.: Doubleday, 1975), p. 331.

[140] Sprague de Camp, *Lovecraft,* pages 253–54.

[141] S. T. Joshi, *H. P. Lovecraft: A Life.* West Warwick, Rhode Island: Necronomicon Press, 1996.

[142] All quotations from Joshi are from *H. P. Lovecraft: A Life,* page 647.

[143] The same conclusion is reached by a writer, Michel Houellebecq, who comes to his study of Lovecraft (Houellebecq 2005) with very different interests from mine. He writes (page 24) of Lovecraft's "obsessive racism," and speaks of him (page 97) as a "conservative anti-Semite" (meaning not that he was conservative in his anti-Semitism, but that he was both a conservative and an anti-Semite). He goes on to devote an entire chapter of his slim book ("Racial Hatred," pages 105–113) to the subject.

[144] Anthony Thwaite (ed.), *Selected Letters of Philip Larkin.* Faber & Faber, 1992.

[145] Andrew Motion, *Philip Larkin: A Writer's Life.* Faber & Faber, 1993.

[146] Martin Amis, "Don Juan in Hull," *The New Yorker* (July 12, 1993), pages 74–82. Amis's father, Sir Kingsley, made a similar comment elsewhere: "… when Philip Larkin used such [four-letter] words in letters to contemporaries he was not being 'misanthropic' or 'foul-mouthed' but being very mildly subversive and, like a good letter-writer, encouraging the recipient to feel he was

a member of the same secret army as the sender. And what I was principally doing, by including in a letter to him a whole page of scurrility directed at our common publisher, was trying to entertain a friend."

147 Christopher Hitchens, "D.W.E.M. Seeks to R.I.P.," *Vanity Fair* (April 1993), pages 80–88.

148 Robert Graves, *Lars Porsena, or The Future of Swearing* (London: Kegan Paul, 1927), page 16.

149 Tony Judt, "The Information," [review of Martin Amis' *Koba the Dread*], *The New Republic* (November 4, 2002), pp. 23–27, at p. 26.

And from an anonymous review in *The Economist* (April 5, 2003), pages 75–76, of Anne Applebaum, *Gulag: A History* (Penguin/Allen Lane, 2003): "In post-Communist Prague you can buy Soviet mementoes: red stars, hammers and sickles, portraits of Lenin. So at least Anne Applebaum discovered one day while crossing the Charles Bridge. She reflected that selling swastikas and portraits of Hitler would rightly be considered an outrage. What was the difference? Why does western public opinion seem so indifferent towards the legacy of the Soviet concentration camps while continuing to regard the Nazi ones with justified abhorrence?"

150 Martin Malia, "Judging Nazism and Communism," *The National Interest* (Fall 2002), pages 63–78.

151 A British psychologist has now made this a scientific hypothesis: Dr Patrick Leman of the University of London has told the 2003 annual meeting of the British Psychological Society that "humans have an innate tendency to try to link major events with major causes," and "there is some underlying process in human psychology that assumes that the bigger the effect is, the bigger the cause must have been." See "Who shot the president?" *The Economist* (March 22, 2003), page 74.

152 German Justice Minister Herta Daeubler-Gmelin, speaking on or about September 19, 2002.

153 The archetype of all intellectuals is Hamlet; the archetype for our time is Jean-Paul Sartre.

154 Quoted in S. Benardete (ed.), *Leo Strauss on Plato's Symposium* (U. of Chicago Press, 2001), page 4.

155 Plato, *The Republic* (Shorey translation), I, 347c.

156 The allusion is to T. S. Eliot, "Choruses from 'The Rock'," vi, 23: "… dreaming of systems so perfect that no one will need to be good."

157 See, for example, Reuben Hersh, *What is Mathematics, Really?* (Oxford U.P., 1997), page 38.

158 See, for example, Alan R. Malachowski (ed.), *Reading Rorty.* Oxford & Cambridge (Mass.): Basil Blackwell, 1990, and Robert B. Brandom (ed.), *Rorty and His Critics.* Blackwell, 2001.

159 Among them Barbara Herrnstein Smith, *Belief and Resistance* (Harvard U.P., 1997), a book that, as its title implies, does not so much try to argue for PM as to offer a study of how and why people resist, in the psychoanalytical sense, the PM ethos.

160 Clive James, review of John Bayley's *The Power of Delight*, in *TLS* (May 27, 2005).

161 "Solidarity or Objectivity?" in *Objectivity, Relativism, and Truth* (Cambridge U.P., 1991), page 178.

162 *Philosophy and Social Hope* (N.Y.: Penguin Books, 1999), page 87.

163 Mark Halpern, "The Meaning of Post-Modernism in an Age of Terrorism," *The Vocabula Review*, July 2002.

164 "Priority of Democracy to Philosophy," in *Objectivity, Relativism, and Truth* (Cambridge U.P., 1991), pages 187–188.

165 "On Ethnocentrism," in *Objectivity, Relativism, and Truth*, page 207. Words in square brackets are mine, not Rorty's.

166 "Solidarity or Objectivity?", page 25.

167 See (Hoffer 2004) for an account of the most prominent of the plagiarism cases.

168 (www.law.uchicago.edu/news/posner-r-plagiarism.html)

169 (http://www.theatlantic.com/cgi-bin/send.cgi?page=http%3A//www.theatlantic.com/issues/2002/04/posner.htm)

170 Her two-part piece "Annals of Scholarship: Trouble in the Archives" ran in the *New Yorker* on December 5 and 12, 1983; the book is *In the Freud Archives* (NY: Knopf, 1984).

171 Quoted in Andrews, *The New Penguin Dictionary of Modern Quotations,* page 428.

172 "The desire shared by many linguists to be a member of the illustrious circle of natural scientists has driven some to dream up rather grotesque theories." — Keller, page 142.

173 What might be in order is a language-usage equivalent of the Underwriter's Laboratory: an institution with no enforcement powers, but with the power to award an emblem showing that a test article has been considered by that independent and disinterested body, and found to pass certain tests. No official penalty whatever would be imposed on those who chose to disregard the Usage U.L.; the only possible penalty that might be incurred by non-conformers is that some readers might refuse to read a book that did not bear the U.U.L. emblem. But writers and publishers would soon come to think of the U.U.L. as electrical appliance manufacturers now think of the present U.L. — as a helpful, indeed indispensable, adjunct to their business.

174 The last two lines of Emerson's "Give All to Love" are "When half-gods go,/ The gods arrive."

175 Stephen 1991, page 176.

176 Glanvill's text reads "So they [the dogmatists] that never peep't beyond the belief in which their easie understandings were at first indoctrinated, are indubitately assur'd of the Truth ... while the larger Souls, that have travail'd the divers *Climates of Opinion,* are more cautious in their resolves, and more sparing to determine." Quoted in Elisabeth Noelle-Neumann, *The Spiral of Silence,* 2nd ed. (U. of Chicago Press, 1993), page 78.

177 Schauer 2003, page 283.

178 *The New York Review of Books* (December 1, 2005), page 2.

179 The story of how the study of natural phenomena rose in prestige as it went from success to success, and how students of other subjects aspired to have their studies, too, called *science,* is slightly complicated by a shift in English terminology in the first half of the 19th century. In 1840 William Whewell proposed the term *science* as the name for the investigation of *natural phenomena,* to

replace *natural philosophy* or *natural theology;* until then, *science* had been a highly general term, almost synonymous with *knowledge.* But none of this is relevant to my argument, where I am concerned not with names, but the things they stand for. If what we today call *science* were still called "natural philosophy," *that* would be the label that many would want awarded to their studies.

180 A practice perhaps traceable, in its turn, to the careless translation as "science"of *wissenschaft,* a term often used by German philologists and other humanistic scholars in referring to their own disciplines.

181 "The Application of Thought to Textual Criticism," in *Collected Poems & Selected Prose* (ed. Ricks), page 325.

182 Housman 1969 (1911), page 16.

183 One linguist has suggested to me that linguistics, rather than being *no* science, is *several* sciences. If true, this would only explain just how linguistics' claim to be a science is false, not vindicate that claim.

184 The motto proudly adapted from Terence by Roman Jakobson (Jakobson 1990), *Linguista sum; linguistici nihil a me alienum puto* (I am a linguist and I consider nothing having to do with language as foreign to me) testifies at the same time to Jakobson's catholicity as a philologist and to the reason why linguistics cannot be a science.

185 Chomsky 1979, page 46.

186 Chomsky 1977, pages 132–3.

187 Turing 1950.

188 In a *Wall Street Journal* story (Michael W. Miller, "Fujitsu Can Legally Clone IBM Software; The Question Now: Will It Be Able To?" [December 1, 1988], page B1), reverse engineering is described thus: "To avoid any accusations of breach of copyright, Phoenix uses two sets of programmers to clone the BIOS. One set picks apart IBM's product and makes a list of all the tasks it does, but not how it does them. The other set, known inside Phoenix as the virgins, takes that list and creates a new product that does all those tasks."

[189] Chomsky has occasionally commented on AI and the Turing Test, but never, to my knowledge, at length or in great depth. The most recent comment by him on the Turing Test is his note "Turing on the 'Imitation Game'," in (Shieber 2004), pages 317–321. This piece is brief, perfunctory, and uncharacteristically ill-written — one seldom comes away from anything written by Chomsky uncertain about what he was saying, but this note is disappointingly turbid. In it, he seems to deny that a successful performance of the Test would tell us anything about human thinking, and to agree with the position taken by John Searle in his well-known "Chinese Room" thought experiment.

[190] The first and best-known metalanguage is "Backus Normal Form" (BNF), named for its principal designer, John Backus of IBM; later "BNF" was redefined as "Backus Naur Form" in order to honor the Danish computer scientist Peter Naur, who had contributed to its design.

[191] John Searle, professor of philosophy, University of California at Berkeley; Hilary Putnam, emeritus professor of philosophy at Harvard; Willard Van Orman Quine (1908-2000), late professor of philosophy at Harvard; Sir Michael Dummett, emeritus professor of logic at Oxford.

[192] "The actual systems called 'languages' in ordinary discourse are undoubtedly not 'languages' in the sense of our idealizations ..." (Chomsky 1980, page 28).

[193] Chomsky 1976, pages 56–57.

[194] Chomsky 1980, pages 229–230.

[195] Chomsky 1980, page 230.

[196] A recent news story is relevant: "Being bilingual produces changes in the anatomy of the brain, scientists said on Wednesday in finding that could explain why children are so much better than adults at mastering a second language. They found that people who speak two languages have more gray matter in the language region of the brain. The earlier they learned the language, the larger the gray area." Excerpted from Patricia Reaney, "Learning 2nd Language Changes Brain Anatomy: Study," London

(Reuters), October 13, 2004. The research report on which this story is based is Andrea Mechelli *et al.*, "Neurolinguistics: structural plasticity in the bilingual brain," *Nature* (2004 Oct 14); 431(7010):757. Another suggestive fact is that "feral children" — children who in their formative years had no exposure to language — are not merely inarticulate, but seem when examined in adolescence or later to be so mentally unformed as to be only imperfectly human. Of course the feral child, in missing socialization, has missed more than language, so his state cannot be ascribed exclusively to language deprivation — hence my calling this fact no more than suggestive.

197 But Lucian Endicott calls my attention to *you-uns,* which the *American Heritage Dictionary of the English Language* gives as a Vermont equivalent of *you all.*

198 To clarify this point: once a mathematical object has been defined in natural-language terms, it may be described in more technical and advanced mathematical terms, and many such descriptions may be formulated, each highlighting a different aspect of it. For example, some primitive mathematical operations and objects, originally defined in ordinary words, have been redescribed in terms of sets and operations on sets. But these more advanced descriptions cannot be formulated until the elementary, natural-language definitions have been absorbed, any more than a penthouse can be built until the basement and foundations have been constructed. The more advanced descriptions can be very useful, and may disclose some profound properties and interesting connections of the objects they deal with, but they must not be mistaken for original definitions. To describe zero as the cardinality of the null set, for example, may reflect or lead to some valuable insights, but that description is not the way zero entered the world of mathematical thought.

199 Robert S. Strichartz, professor of mathematics at Cornell, has proposed the development of a universal intermediate language, "Intermath," to facilitate the translation of from one national language to another of mathematical papers. Intermath, a highly

simplified and stereotyped abstraction from that part of natural language that is commonly used in the mathematical literature, would play a role in such translation analogous to that played by UNCOL in programming-language translation. Stichart explains the occasion for his proposal as follows (Strichartz 1989, page 12):

> Recently, the mathematics library at Cornell suggested the possibility of dropping its subscriptions to some translated Russian journals in order to save money. The reasoning is that these journals are not frequently used, and we already receive the Russian-language originals, so our collection would remain complete. Alas, only the Russian-born among us can read them.

But Strichartz concedes (page 13) that even if his proposal were adopted, the result might not be fully satisfactory, since mathematical papers use more of natural language's resources than Intermath would offer:

> ... a portion of the text, especially in the introduction and its motivating remarks, may be beyond the reach of the Intermath language.

[200] (Ross 2005).

[201] (Ross 2005), page 41.

[202] "Abstracting from an actual program" does not imply that working code need be written first; the abstract model may well be created first. But the order in which these steps are taken is immaterial for present purposes.

[203] (Nelson 2003).

[204] Geoffrey Wheatcroft, "How Seeds of Evil Germinated and Bore Deadly Fruit," *The New York Times* (March 17, 2004).

[205] "They stooped to conquer," *The Economist* (October 29, 2005), page 88.

Index

375